How to Improve the World

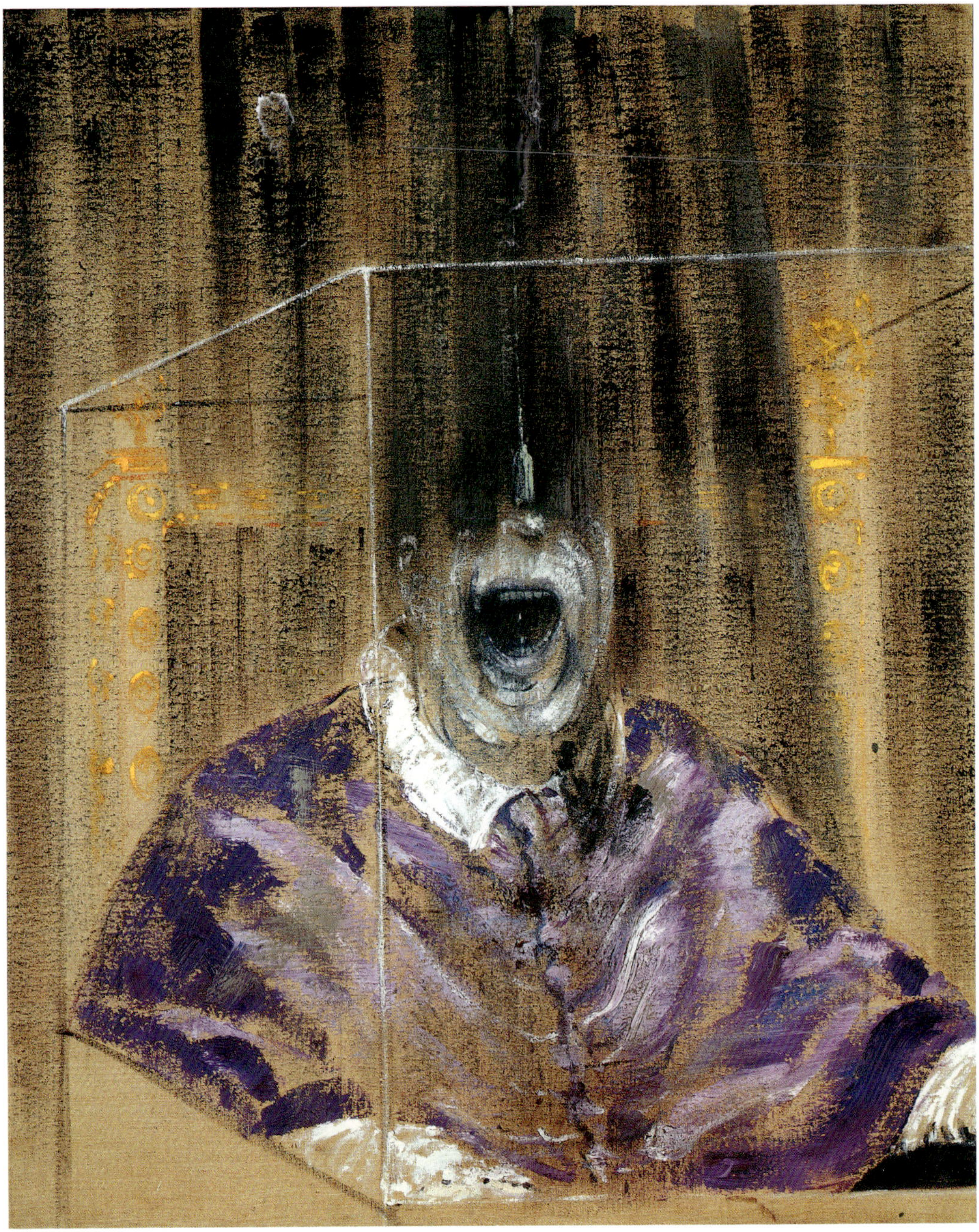

Roger Ackling
Rasheed Araeen
Kenneth Armitage
Keith Arnatt
Art & Language
Frank Auerbach
Gillian Ayres
Francis Bacon
Anna Barriball
John Berger
Bruce Bernard
Zarina Bhimji
Peter Blake
David Bomberg
Henry Bond
Christine Borland
Jane Bown
Martin Boyce
Ian Breakwell
Stuart Brisley
Glenn Brown
Angela Bulloch
Victor Burgin
Reg Butler
Gillian Carnegie
Anthony Caro
Patrick Caulfield
Lynn Chadwick
John Coplans
Tony Cragg
Michael Craig-Martin
Martin Creed
Ian Davenport
Enrico David
Richard Deacon
Jeremy Deller
Harry Diamond
Peter Doig
Zoë Dominic
Tracey Emin
Rose Finn-Kelcey
Barry Flanagan
Lucian Freud
Terry Frost
Gilbert & George
Liam Gillick
Douglas Gordon
Gregory Green
Lucy Gunning
Sunil Gupta
Richard Hamilton
Ian Hamilton Finlay
Siobhán Hapaska
Mona Hatoum
Tim Head
Nigel Henderson
Barbara Hepworth
Patrick Heron
Susan Hiller
Roger Hilton
Roger Hiorns
Damien Hirst
David Hockney
John Hoyland
Paul Huxley
Anish Kapoor
Mary Kelly
Balraj Khanna
Phillip King
Leon Kossoff
Jim Lambie
John Latham
Bob Law
Mark Leckey
Andrew Logan
Richard Long
Camilla Løw
Colin Lowe
Sarah Lucas
Kenneth Martin
Mary Martin
Bruce McLean
Steve McQueen
Gustav Metzger
Henry Moore
David Musgrave
Rosalind Nashashibi
Mariele Neudecker
Ben Nicholson
Lucia Nogueira
Chris Ofili
Julian Opie
Otolith Group
Horace Ove
Eduardo Paolozzi
Victor Pasmore
Oliver Payne
Peter Peri
Keith Piper
Ingrid Pollard
Kathy Prendergast
Nick Relph
Bridget Riley
David Robilliard
Donald Rodney
Eva Rothschild
Karin Ruggaber
Tim Scott
William Scott
David Shrigley
Maud Sulter
Roddy Thomson
Mark Titchner
William Tucker
Keith Tyson
Euan Uglow
Mark Wallinger
Gary Webb
Richard Wentworth
Rachel Whiteread
Alison Wilding
Cathy Wilkes
Victor Willing
Richard Wilson
Isaac Witkin
Bill Woodrow
Cerith Wyn Evans
Carey Young

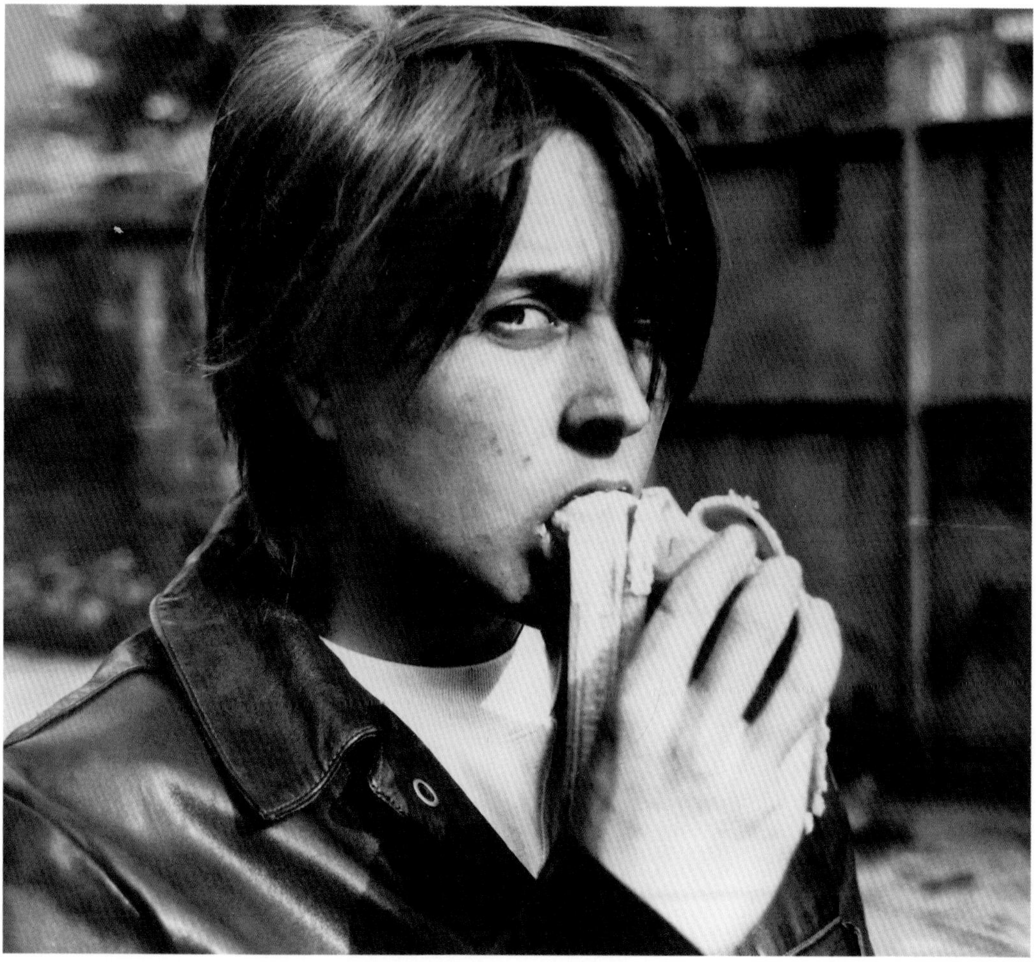

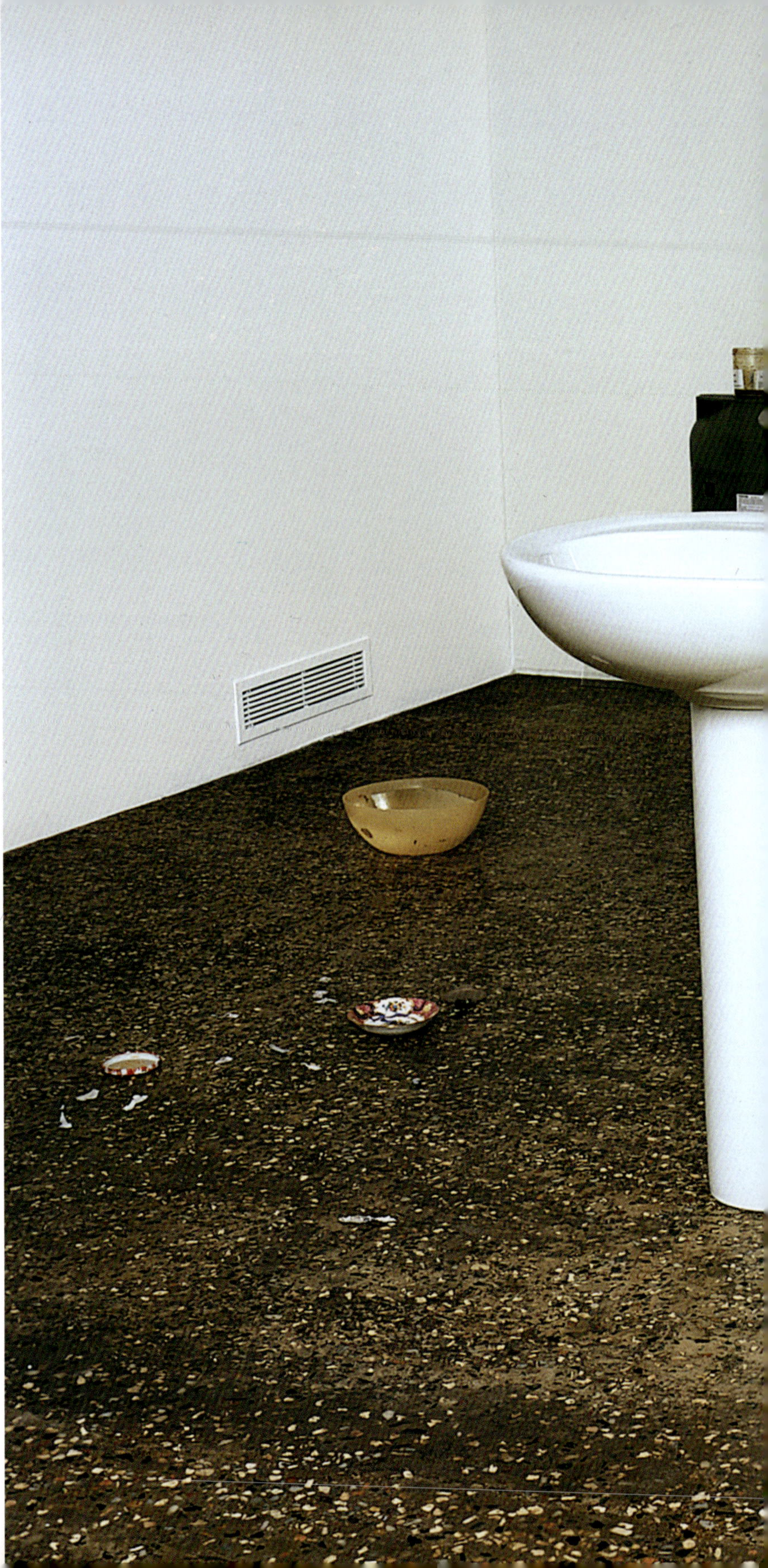

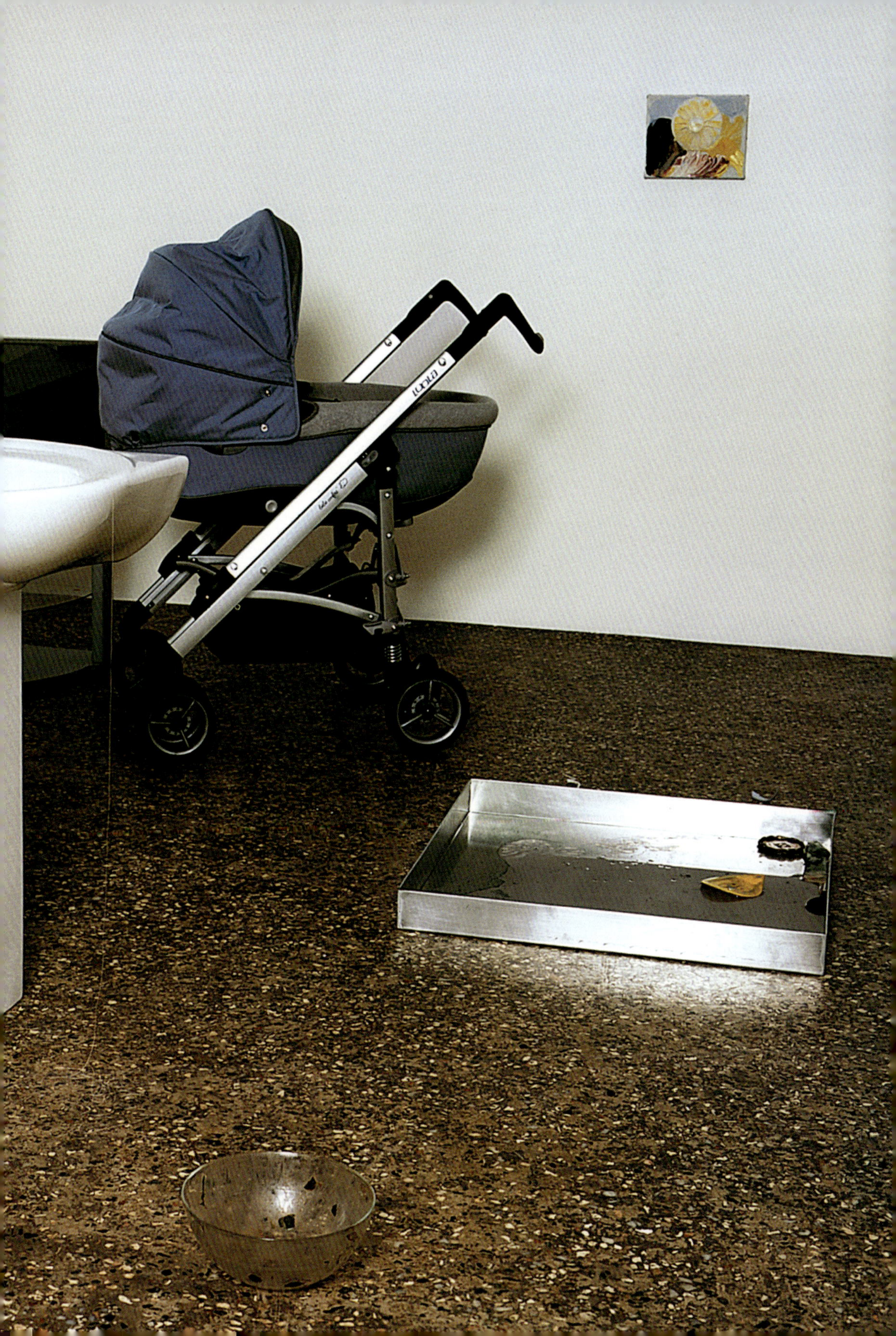

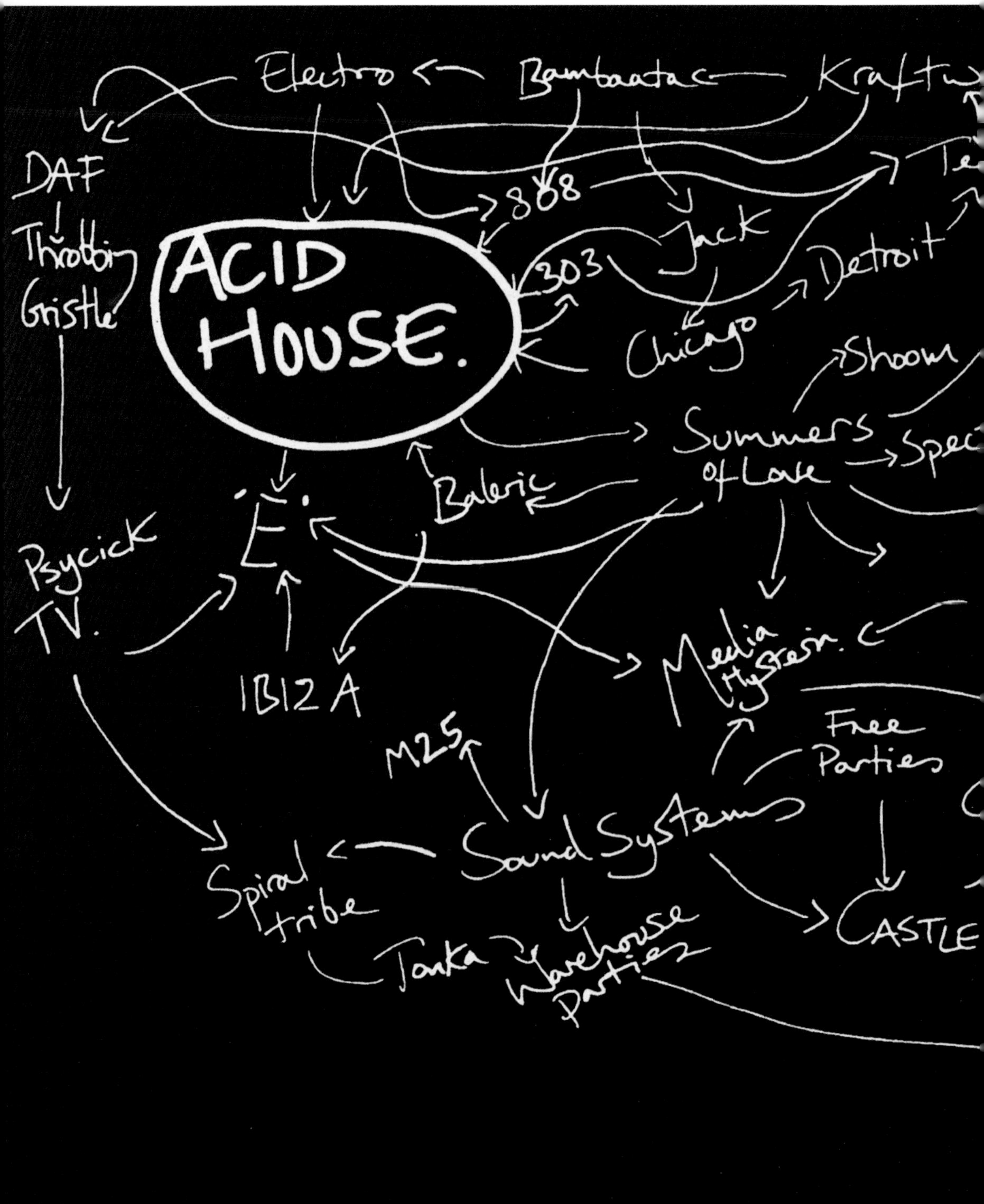

Electro
Bambaataa
DAF
Throbbing Gristle
888
Jack
ACID HOUSE.
303
Detroit
Chicago
Shoom
Summers of Love
Balearic
E
Psycick TV.
Media Hysteria.
IBIZA
Free Parties
M25
Sound Systems
Spiral tribe
Tonka
Warehouse Parties
CASTLE

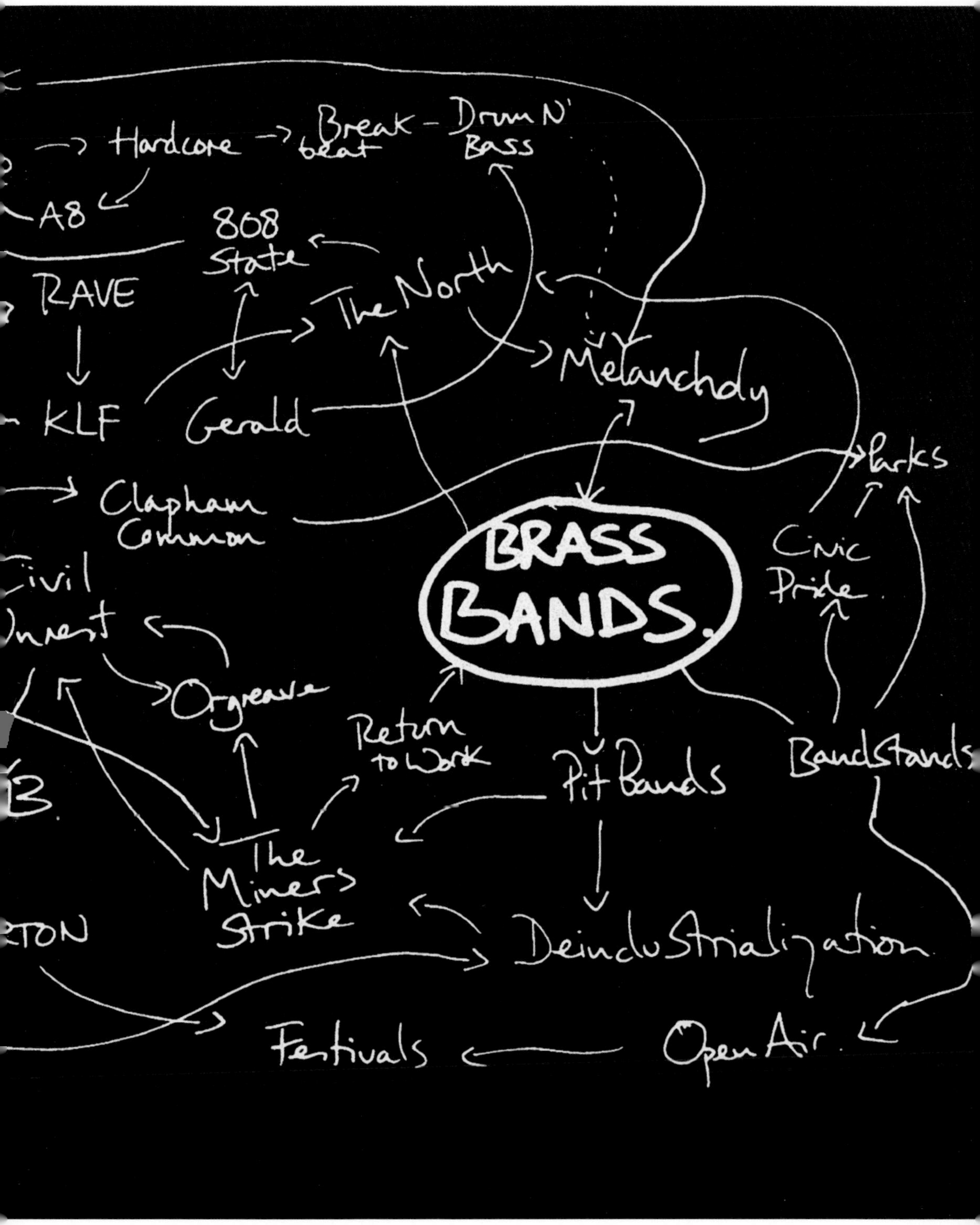
Hardcore
Break beat
Drum N' Bass
A8
808 State
RAVE
The North
Melancholy
KLF
Gerald
Clapham Common
Parks
Civil Unrest
BRASS BANDS.
Civic Pride
Orgreave
Return to Work
Pit Bands
BandStands
The Miners Strike
Deindustrialization
Festivals
Open Air.

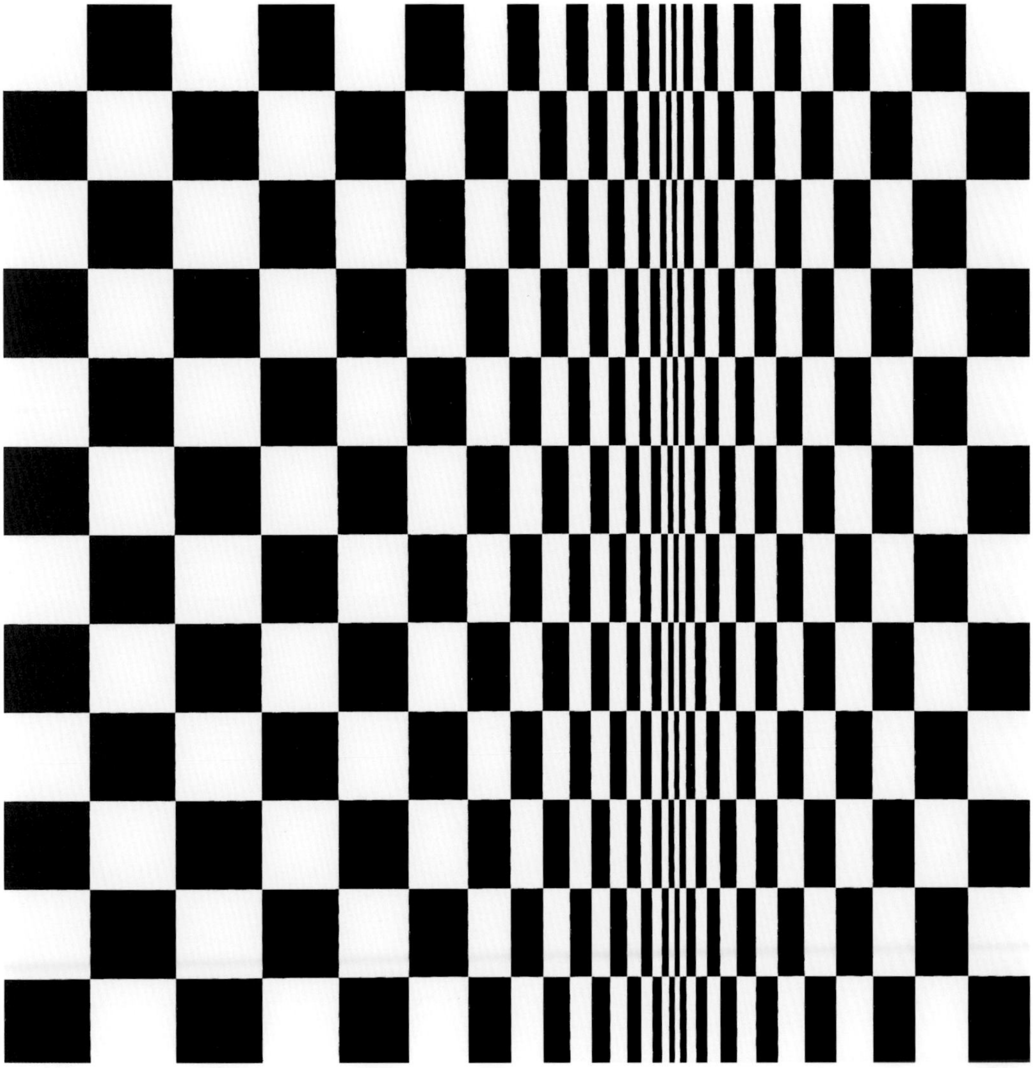

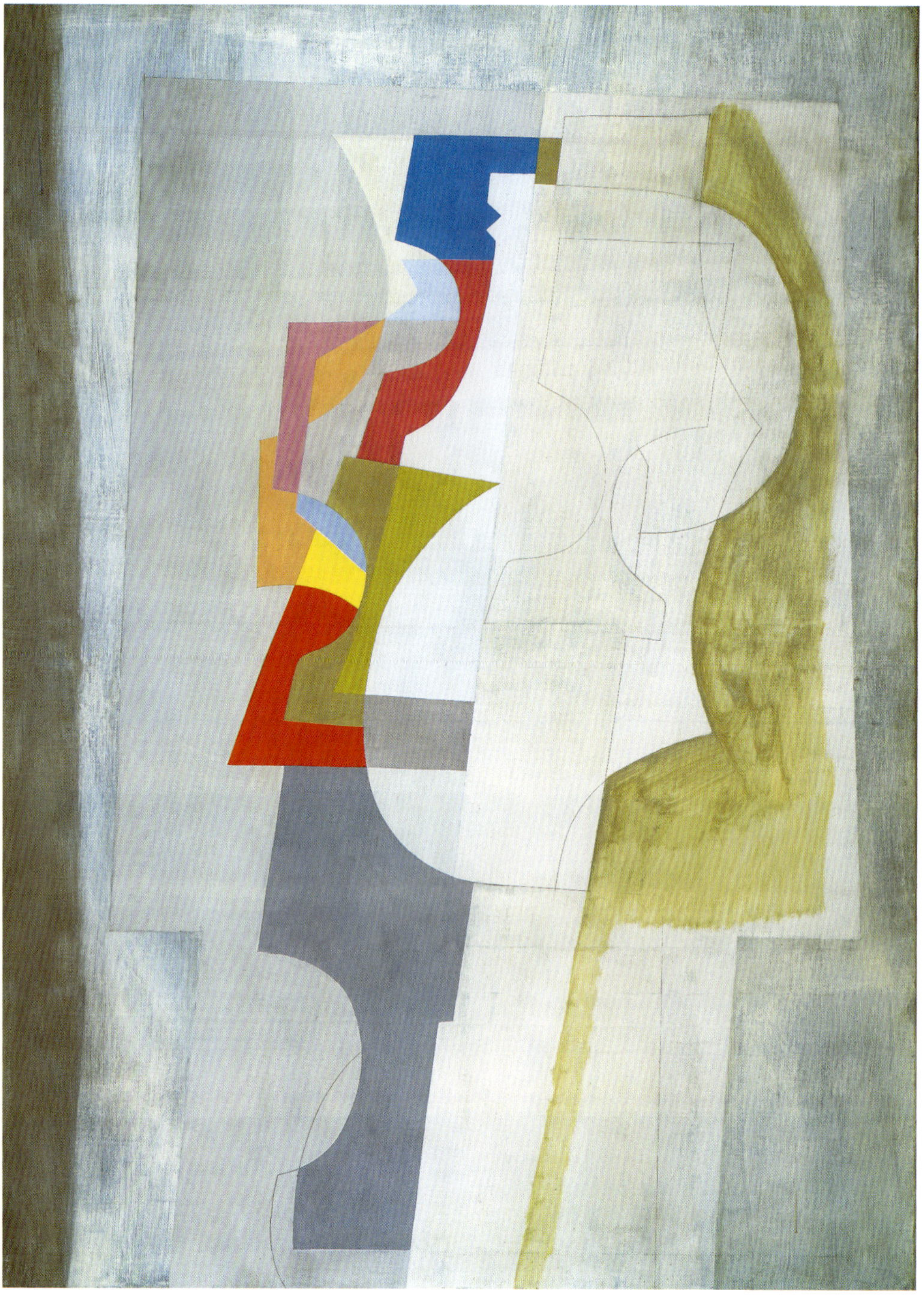

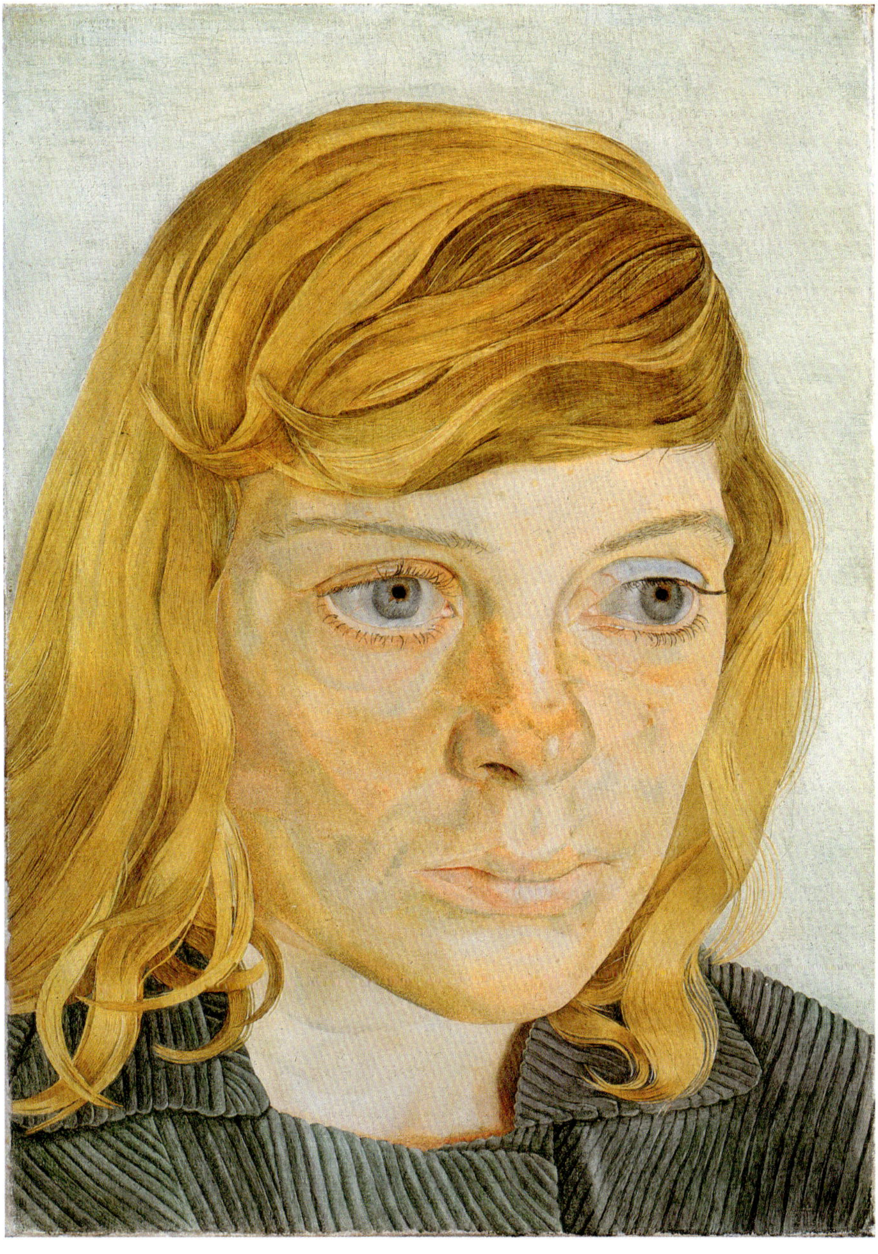

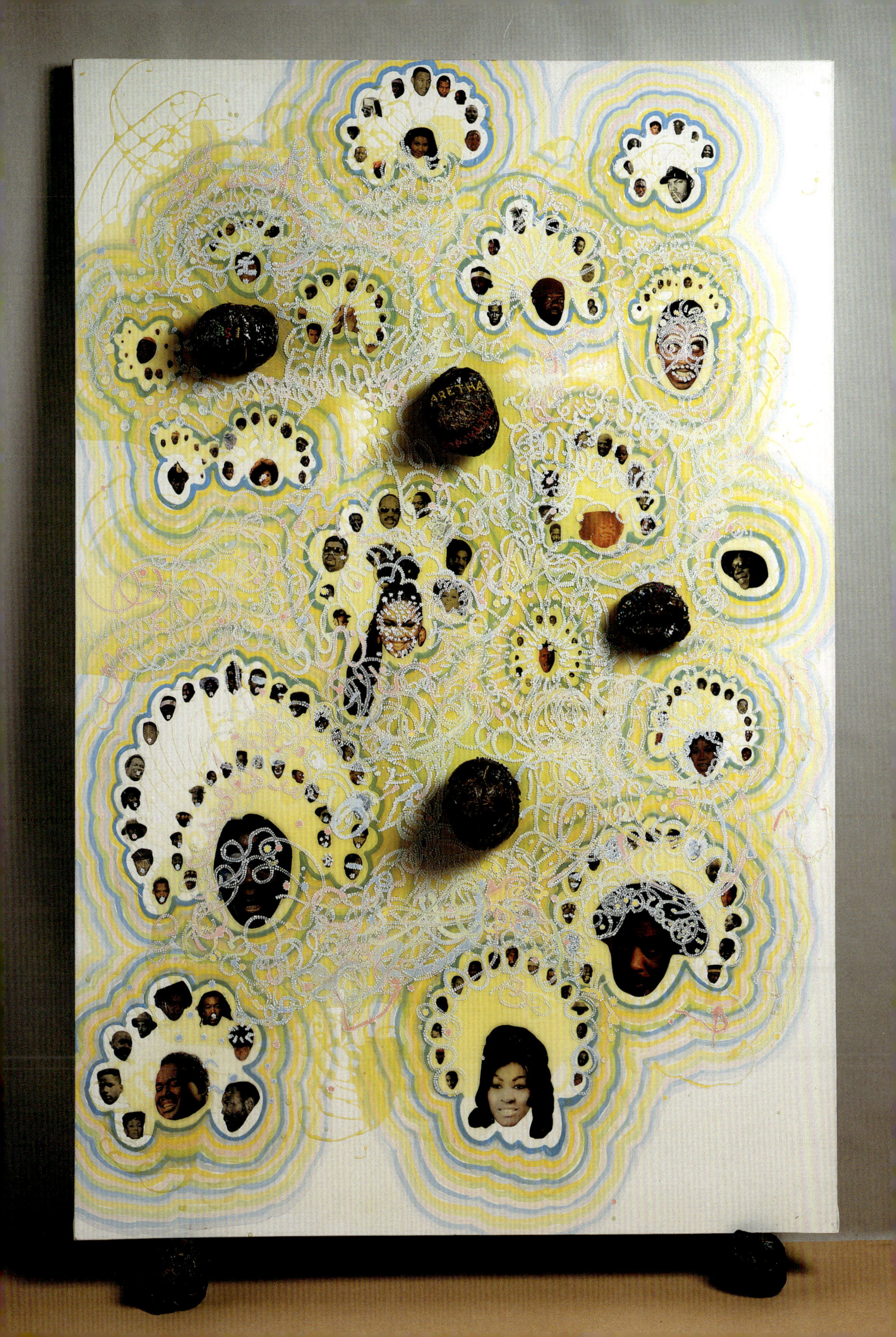
ARETHA

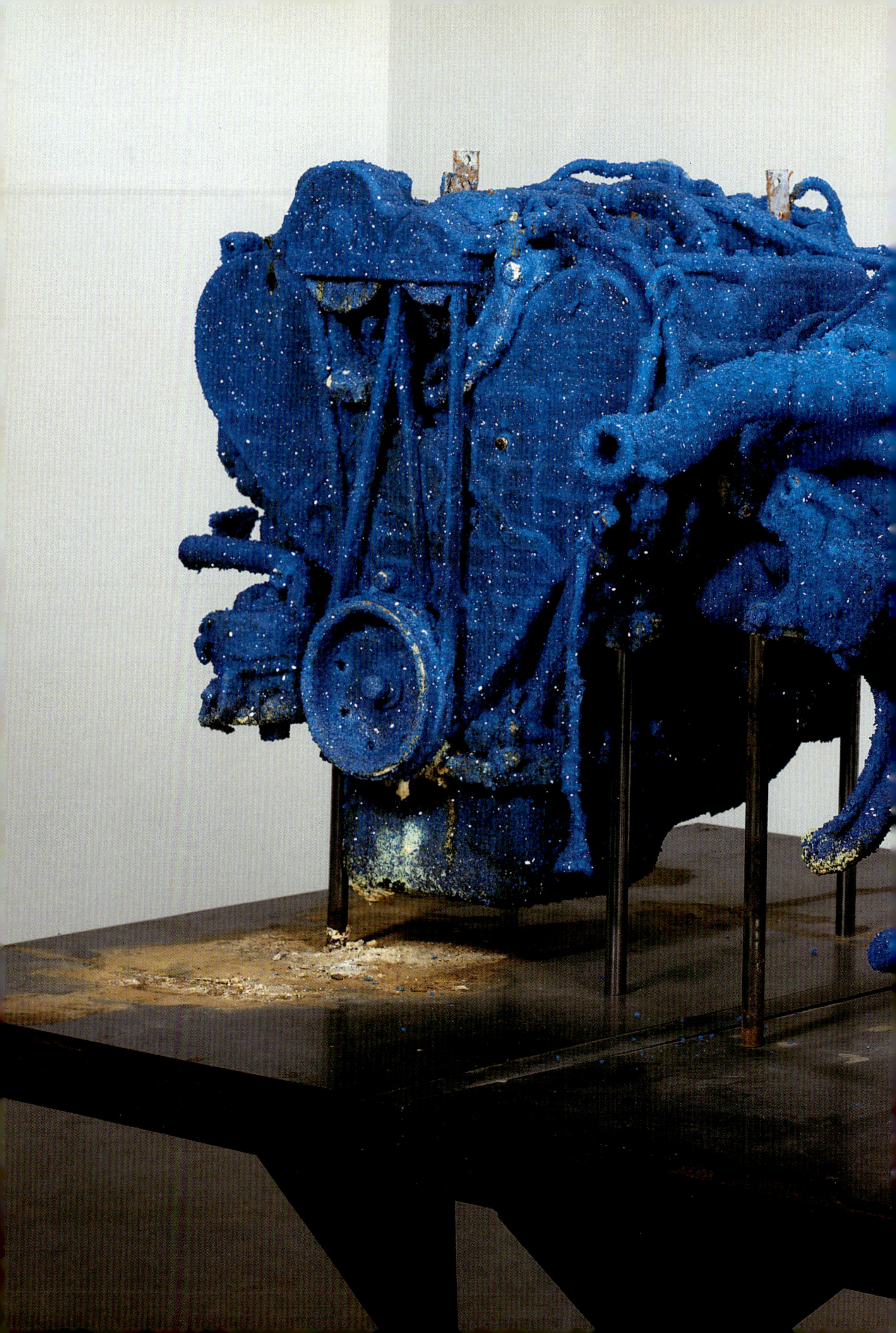

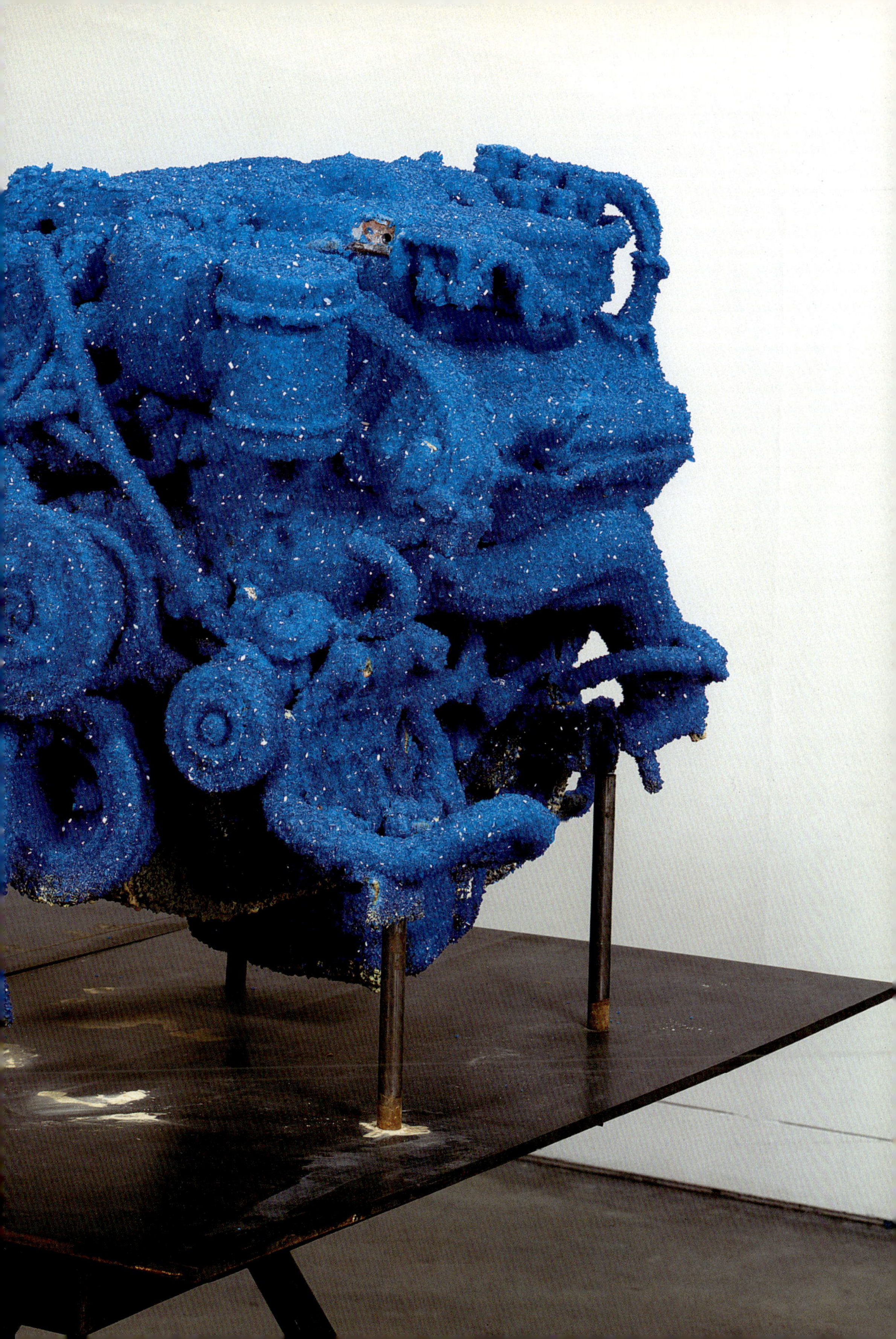

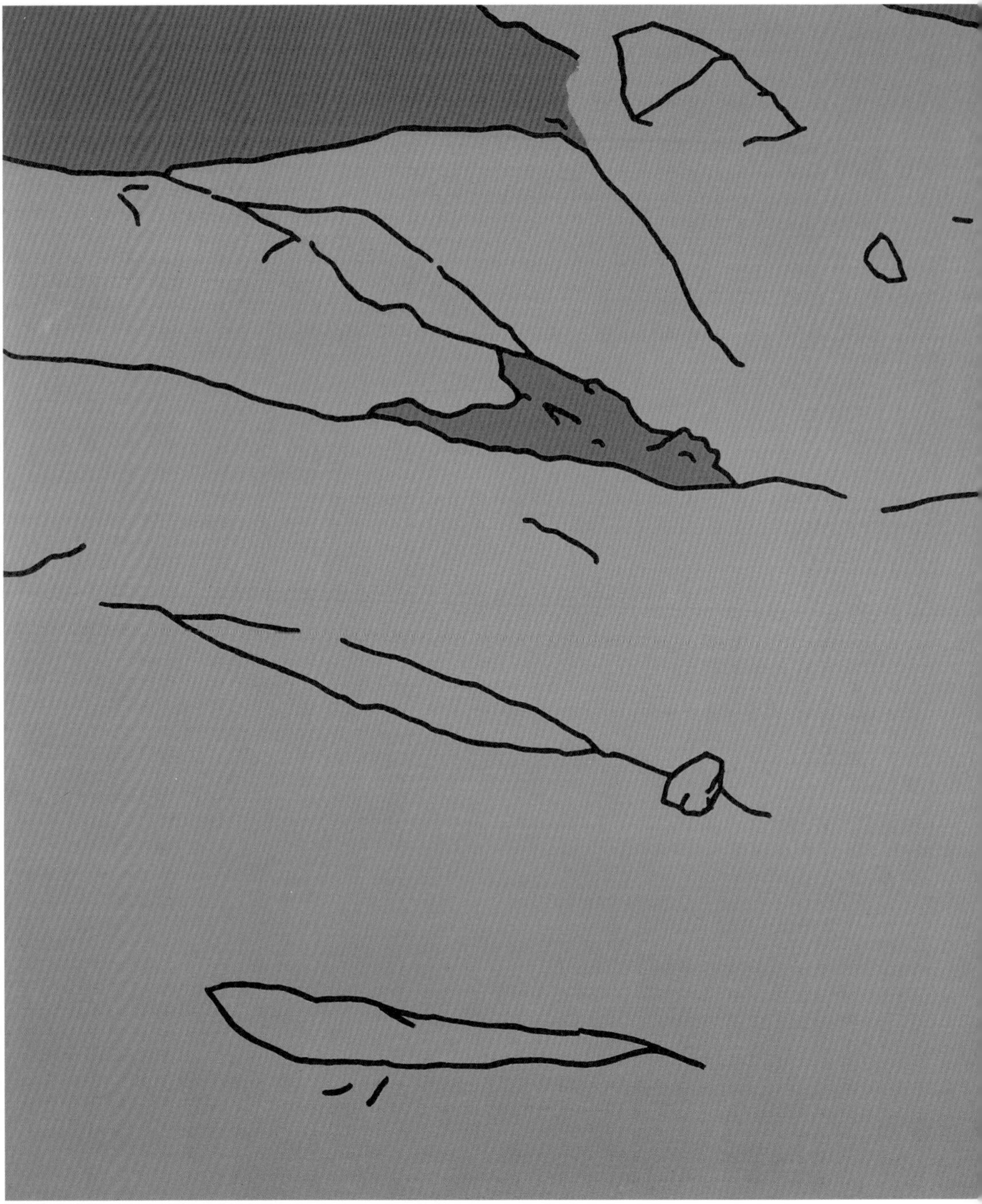

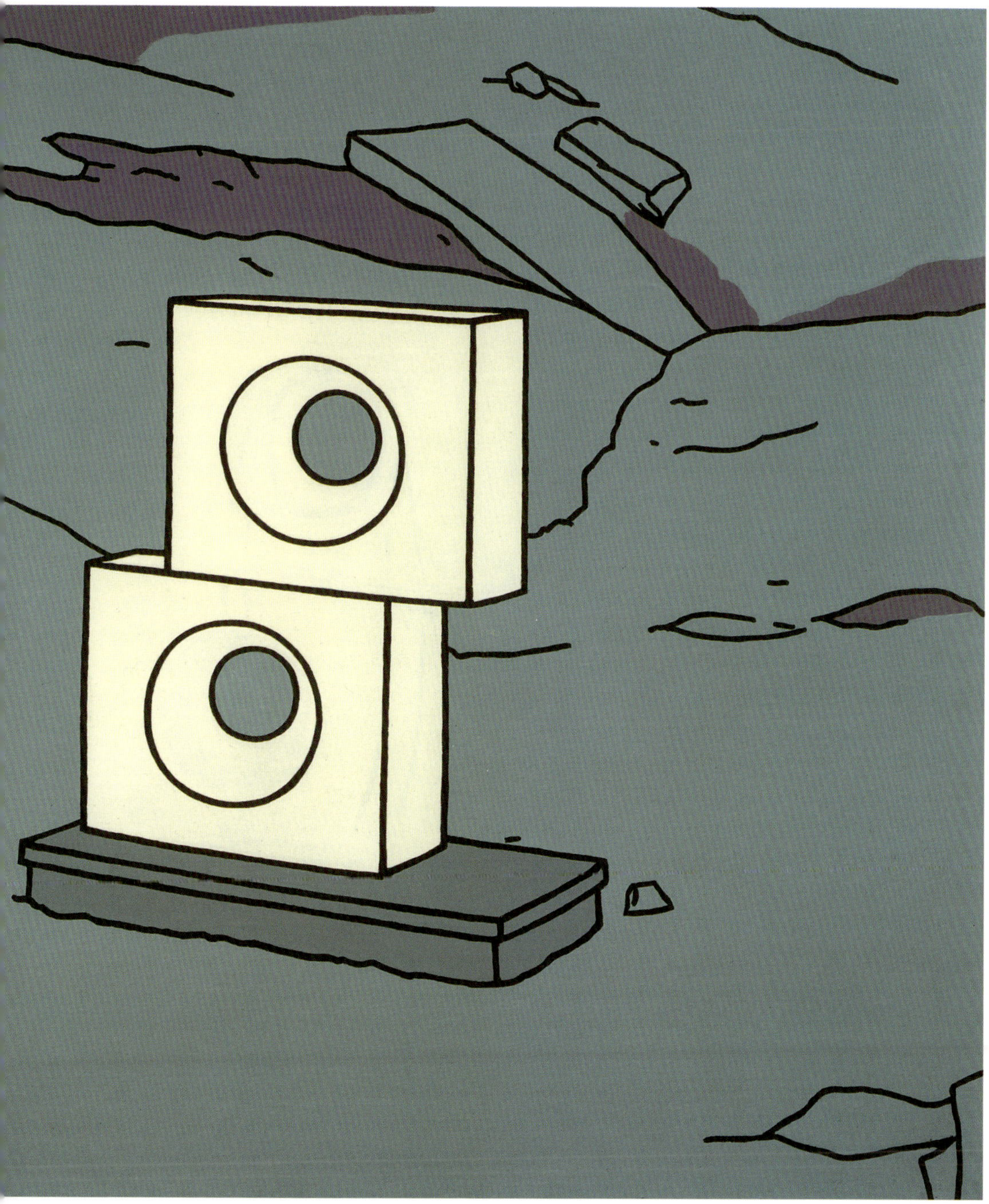

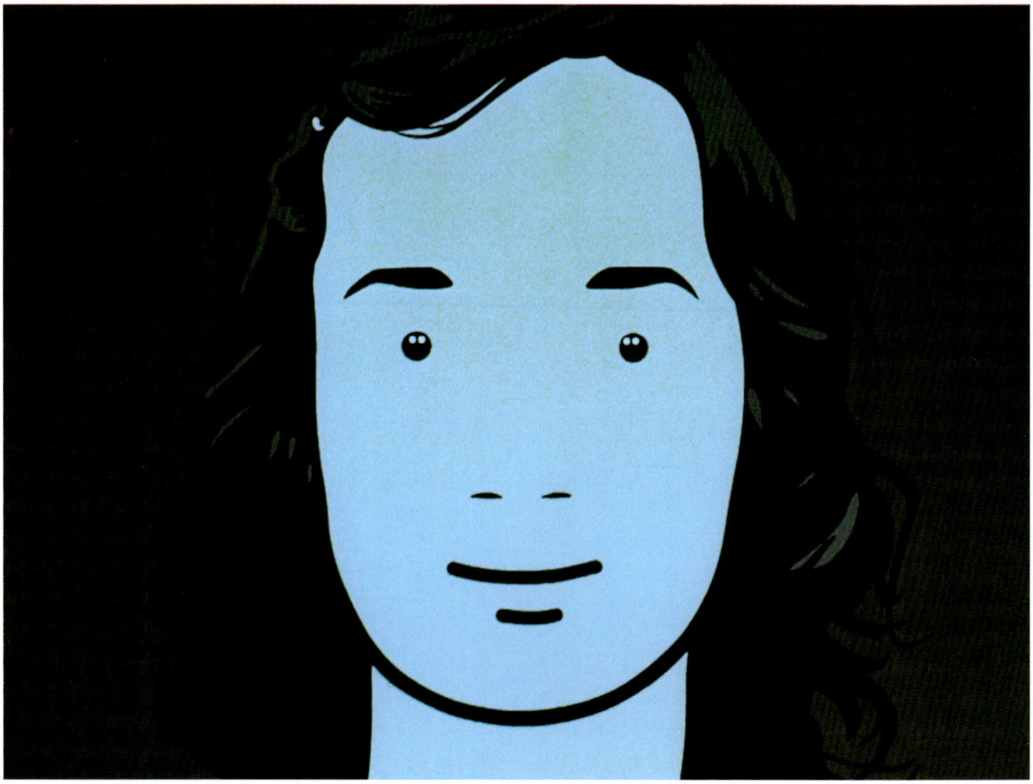

How to Improve the World

60 Years of British Art

Arts Council Collection

Michael Archer
Marjorie Allthorpe-Guyton
Roger Malbert

HAYWARD GALLERY
SOUTH BANK CENTRE · LONDON

Published on the occasion of the exhibition *How to Improve the World: 60 Years of British Art*, Hayward Gallery, London, 7 September – 19 November 2006

Exhibition curated by Michael Archer
and Roger Malbert

Exhibition organised by Roger Malbert
with Jill Constantine, assisted by
Marianne Mulvey and Charu Vallabhbhai

Exhibition sponsored by a consortium
of Hayward Gallery Corporate Members

Construction by Sam Foster
Lighting by John Johnson

The Hayward Gallery would like to thank
Arts Council England for their generous
contribution to the catalogue.

Art Publisher: Charlotte Troy
Publishing Co-ordinators: Shela Sheikh
and Oriana Fox
Sales Manager: Deborah Power
Catalogue and typeface design: A2/SW/HK

Published by Hayward Gallery Publishing,
South Bank Centre, London SE1 8XX, UK
www.hayward.org.uk

Hayward Gallery Publishing titles are distributed outside North and South America by
Cornerhouse Publications
70 Oxford Street
Manchester M1 5NH
T +44 (0)161 200 1503
F +44 (0)161 200 1504
email: publications@cornerhouse.org
www.cornerhouse.org/books

ISBN 1-85332-257-1 / 978-1-85332-257-0

Printed and Bound in the UK, with kind thanks to F&G

Preceding pages:

page 2 **Francis Bacon** Head VI, 1949
page 5 **Sarah Lucas** Eating a Banana, 1990, from the series Self Portraits, 1990–1998
page 6–7 **Cathy Wilkes** She's Pregnant Again, 2005
page 8–9 **Jeremy Deller** The History of the World, 1998
page 11 **Bridget Riley** Movement in Squares, 1961
page 12 **Ben Nicholson** Contrapuntal, Feb 25 – '53, 1953
page 13 **Lucian Freud** Girl in a Green Dress, 1954
page 15 **Chris Ofili** Popcorn Shells, 1995
page 16–17 **Roger Hiorns** Nunhead, 2004
page 18–19 **Patrick Caulfield** Sculpture in a Landscape, 1966
page 20 **Julian Opie** This is Fiona, 2000

overleaf **Tim Scott** Round Midnight, 1961

endpiece **David Musgrave** Overlapping Figures, 2001

Arts Council England
sixty years celebrating the arts

Arts Council Collection

Contents

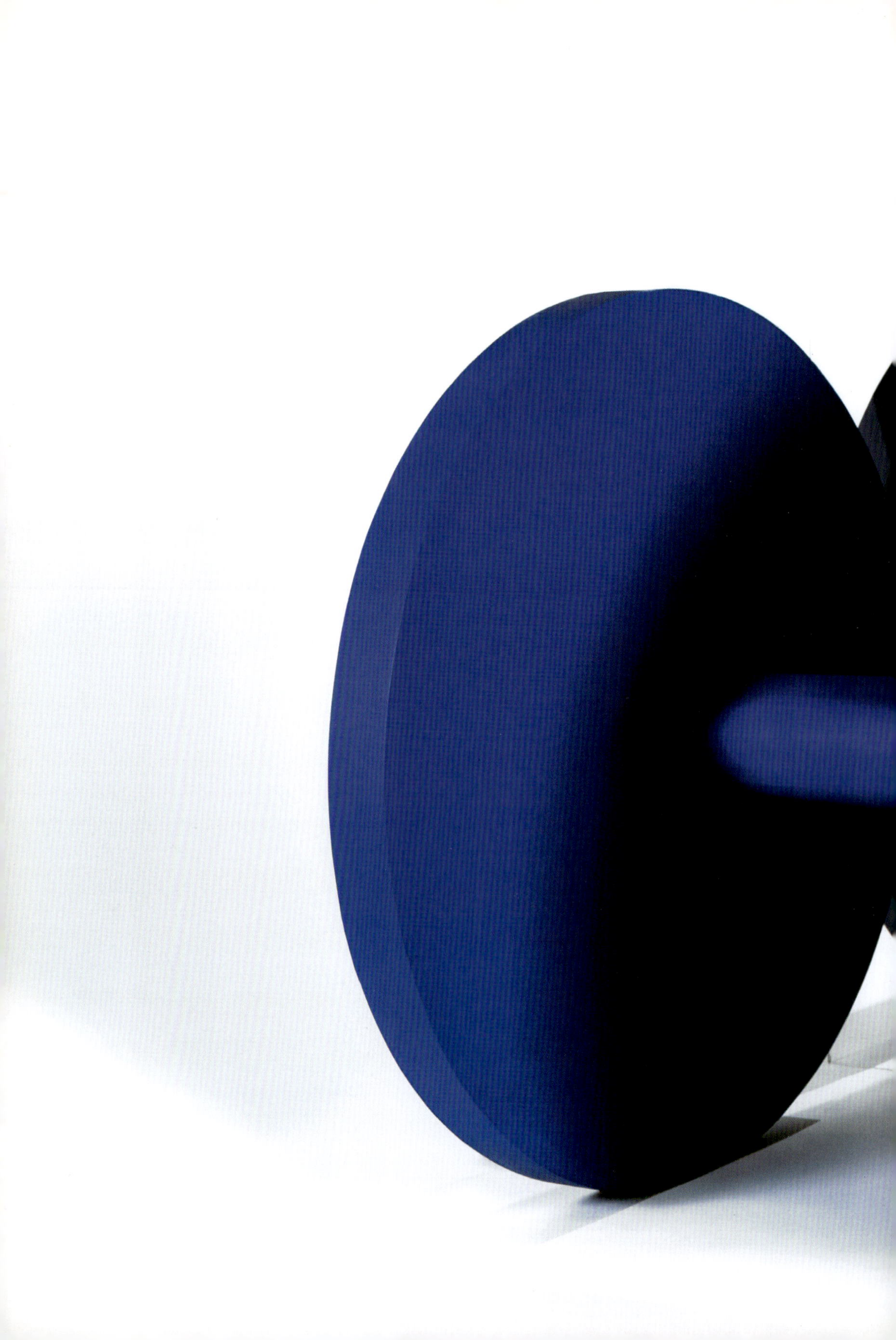

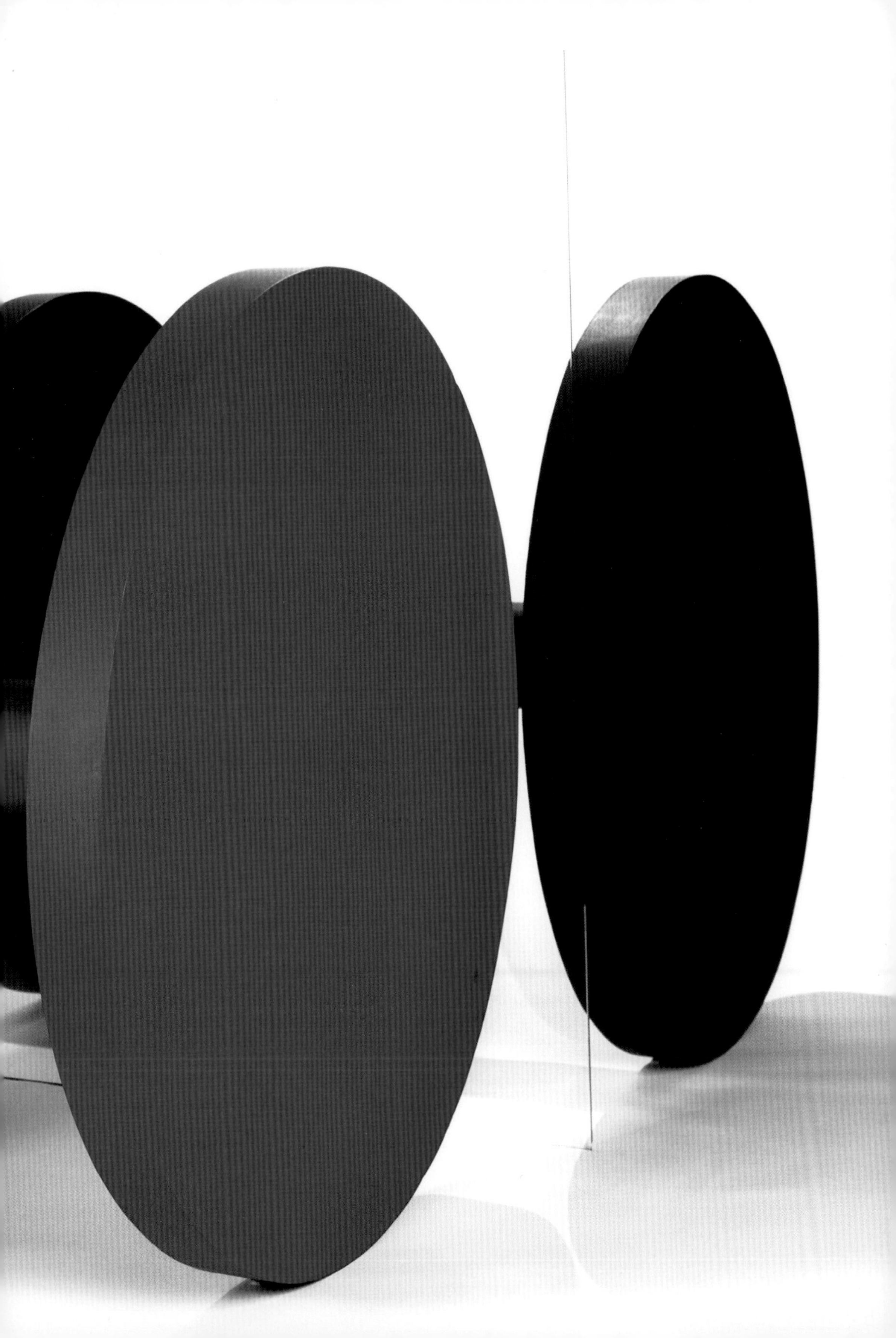

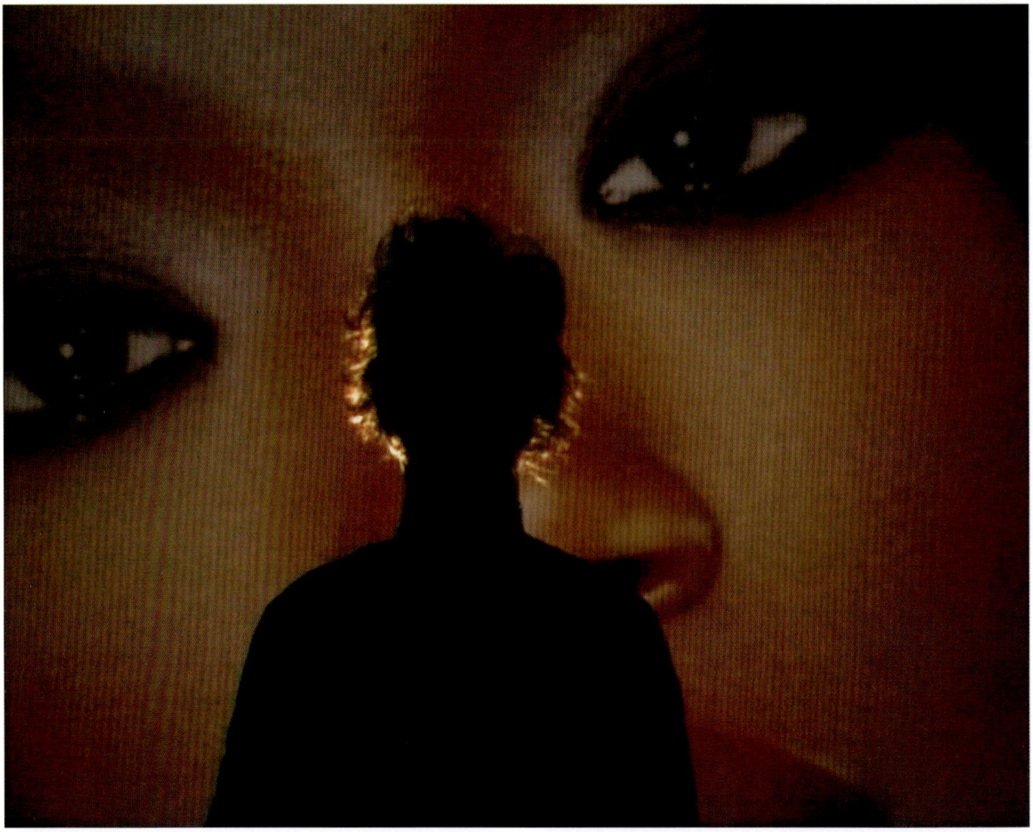

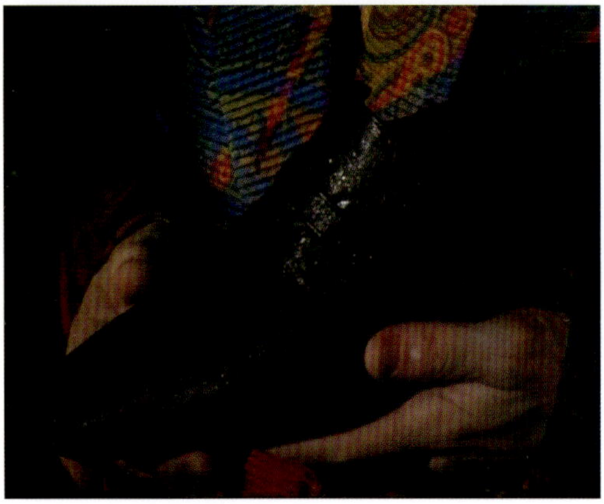

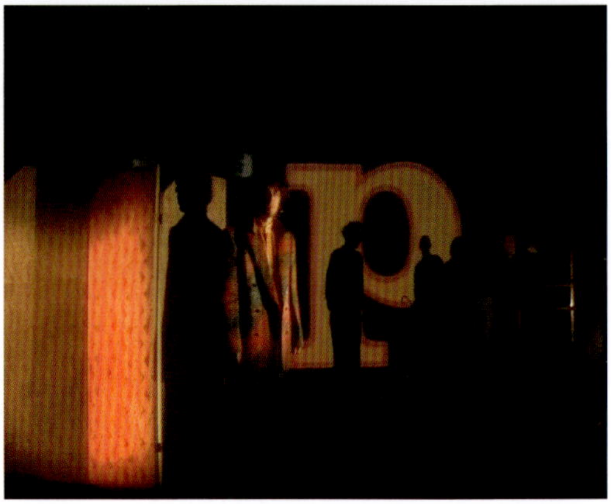

Mark Leckey Parade, 2003

Foreword

by Ralph Rugoff
Director, Hayward Gallery

The Arts Council Collection is one of the UK's foremost national collections of post-war British art. It is also, importantly, the most widely circulated collection of its kind. The idealistic, yet utterly empirical, goal of establishing such a national collection in 1946 was partly to ensure that the visual arts might have a lively presence in all corners of the nation, as well as to support the ongoing production of art as a significant social resource. To borrow the title of this exhibition, the Collection was seen as a vehicle for 'improving the world' by creating a cultural opportunity designed to be available to all in Britain. Celebrating the Collection's success in fulfilling this mission, *How to Improve the World: 60 Years of British Art* presents key works by 131 artists, while reflecting on a period in which British art has arguably exerted an international impact unparalleled in its history.

By its nature, such an exhibition – the broadest display of works from the Collection since an earlier show at the Hayward in 1980 – can represent only a small fraction of what has been purchased and preserved over the years. Managed by the Hayward Gallery on behalf of the Arts Council since 1986, the Collection now boasts over 7,500 works by close to 2,000 artists. Operating as a kind of 'museum without walls', the Collection is manifested publicly in several ways: through loans to museums, galleries and other public buildings throughout Great Britain; in exhibitions and displays focused on single artists or historical movements, organised for touring nationally by the Hayward; and in the ACC *Select* programme, for which curators from museums and galleries, mostly outside London, are invited to conceive and organise exhibitions drawn from the Collection. Over 60 exhibitions in this last category have taken place since the programme was set up in 1997. At any one time, meanwhile, approximately 2,500 works from the collection are circulating to institutions across the country.

One of the distinguishing traits of this particular collection is its highly democratic selection process. Whereas institutional collections are generally put together by small groups of internal curators, the Arts Council Collection has been assembled by a rotating panel, whose members have been drawn from all parts of Great Britain. Over the past decades, the acquisition team has included some of the country's leading artists, writers, critics and independent curators, as well as a changing cast of curators from the Arts Council and the Hayward. Their passion and commitment to the highest critical standards, as well as the diversity of their viewpoints and values, has ensured that the Collection has developed as a truly representative sampling of the best of British art from the past 60 years. Given a limited purchasing budget, these selection panels have also had to make consistently shrewd choices, often buying works by emerging artists. Many of their selections – by once 'emerging' artists such as Francis Bacon, Lucian Freud, Bridget Riley and Anthony Caro – demonstrate a remarkable understanding of the moment in which a purchase was made. This tradition is very much alive today as the Collection continues to have an active relationship with contemporary artists, including the development of new commissions (for instance, the cover of this book, created by Bob & Roberta Smith, and Liam Gillick's project in the Hayward foyer).

To create an exhibition from over 7,500 works spanning 60 years is a daunting task that requires a broad historical purview as well as an acute understanding of the contemporary landscape (not to mention a certain amount of courage). And inevitably such an exhibition requires a longer list of acknowledgements than space allows for here. First of all, of course, we are indebted to all of the artists in this exhibition, and in the entire Collection, for their inspiring work. We are also very grateful to guest curator Michael Archer and Roger Malbert, Senior Curator Hayward Touring Exhibitions, for organising an exhibition that challenges, delights and provokes us. Michael's broad historical knowledge and acute aesthetic and intellectual insights into British art from the past 60 years are apparent in his fresh reading of the Collection, articulated in his thoughtful essay. Roger's perceptive and informative text highlights the Collection's diversity and strengths as well as the controversies that can surround the collecting of contemporary art. Together Michael and Roger have assembled an exhibition that allows us to engage with both the enormous range of post-war art as well as with individual works that carry out 'conversations wholly relevant to the present moment', to borrow a phrase from Michael's essay.

How to Improve the World is the culmination of several exhibitions that have been organised elsewhere in Britain this year. *60*, at Longside Gallery, the Collection's sculpture base in Yorkshire Sculpture Park, presented 60 sculptures and video works by some of the leading figures and rising stars of British art, a number of which have also been included in *How to Improve the World*. *Material World*, another major sculpture show, is currently on display at the Gallery of Modern Art in Glasgow, and features works by Richard Deacon, Shirazeh Houshiary, Tony Cragg and Rachel Whiteread that might otherwise have been included in *How to Improve the World*. Finally, *Revelation*, which highlighted the Collection's ability to acquire work by artists during their emerging years, was presented at the Laing Art Gallery in Newcastle upon Tyne to coincide with the opening of *British Art Show 6* at Baltic, Gateshead, and then toured to the Lowry in Salford and the Graves Art Gallery, Sheffield. Loans to still other exhibitions during this period, including major works by David Hockney and Howard Hodgkin, account for a few significant omissions from *How to Improve the World*.

The idea for this exhibition was initiated by Susan May during her tenure as Head of the Collection, with valuable input from Polly Staple, a member of the current acquisitions Committee. It has since evolved under the guidance of Jill Constantine, Senior Curator and Acting Head of ACC, whose intimate knowledge of the Collection and good judgment have been essential to its success. We would like to thank our colleagues at the Hayward Gallery, the South Bank Centre, Arts Council England and the Arts Council

Collection, in particular, Ann Jones, Helen Luckett, Marianne Mulvey, Natalie Rudd, Charu Vallabhbhai. We are also grateful to the following individuals without whose help the exhibition and this catalogue would not have been possible, Marjorie Allthorpe-Guyton, Lise Connellan, Robin Footitt, Kit Grover, Isobel Johnstone, Henrik Kubel, Shela Sheikh, Bob and Roberta Smith and Scott Williams. Finally we would like to express our gratitude to the consortium of Hayward Gallery Corporate Members who have given their further support to this exhibition.

overleaf **Susan Hiller** Wild Talents, 1997

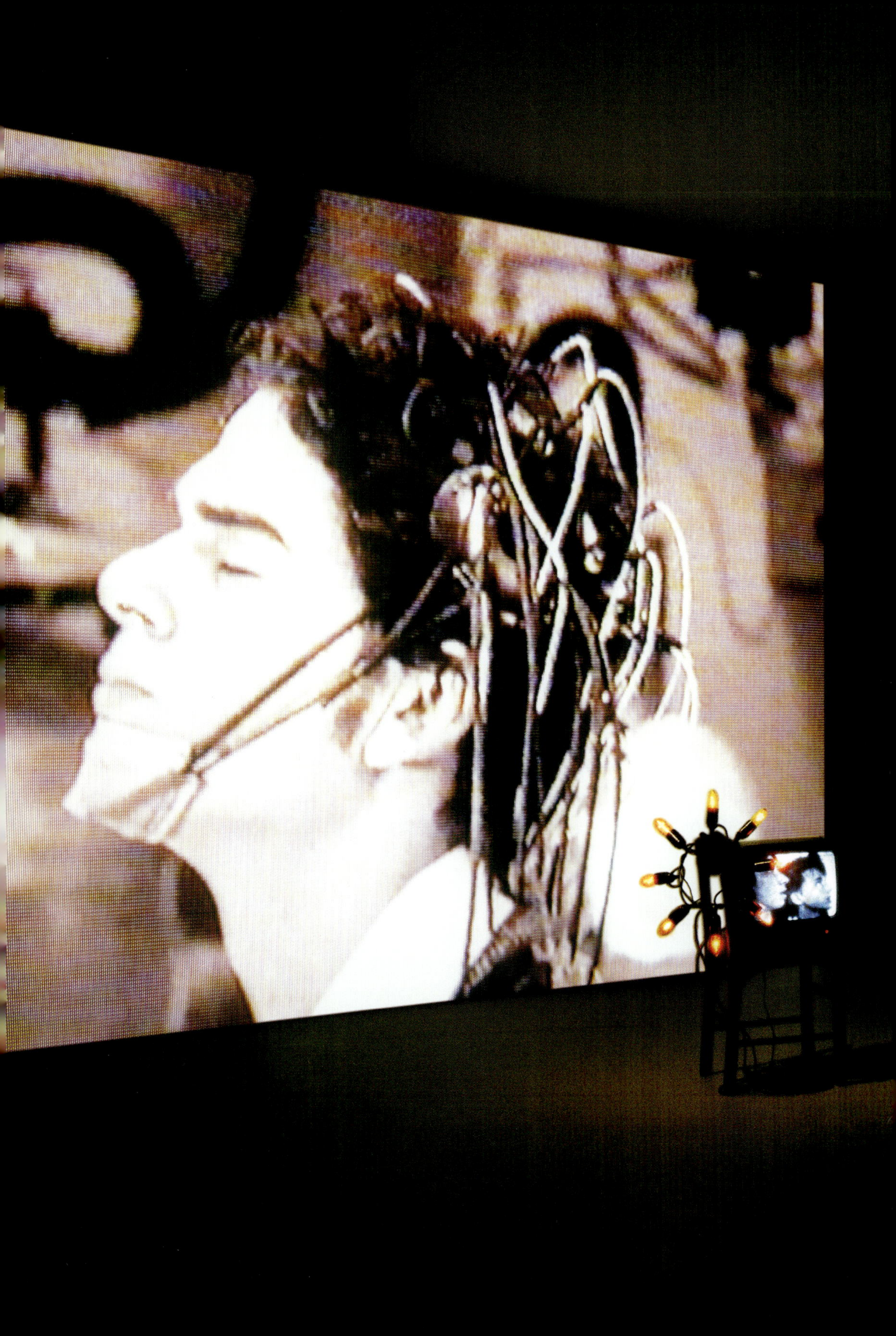

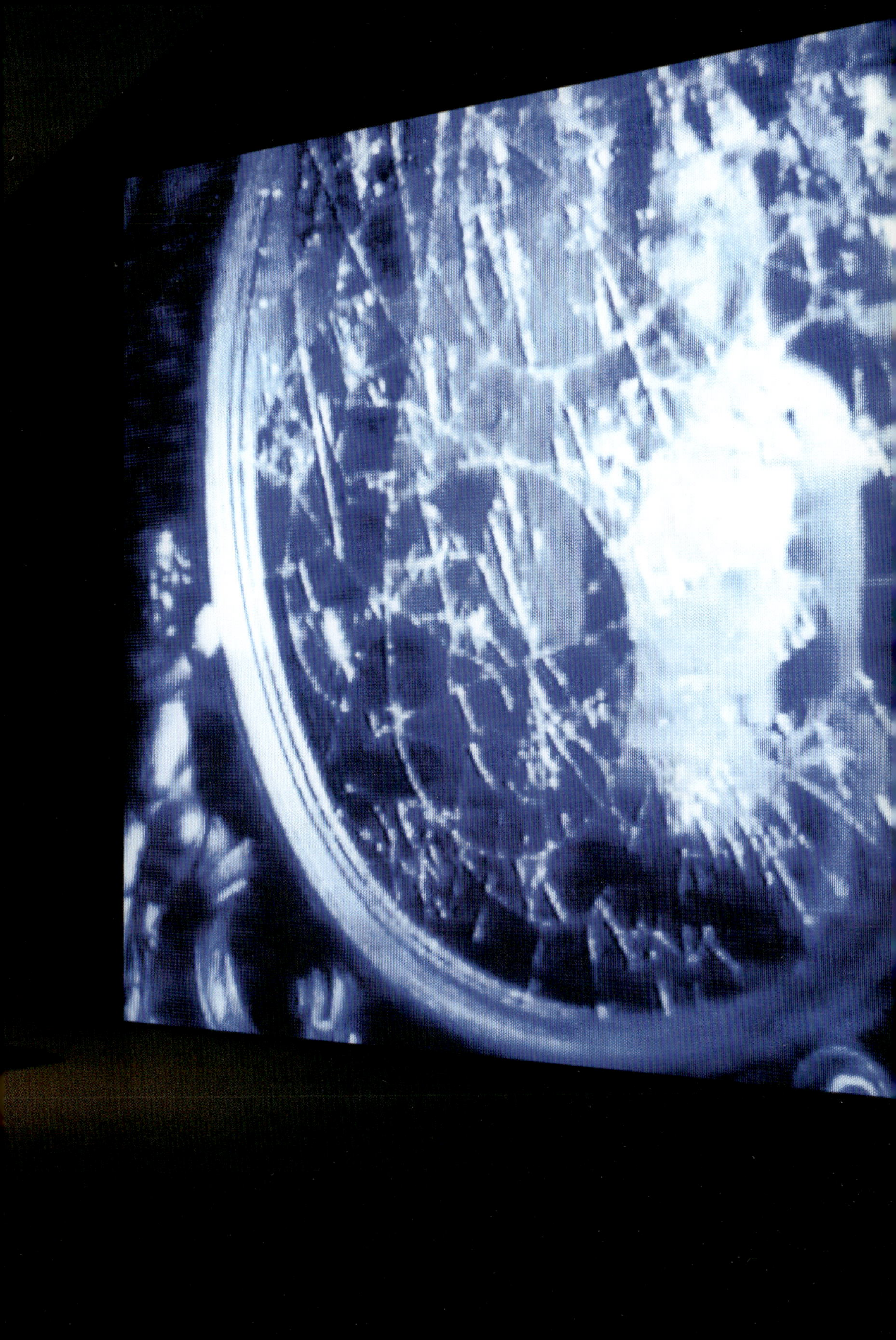

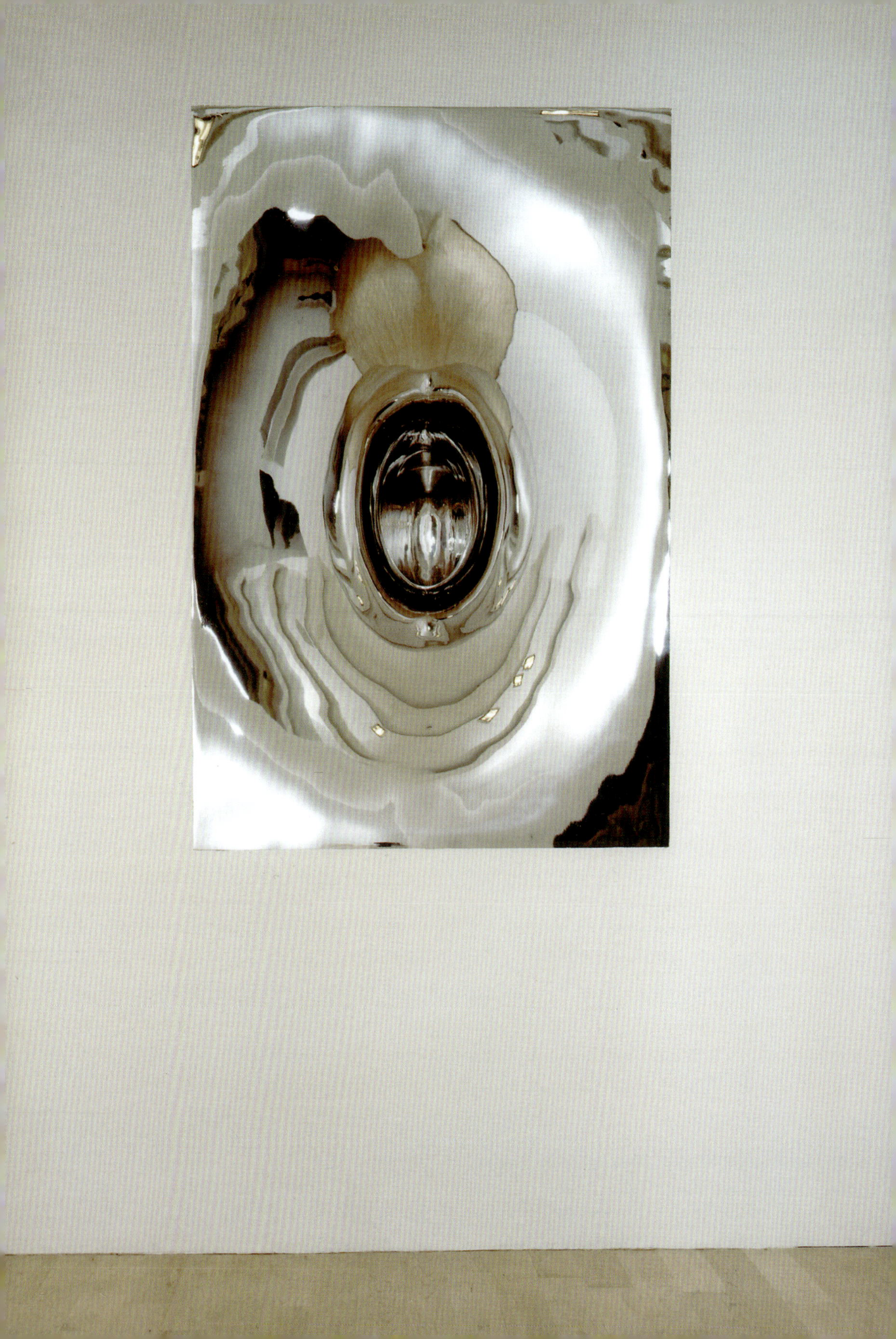

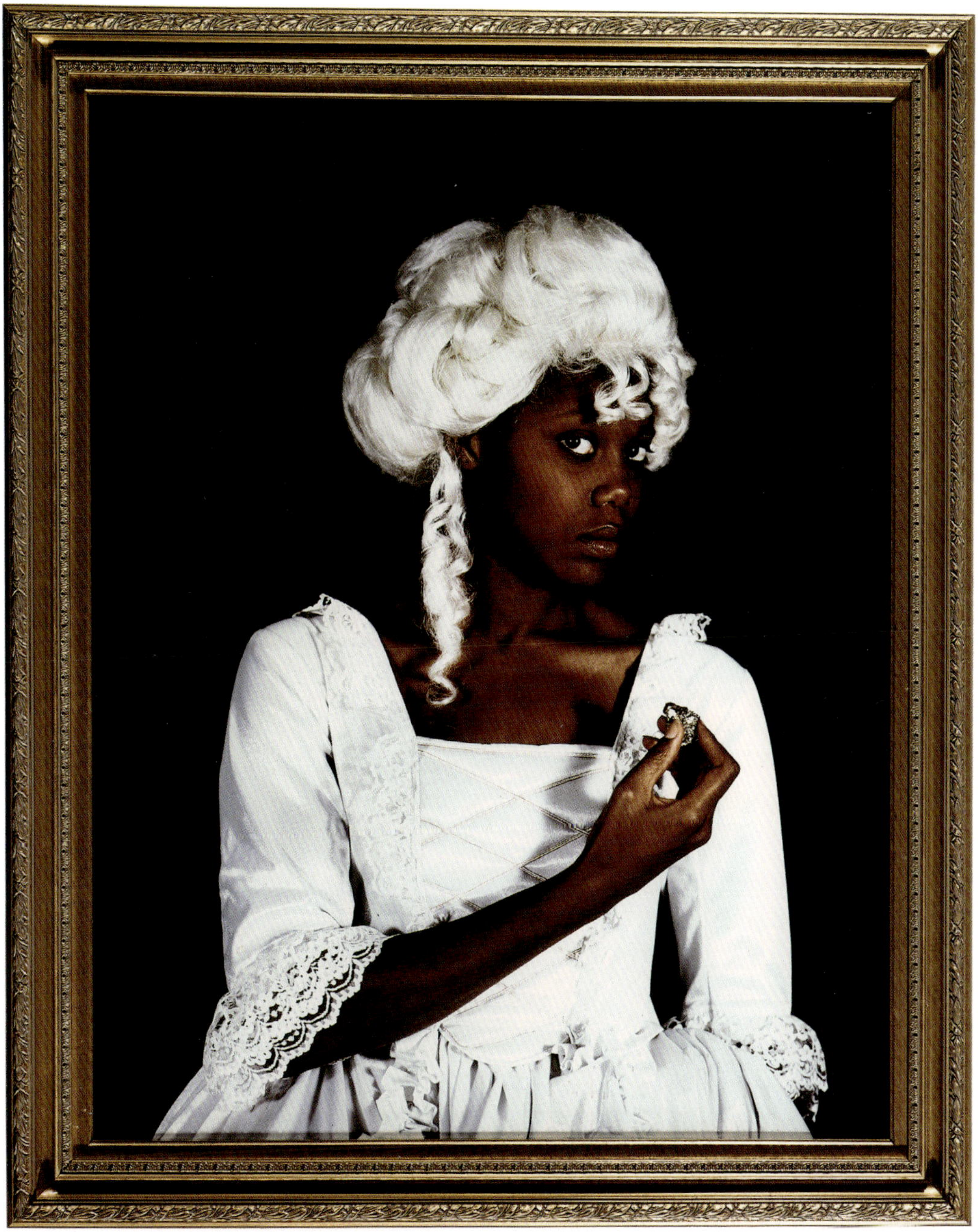

opposite **Anish Kapoor** Untitled, 1995

above **Maud Sulter** Calliope from the series 'Zabat', 1989

A SPECIFICATION FOR AN ART CONDITION:

The information presented in this text specifies those circumstances in which the art condition may be said to be actualised; neither the information expressed in the text, nor the text itself, is to be construed as part of the art condition being actualised.

It will become apparent that this information, both in its present form, that is, expressed in an exhibited text, and in any other form which it could take, creates an obstacle to the actualisation of the art condition.

Let me explain. In the context of this exhibition, or if similarly presented in any other context, this information needs to satisfy a certain requirement such that it can properly be said to be information about the art condition. This is that this information be such as to be conveyable to at least one person; that is, this information must be presentable to a spectator such that he is able to see it, read it, consider it, understand it, or otherwise stand in a cognitive relation to what is expressed in the text. To this end the information is expressed in the form of a written text which exists continuously with, and can be seen, read, etc. at any time throughout, the duration of this exhibition. This is not to preclude other ways of presenting this information; for instance, there could be a tape of the information being read, or a slide projection of this text, or the artist could read out this information, etc.

The obstacle mentioned above concerning the actualisation of the art condition arises just because such a requirement, as stated in the preceding section, needs to be met. For part of this information is the following condition, which must be satisfied for the art condition to be actualised:

THAT NO INFORMATION, IN ANY FORM WHATSOEVER, WHICH SPECIFIES THOSE CIRCUMSTANCES IN WHICH THE ART CONDITION IS ACTUALISED, EXISTS AT THE SAME TIME AS THE ART CONDITION.

Thus, the requirement which needs to be satisfied for the art condition to be actualised is that there exists in no form any information which specifies those circumstances in which the art condition may be said to be actualised. In short, the existence of information about the art condition is incompatible with the art condition being actualised.

To secure the satisfaction of this requirement, two further conditions need to be met:

WHEN THIS INFORMATION IS SEEN, READ, CONSIDERED, UNDERSTOOD, OR OTHERWISE MENTALLY ACKNOWLEDGED BY THE PRESENT READER, THE ART CONDITION CANNOT TAKE PLACE.

ANY RECOLLECTION, OR ANY RETRIEVAL IN ANY FORM, BY A PAST READER OF THIS INFORMATION, IS INCOMPATIBLE WITH THE ACTUALISATION OF THE ART CONDITION.

From the above we can derive the following conclusion:
The art condition may be said to be actualised if and only if

a) NO PERSON IS PRESENTLY EITHER SEEING, READING, UNDERSTANDING, OR OTHERWISE STANDING IN A COGNITIVE RELATION TO THIS INFORMATION.
b) NO PERSON IS PRESENTLY EITHER REMEMBERING, RECALLING OR OTHERWISE RETROSPECTIVELY CONTEMPLATING THIS INFORMATION.
c) THIS INFORMATION, EITHER IN ITS PRESENT FORM OR IN ANY OTHER FORM POSSIBLE, DOES NOT EXIST.

KEITH ARNATT, 1970

Keith Arnatt Is it Possible for me to do Nothing as my Contribution to this Exhibition?, 1970

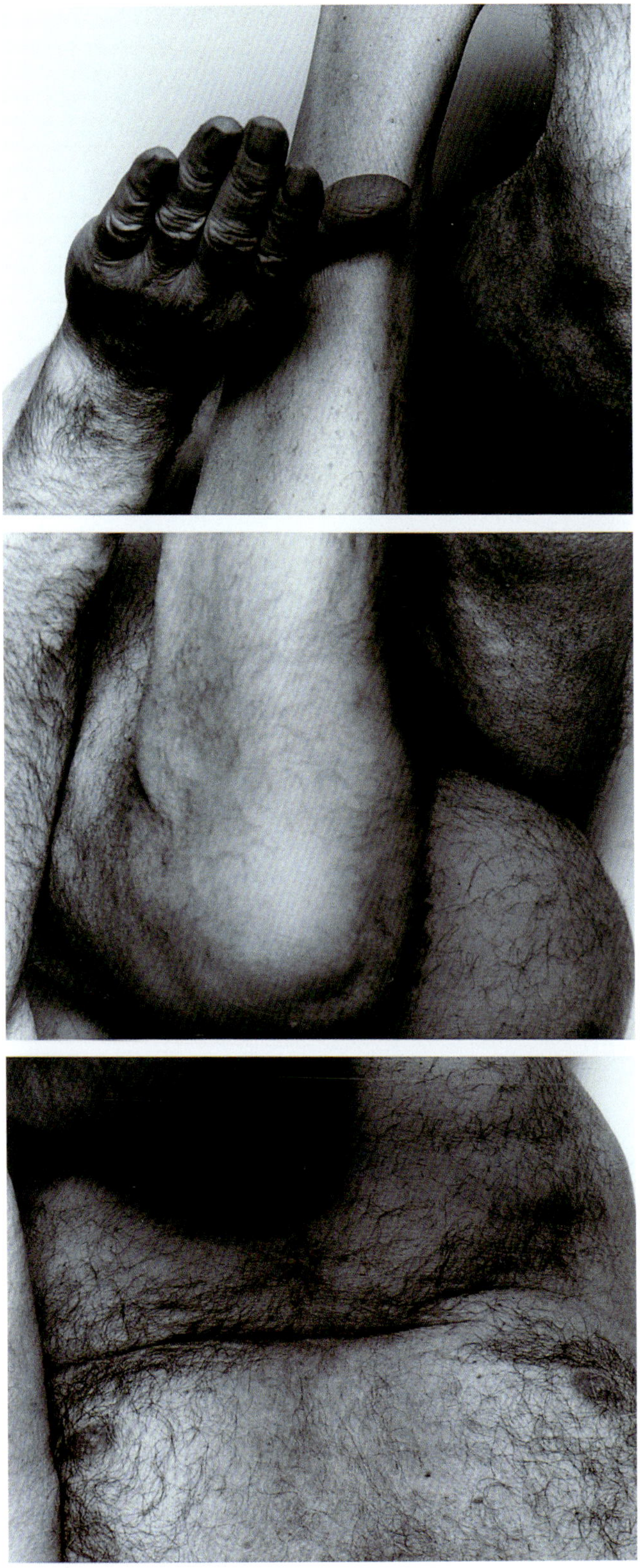

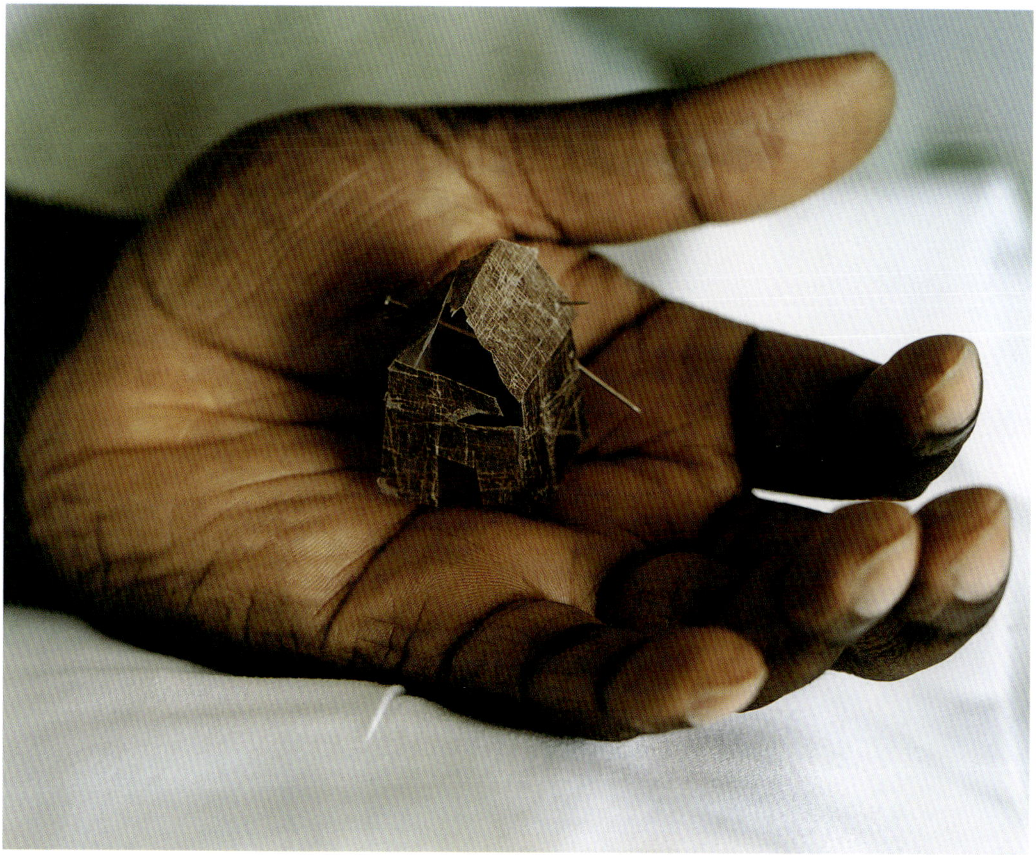

opposite **John Coplans** Self Portrait (Upside Down No.1), 1992
above **Donald Rodney** In the House of My Father, 1997

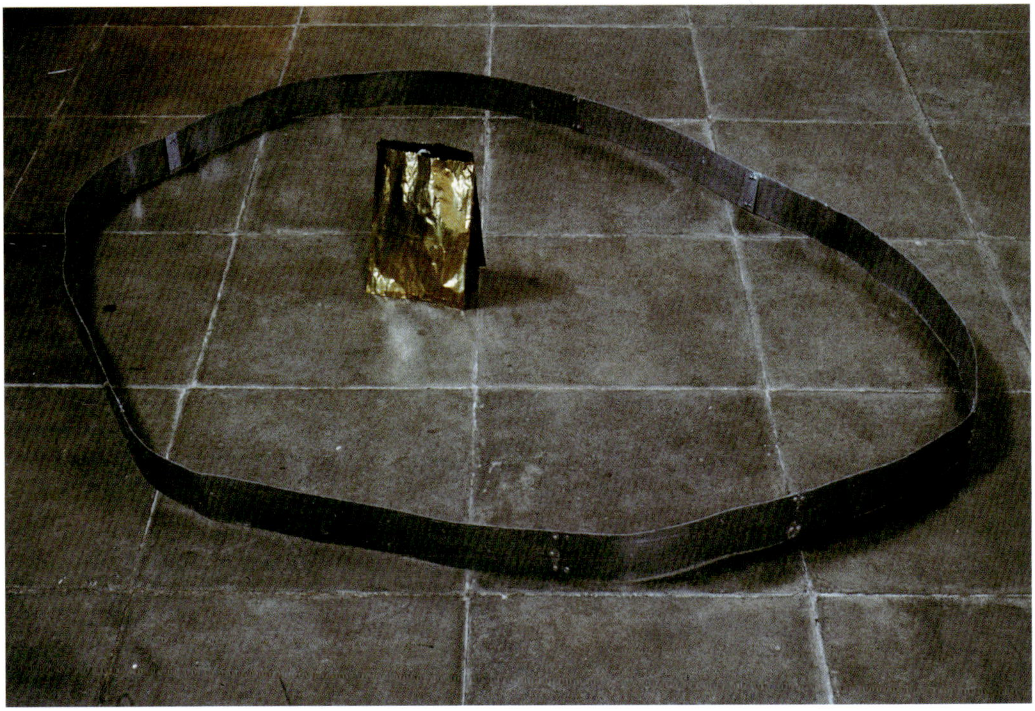

Alison Wilding Untitled, 1980

Overlapping Figures

by Michael Archer

How to improve the world? You may think the ironic overtone inescapable, but it is none the less a question that fits the Arts Council. Established 60 years ago, the Arts Council has made it its business never to rest content with the long-trusted and already-accepted, but rather to encourage experimentation and exploration, and to support the emergent in art. Allied to this has been a policy of making as much art as possible available to all parts of Britain. The Arts Council Collection, founded in that same year, 1946, bears witness to these aims. It is now the country's great 'museum without walls', lending works to innumerable exhibitions, siting others on long-term loan in public institutions, and initiating through Hayward Gallery Touring Exhibitions many shows of its own.

There have been many exhibitions featuring aspects of the Arts Council Collection since its inception. For the most part these have tended either to concentrate on works purchased within a short period, sometimes just the previous year or two, or featured works grouped around a specific theme. On several occasions up until the late 1970s, in fact, works were purchased specifically for the latter purpose by the curator concerned. The only other full-scale show containing a range of works in all media purchased across the whole period of the Collection's existence took place over a quarter of a century ago in 1980. It was staged at the Hayward Gallery, which at that time was directly under the control of the Arts Council's Visual Arts Department as well as being the administrative and physical base for the Collection. Although the Hayward is now part of the South Bank Centre, it continues to be integral to the Collection's life as the distribution point for the many Hayward Gallery Touring Exhibitions that draw upon its holdings, and the *Spotlight* shows, each of which focuses on an individual artist in the Collection. It is therefore fitting that this exhibition, *How to Improve the World: British Art, 60 Years of British Art*, should also fill the Hayward.

Looking through many articles, biographies and catalogue entries in preparation for the show, one small piece of information snags my attention. In one respect it is unremarkable, merely a statement about the fact that an artist went to art school – which, give or take a very small percentage, they all did. Yet viewed from another perspective it reveals a connection whose character lends a defining quality to the cultural space within which *How to Improve the World* is able to take place. That space is a complex one, formed as much by international as by domestic social, political and economic forces. It is dynamic, constantly in flux, and it is energised by an artistic community whose members are not merely dispassionate observers of those events and changing circumstances, but active participants in them. The snippet of information that detains me is that Gustav Metzger went to the Borough Polytechnic, where he was taught by David Bomberg. Both Berlin-born Frank Auerbach and Leon Kossoff, London-born of Russian parents, also attended Bomberg's drawing classes. Together with Lucian Freud, also born in Berlin,

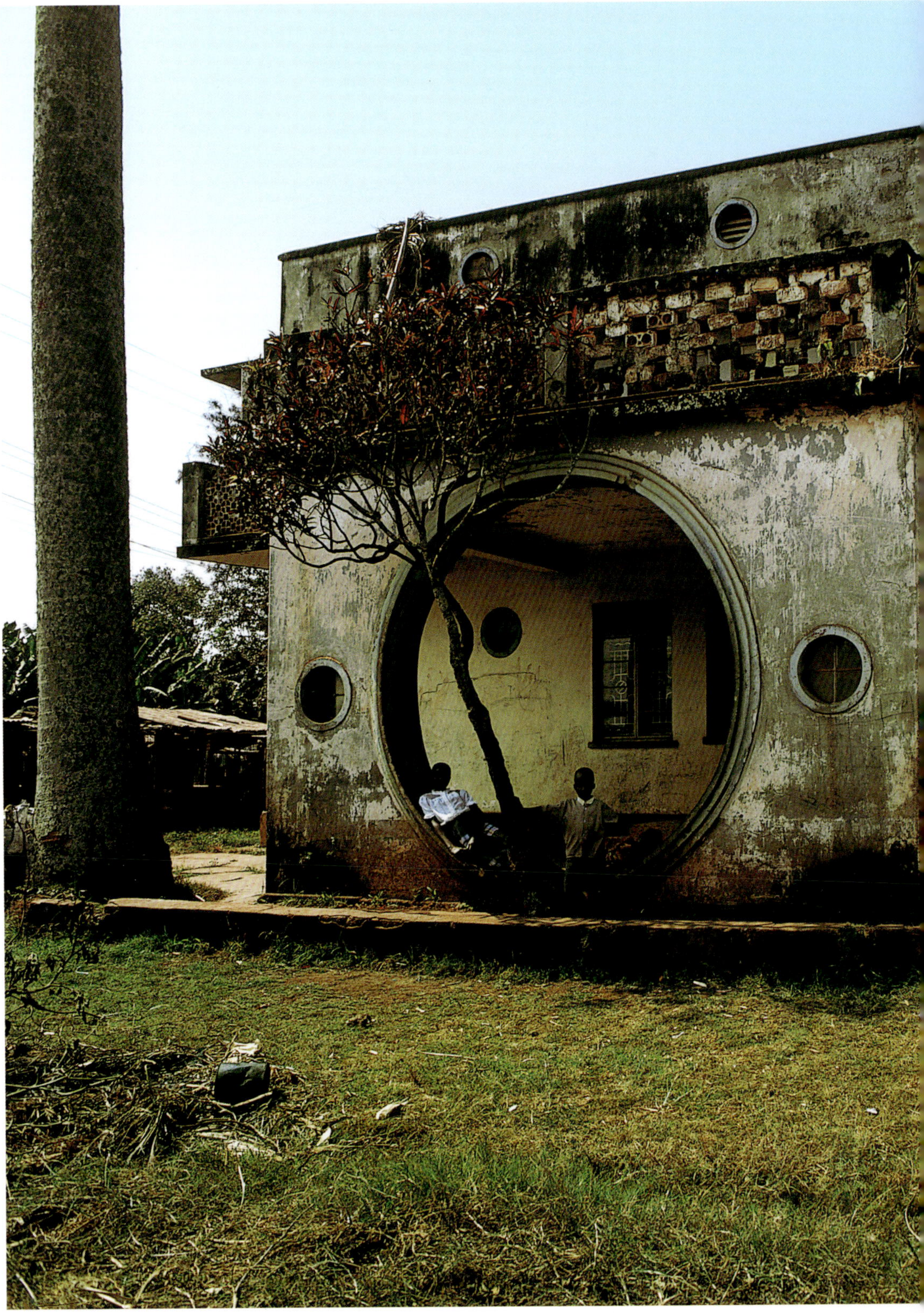

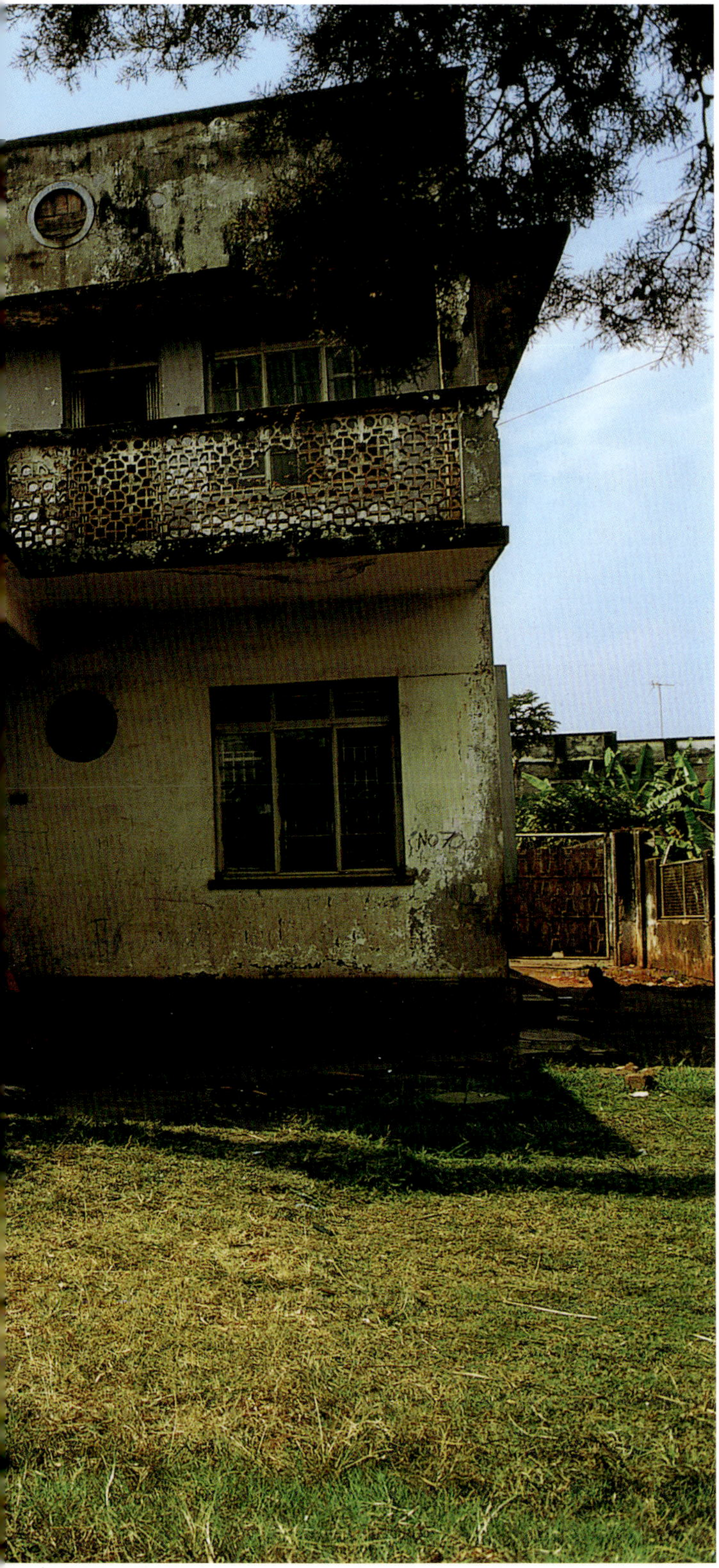

Zarina Bhimji

Here was Uganda, as if in the vastness of India, 1999–2000

and Dubliner Francis Bacon, these artists have made major, sustained contributions to the art of painting in this country over the past half century.

The situation regarding the diverse backgrounds of the artists being brought into the Collection is, if anything, even more varied today than it was when it began in the middle of the last century. For example, the 2005–2006 *British Art Show 6*, a Hayward Gallery Touring Exhibition, includes works by more than 50 contemporary artists living and working in Britain, of which half were born elsewhere. Of these, the Arts Council has acquired works by artists born in Brazil, Canada, China, Croatia, France, Germany, Poland, Turkey and USA.[1] *How to Improve the World* provides an accurate reflection of this state of affairs, with more recent purchases in the exhibition including works by Zarina Bhimji (Uganda), Mona Hatoum (Lebanon), Susan Hiller (USA), Anish Kapoor (India), Camilla Løw (Norway), Mariele Neudecker (Germany), Lucia Nogueira (Brazil) and Eva Rothschild (Ireland).

In the early 1950s Metzger was part of the Borough Bottega, the successor to the Borough Group of artists of 1947–1949 that had formed around Bomberg. At that time Metzger was still a painter, but before the end of the decade he was to publish his first manifesto of Auto-Destructive art. Two years later, in July 1961, Metzger gave a demonstration of Auto-Destructive art on the South Bank. For this, he sprayed hydrochloric acid on to a black, a white and a red nylon sheet stretched on a metal frame, causing them to dissolve within the space of 20 minutes. A poster handed out at the event carried among other material a reprint of that first manifesto, which begins: 'Auto-destructive art is primarily a form of public art for industrial societies'. Both Bomberg and Metzger are represented in the Arts Council Collection, itself, perhaps, a substantial instance of public art for an industrial society. Work by Bomberg was acquired in 1947, early in the Collection's life though late in the career of an artist who had started, before experiencing the horrors of the First World War, by championing the glories of the machine. That painting,

1. *British Art Show 6* is the most recent in a series, which began in 1979, of touring survey exhibitions devoted to contemporary art in Britain. With few exceptions, the shows have been staged at venues outside London. Organised by Hayward Gallery Touring Exhibitions, the 2005–06 show opened at Baltic, Gateshead, and travelled to Manchester, Nottingham and Bristol. The Arts Council Collection has made many purchases from these exhibitions over the years. *British Art Show 6* is no exception in this respect.

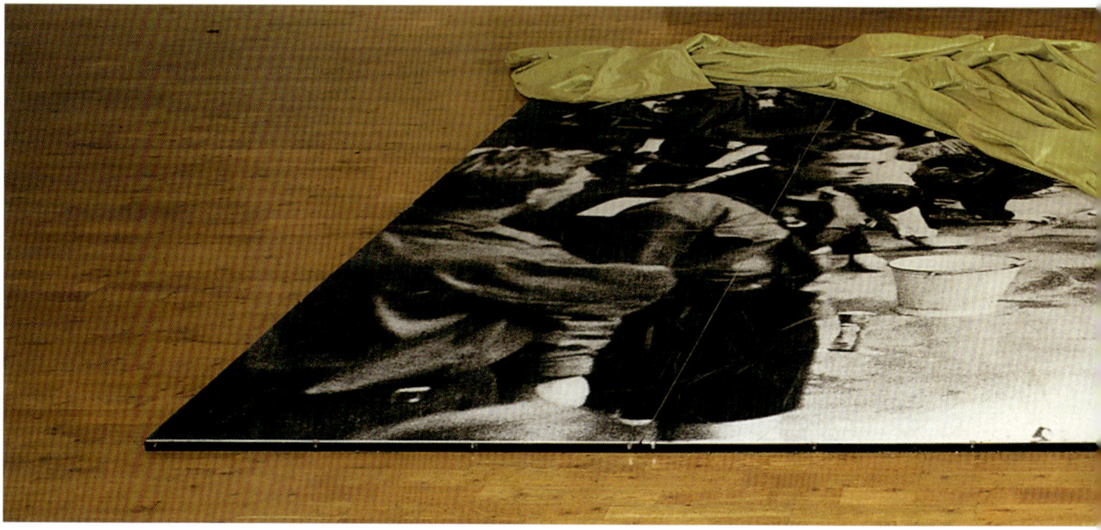

Trendrine, Cornwall, is in fact the earliest work in this exhibition. Despite his seniority and a career spanning the intervening half century and more, it would be another 50 years before Metzger's *Historic Photographs: To Crawl Into – Anschluss, Vienna, March 1938* was purchased for this same Collection.

Bomberg, though himself born in Birmingham at the end of the nineteenth century, was the son of Polish immigrant parents, and Metzger, born in Nuremberg, came to Britain shortly before the Second World War. A report on the 'Destruction in Art Symposium' held in London in 1966 and organised by Metzger appeared in *Studio International* in December of that year. In it, among the biographical details provided on the participants, Metzger describes himself as 'Stateless'.[2] Nowadays Metzger shows regularly and widely, and his reputation among and influence on students and young artists grows steadily. In this one biographical detail then, lies a connection that allows us to arc across the whole of the last century and into this one, to acknowledge the ambivalent relationship that modern art has maintained with technological advance, and to witness the profound impact of the major military conflicts and art's struggle to come to terms with their consequences. Through it we grasp the Collection's potential to help us engage with that history. It also demonstrates with clarity that to speak of a national collection is to deal with something porous, something open and endlessly receptive towards what lies beyond it.

2. 'Excerpts from selected papers presented at the 1966 Destruction in Art Symposium', *Studio International*, December 1966, p. 282.

The title of this exhibition is derived from the 2003 work by Cerith Wyn Evans (who in turn borrowed it from John Cage: *'Diary: How to Improve the World (You Will Only Make Matters Worse) Continued 1968 (Revised)' from 'M' Writings '67–'72 by John Cage*). I should declare an interest and state that I was on the purchasing panel that acquired the work for the Collection, and was as enthusiastic as my fellow members about seizing the opportunity to buy it. In an interview that same year, Wyn Evans speaks of how important Cage has been to him as someone to whose practice the notion of polyphony

Gustav Metzger
Historic Photographs: To Crawl Into – Anschluss, Vienna, March 1938, 1996–1998

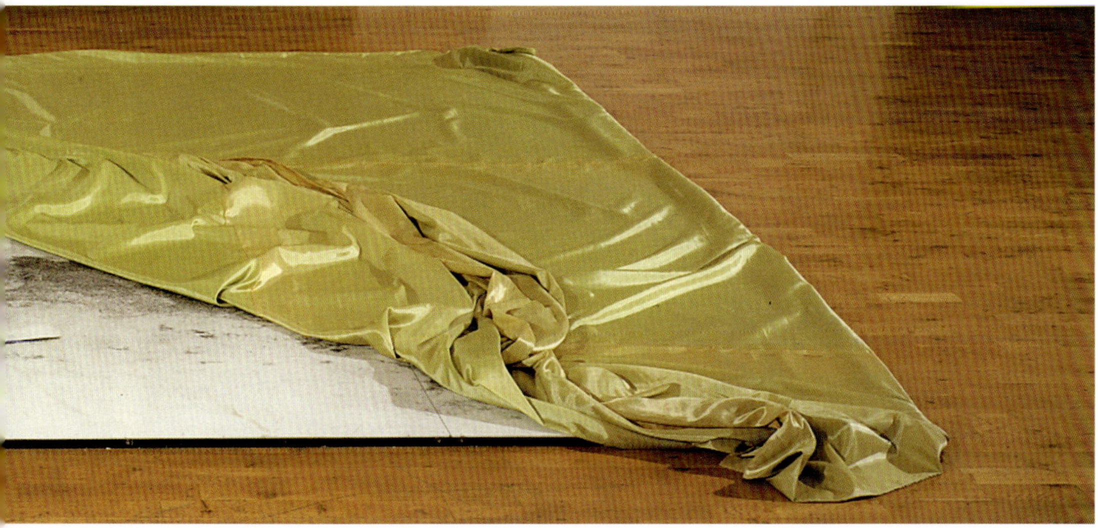

has been of central significance. Having already snaffled Wyn Evans' title, I feel compelled to prevail on him further and to emphasise that polyphony is also of great relevance to an exhibition such as this present one. Making an exhibition by drawing on a collection that, though of substantial size, does not have a permanent display venue of its own is a delight. There is no pre-existent identity to which one needs to pay due deference. This is the Collection's great strength – that it is not one thing, but is, rather, open to countless selections, framings, explorations and revisitings. It contains many potential points of focus, and allows for the deep look as much as the broad overview.

Cerith Wyn Evans
'Diary: How to improve the world (you will only make matters worse) continued 1968 (revised)' from 'M' writings '67–'72 by John Cage, 2003

The temptation might be to see the Collection as an oversize bag of sweets out of which one could feel free to pick a few favourite flavours. It is, though, nothing of the sort. It is an entity that invites more thoughtful engagement, an engagement that continually raises the question as to what selections are being made, with what aim, and under what circumstances. One such circumstance is practical and inescapable: you are never alone. Which is to say that the Collection, because it is a public resource predicated on the availability of its holdings, is always at work. Chances are that some of the pieces you want are already on loan to exhibitions elsewhere, or are the subject of long-term promises and agreements, so some compromise is always necessary. This, you understand, is a good thing. None the less, the primary circumstance of this exhibition, to mark 60 years of the Council's and the Collection's existence by celebrating the remarkable richness of their inventory, has allowed us great scope in its preparation. One motif in our conversations over the months as Roger Malbert and I looked again and again at the works in the Collection could be indicated by pointing to the title of the 2003 show in which Wyn Evans' piece was first shown:

– Look at that picture . . .
– How does it appear to you now?
– Does it seem to be
Persisting?

Our desire was to make the show in such a way that each work could be seen not just for the place it holds in some putative history of British art, nor simply for the model it might offer of the way things used to be made. Above and beyond these aspects, the works would most significantly be participants in a series of conversations wholly relevant to the present moment. We are after the same jolt of intense engagement as that alluded to by Barry Schwabsky when, in the course of reviewing a recent study of Henry Moore and Barbara Hepworth, he referred to the excitement of a desire 'to look again, more closely and with an impassioned rather than a merely cultured eye' at the work.[3]

For instance, the debate about abstraction among the St Ives artists in the 1950s might not grip us with quite the same vigour today. Roger Hilton's interest in Mondrian and his friendship with the Dutch Cobra artist Constant, William Scott and Patrick Heron's wrestling with the example of Braque and Matisse, Terry Frost's radical simplification of the hull shapes of the local

3. Barry Schwabsky, 'Mum's the Word', a review of *Mother Stone: The Vitality of Modern British Sculpture* by Anne Middleton Wagner, *Bookforum*, April/May 2006, p. 35.

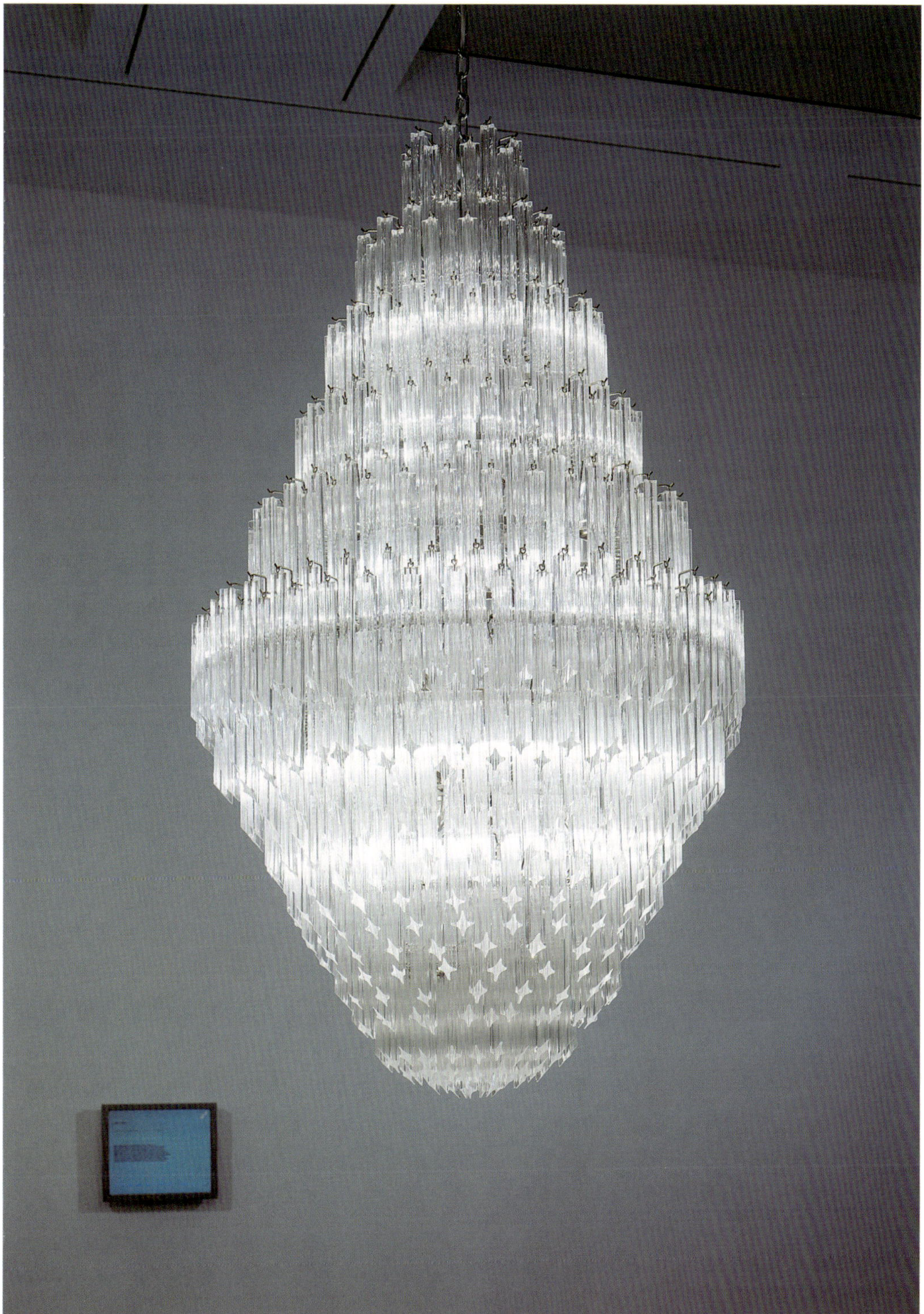

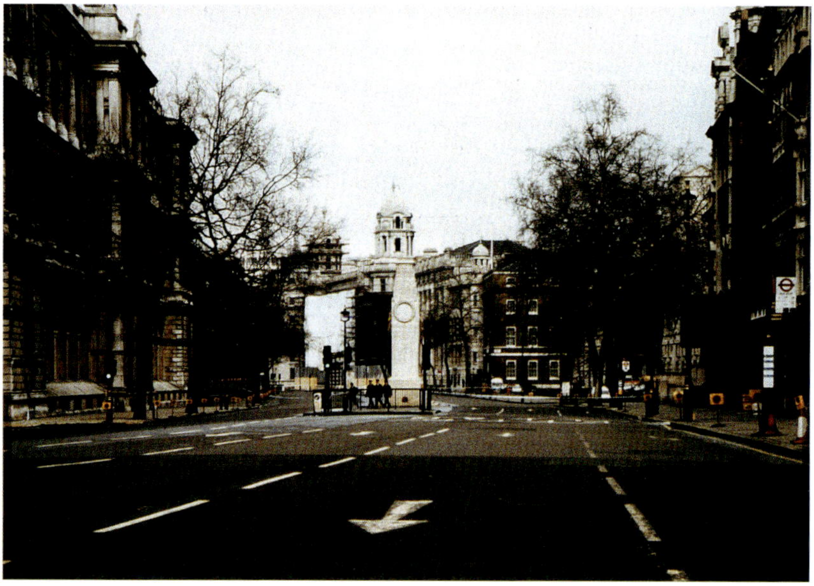

Henry Bond and Liam Gillick
11th February 1992; Evacuation and closure of Whitehall and surrounding area due to discovery of a suspected device. Trafalgar Square, 1992

fishing boats into the crescent form that would preoccupy him throughout the rest of his career – these realities remain, but the strength of works by those artists would be just as likely today to prompt reflection on the inexorable shift of art's prevailing sensibilities into the heart of the metropolis and away from any substantive grounding in rural experience. This theme might be echoed by Tony Cragg's urbanised reworking of Richard Long, and at the same time skewed provocatively back on itself by Ingrid Pollard asking us just why it seems so unusual to encounter a black face in the countryside. And at the other end of the time scale, Henry Bond and Liam Gillick's 'news report' of the closing of Whitehall due to a bomb scare, Christine Borland's pistol in a shopping bag and Gregory Green's pipe bomb all relate to a feature of the world that is current and immediate. Yet, how swiftly the parties concerned change, how rapidly ideologies are superseded, technologies of plan, attack and defence updated. These recent works are salutary precisely because they resonate with conflicts that, if not resolved, at least no longer dominate the headlines.

Though consistently supported throughout its existence by the Arts Council, the funds at the purchasing panel's disposal have never been more than modest. What has been brought together is in large part, though by no means exclusively, work from early in artists' careers. In some instances, those artists have gone on to great success, in which case the Collection owns either a fine example from a person's early period, or a piece that just pre-dates their first substantial mature production. In other instances, the artist's practice has not developed as imagined and the work essentially contributes to a picture of the moment of its purchase. It has never been policy to 'fill gaps' in the Collection, the long-held aim being, rather, to respond to activity in the present. While those looking for a collection that provides a comprehensive overview of UK art since the Second World War might therefore be disappointed, what they will take pleasure in finding is a large group of works that charts the many shifts in social and cultural preoccupation, and the related changes in aesthetic fashion that have occurred since 1946. The Collection, in fact, gives an insight into art in Britain that, in its persistence of vision, attentiveness to developments, and responsiveness to aesthetic debate, is without parallel.

The Arts Council Collection now includes over 7,500 works in a profusion of styles and a wide range of media. Looking at the variety of work contained within the Collection it is evident that those involved in choosing it have maintained a refreshing dislike for privileging certain approaches to art-making above others, including as it does painting, sculpture, performance, video, film, sound, photography, digital media. How, anyway, might rules be drawn up to restrict this range, especially when the Arts Council has itself offered support for the realisation of work across the entire spectrum? What would it mean to stipulate what techniques and media might or might not be legitimate when a decision that, say, performance was uncollectable would signal a narrowing of attention within the range of art-making activity? How much more productive that one address the question of how such work might best be represented and, should it turn out to be resistant to incorporation, examine what the existence of this kind of art might mean for the whole notion of collecting? And nowadays there is the issue of art making use of the internet, as well as more prosaic factors regarding digital and other electronic technology. The means of production, projection and display of works are constantly being upgraded and rendered obsolete. In some cases this fact itself forms part of a work's subject matter – Cerith Wyn Evans, for example, has a chandelier pulsing on and off in a Morse code rendition of Cage's text as it appears on a linked computer screen. Carey Young alludes to the economically aggressive, me-decade of the 1980s in *Lines Made by Walking (after Richard Long)*, a carousel slide sequence of her walking to and fro among the City workers crossing London Bridge. In others, the availability of 'improved' equipment highlights the need to pay due attention to the specifics of what is on offer. If Steve McQueen chooses a certain projection system in part because it is the best available at the time of making a work, what results is a work whose grain is unmistakable. It cannot then be unreasonable to consider whether to show one of his films using different equipment would be to show a different work.

If the Collection has an identity, then, it is one that can only be discerned in and through its variety. And the manner in which its holdings have been assembled has only acted to compound this character. At its inception in 1946 the Collection took over the small group of works already gathered by CEMA (Council for the Encouragement of Music and the Arts), the Arts Council's predecessor, and has continually increased its holdings since then. In the early years, purchases were made according to advice from individuals, or specifically in relation to an exhibition being mounted under the auspices of the Arts Council. Only later was purchasing activity organised under the guidance of a regularly changing panel of Arts Council, Hayward Gallery and external purchasers chaired by the Collection's then curator, Isobel Johnstone.

A panel whose frequently changing personnel are charged with the task

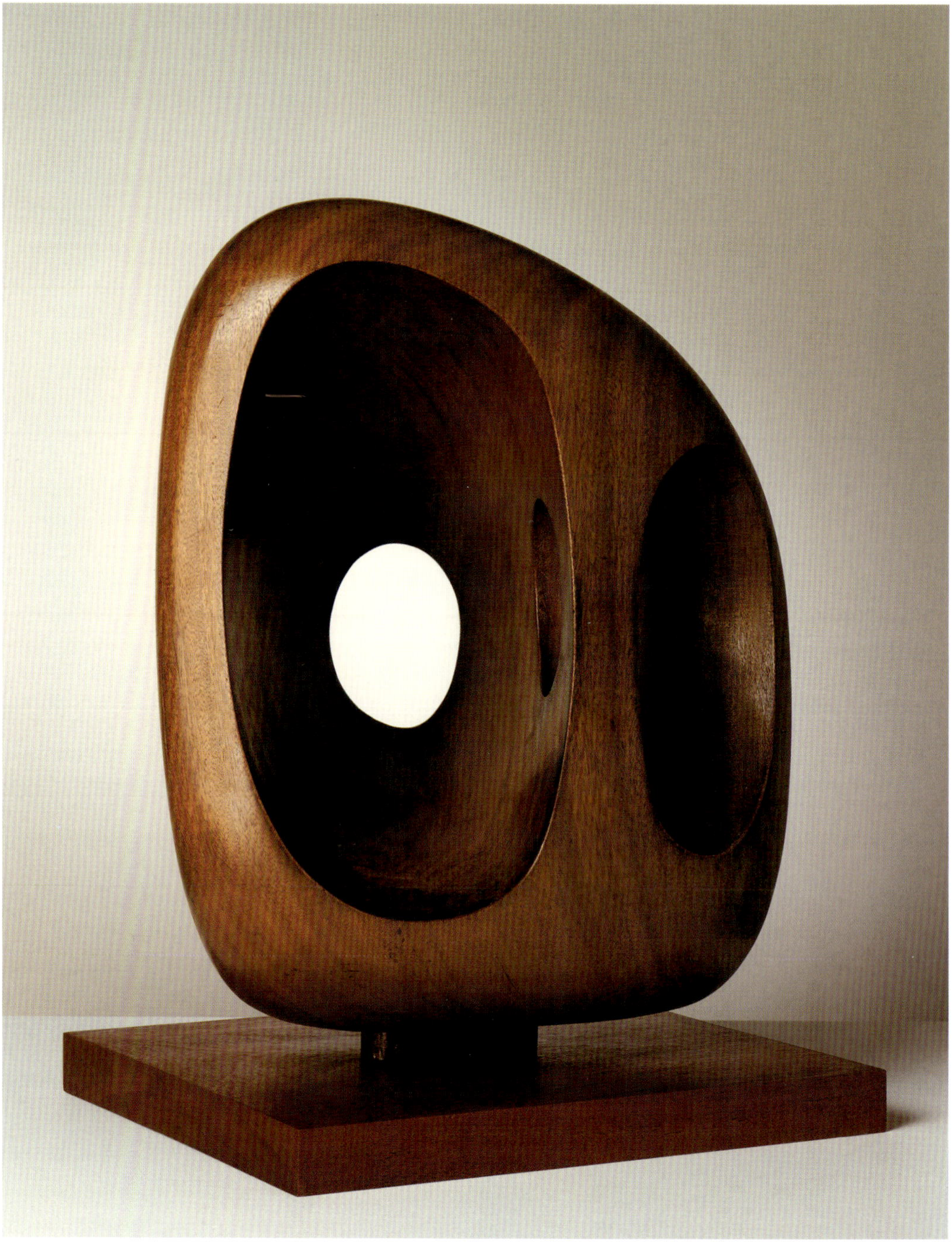

above **Barbara Hepworth** Icon, 1957
opposite **Martin Boyce** Dark Unit and Mask, 2003

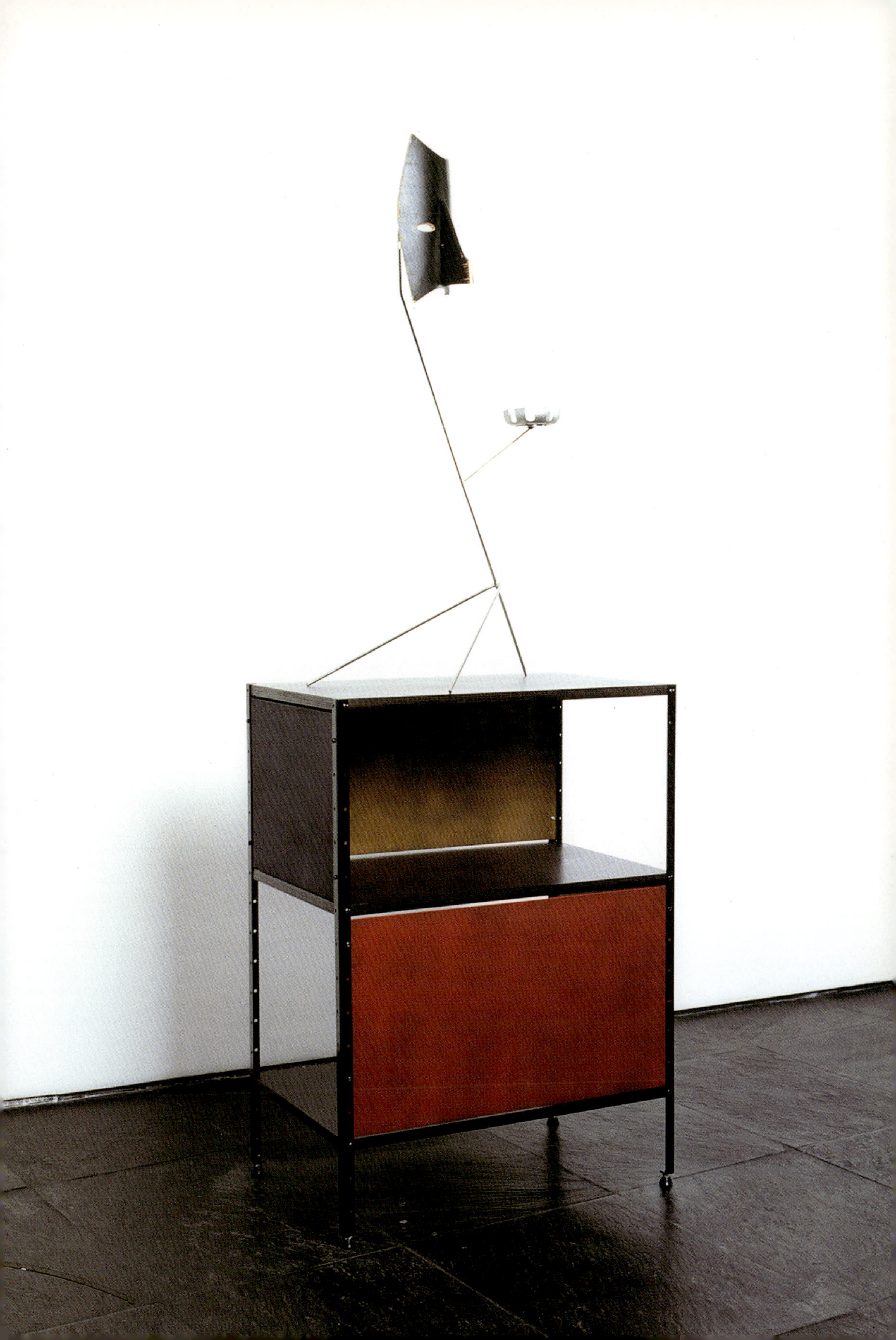

of following their own convictions in seeking out new work of worth and significance must of necessity make purchases that speak to differing sensibilities. Because that panel is explicitly concerned with the activity of the moment, and not with completing a picture or finding appropriate illustrations with which to tell a predetermined story, its role should therefore be understood to be essentially critical rather than art historical. The Collection does not occupy a position – elevated or otherwise – outside of all arguments about what is being made, what is shown and how, what is lionised or decried, what is valued and why. It is, on the contrary, party to all those areas of contention.

We can see this if we begin by proposing a familiar, perhaps expected account of successive phases in British art over the six decades that the Collection currently covers. At the beginning we would place Henry Moore's sculpture, aware as it is of European modernism while being at the same time redolent of the public spirit one also sees embodied in the Arts Council itself. In the first years after the war the focus would be on Ben Nicholson, Barbara Hepworth and the many more based in St Ives. Early in the 1950s are the efforts to reconnect with the European sculptural tradition we see in the work of Reg Butler, Lynn Chadwick, Kenneth Armitage and others so famously dubbed by Herbert Read the 'geometry of fear'.[4] But already by this time Eduardo Paolozzi, Richard Hamilton and Nigel Henderson were turning their attention towards the United States and embarking on the activities that would become known as Pop. The impact of American art from the latter half of the 1950s onwards could be seen in the work of painters and sculptors associated with the Whitechapel Gallery's *New Generation* exhibitions – painters John Hoyland, Bridget Riley, David Hockney and Paul Huxley in 1964, and sculptors Tim Scott, William Tucker and Anthony Caro the year after. Subsequent developments 'beyond painting and sculpture' in the later 1960s and early 1970s are evident in the work of those who contributed to the 1972 Hayward exhibition *The New Art*, such as Art & Language, Gilbert & George, Barry Flanagan and Richard Long. Victor Burgin would show the concern with art for society at a time in the late 1970s when, for instance, the Serpentine Gallery organised a show that asked the question, 'Art for Whom?' The New Sculpture, then incubating at the Royal College and quickly celebrated as part of the 'quiet revolution', Britain's contribution to the experimentalism of post-1960s art, encompassed Richard Deacon, Tony Cragg, Anish Kapoor, Alison Wilding, Bill Woodrow and Richard Wentworth.[5] Then later still there is the generation of Damien Hirst, Sarah Lucas, Angela Bulloch, Henry Bond and Liam Gillick, the earliest of the yBas (young British artists). And the very recent additions to the Collection, such as works by Cathy Wilkes, Eva Rothschild, Mark Titchner, Enrico David, Gillian Carnegie and others, would show us that that phenomenon is already a decade and more old.

All of this newness, all of this youth, as *How to Improve the World* shows, is discernible within the totality of the Collection. But it is by no means the whole story. We have to keep in mind that it is a narrative that must remain endlessly open to question and contestation. What the Collection has to deal with, above all, is the extent to which its decisions are symptomatic of, and

4. The art critic and historian Sir Herbert Read used the phrase 'geometry of fear' in a review of the British Pavilion at the 1952 Venice Biennale. The exhibition of sculpture that year included work by Armitage, Butler, Chadwick and Paolozzi, among others.

5. *A Quiet Revolution: British Sculpture Since 1965* was the title given to an exhibition featuring the work of Richard Long, Barry Flanagan, David Nash, Bill Woodrow, Tony Cragg and Richard Deacon that toured the USA in 1987–88, beginning at the Museum of Contemporary Art, Chicago.

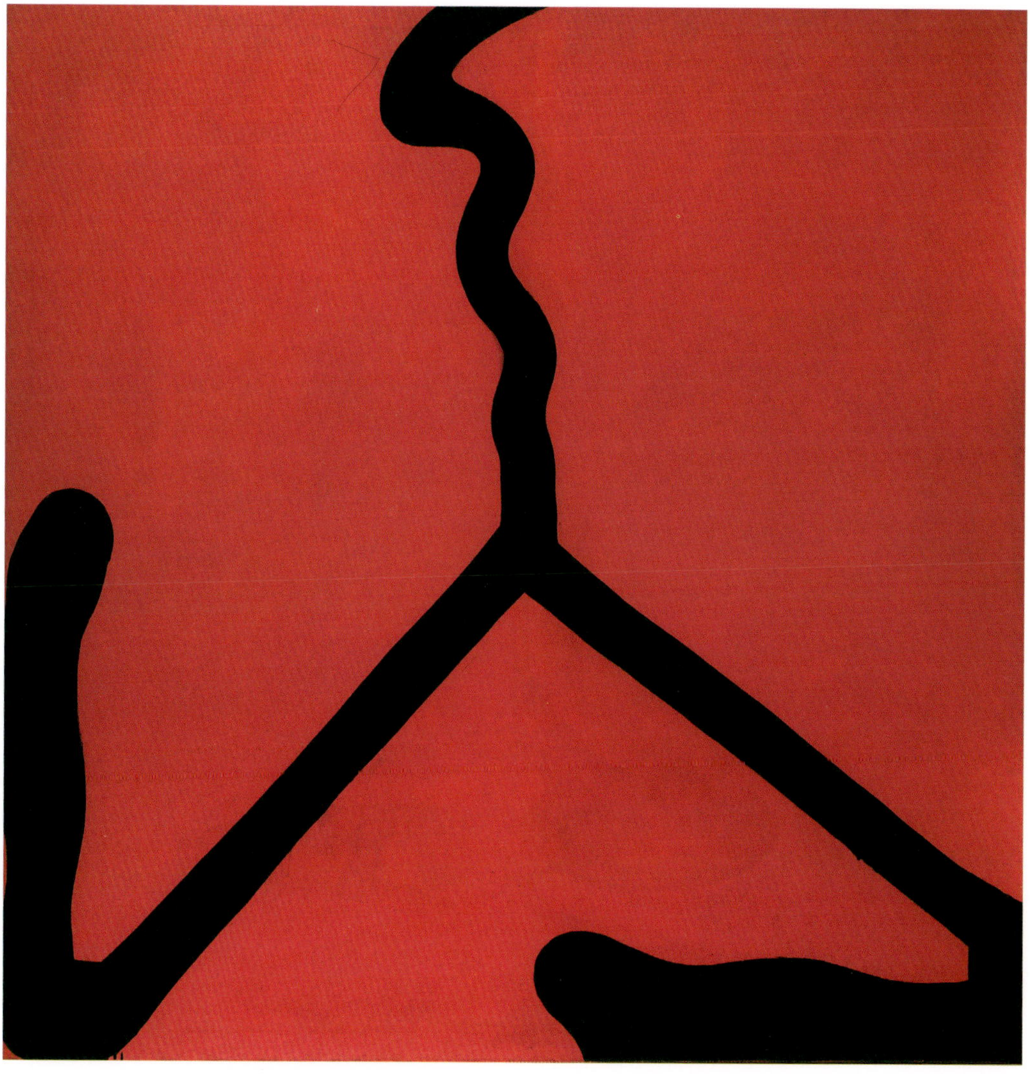

Paul Huxley Untitled No.32, 1964

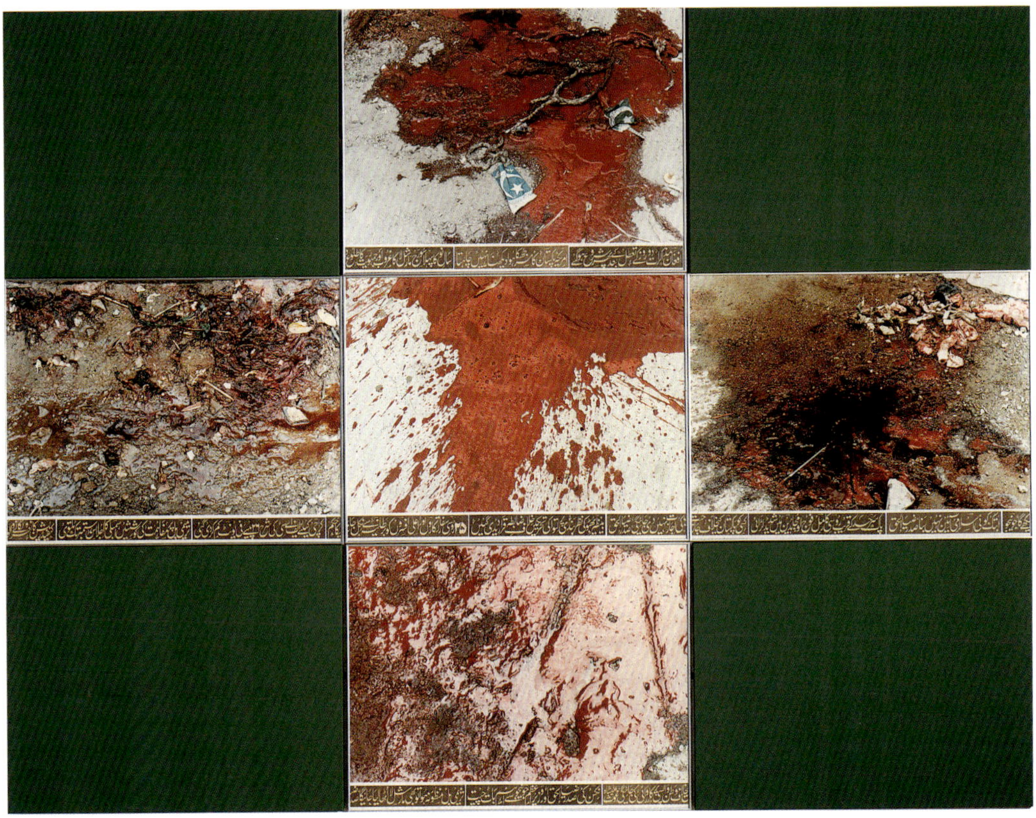

above **Rasheed Araeen** Green Painting 1, 1985–1986

implicated within, the larger social and political realities of the day. Those who have served as purchasers cannot help but reveal their personal and professional concerns in the performance of their duties. Art is not pure. It exists in a culture without the interest of whose members it counts for very little, in a market that sustains it and at the same time steers it in directions it might not otherwise be expected to go. What of practices that avowedly oppose prevailing aesthetic assumptions, activities that cannot be thought of as indicating a tendency so much as a number of critical interventions into the body of art? The feminist practices of Mary Kelly and others in the 1970s, for example, and the work of Rasheed Araeen, Keith Piper, Ingrid Pollard and Maud Sulter in the 1980s which, in its various ways, addressed the cultural marginalisation of black artists. These, too, are part of the history discernible within the Collection, a complex, multivalent history, and one much richer than the succession of key moments sketched out above. Those charged with overseeing the Collection actively seek to place any coherence it might be thought to have in constant jeopardy. Indeed, a mark of its robustness is the many incompatible aesthetic attitudes that distinguish its various works.

The Second World War precipitated significant contact between British artists and a number of figures involved in avant-garde activity on the Continent, often as a result of them passing through Britain en route to the USA. Not least among those who came to this country in this way was Mondrian, who stayed in Hampstead near his friends Barbara Hepworth and Ben Nicholson between 1938 and 1940. When Hepworth and Nicholson left London for St Ives just before the war they begged their friend to accompany them. Though Mondrian did not go, he and Naum Gabo, who was in St Ives for several years, proved influential in stimulating an engagement with the precepts of Constructivism. Started, as the Collection was, in the immediate aftermath of the war, one is able to trace this engagement from its beginnings, not only in the work of Victor Pasmore, Roger Hilton, Hepworth and Nicholson, but also in that of Kenneth and Mary Martin.

That was then, but more recently and now, too, wars make their presence felt as the pressing reality demanding attention, and as the context that defines the possibility of any aesthetic experience at all. Rose Finn-Kelcey humorously deflates the macho pretensions that lead us to conflict in the first place, Mona Hatoum sees the forced separations of war bound up with the generational distance between mother and daughter, and Richard Wentworth meditates on a child's games with toys in the bath in such a way that the outcome resonates with events in the Falklands War. Douglas Gordon paints the words 'Korea goes to war' on a canvas and titles it with the name of a Rothko exhibition at the Betty Parsons Gallery in 1951. That year, coincidentally, was the year of the Festival of Britain and of the inauguration of the South Bank as a cultural centre for London and the nation. John Berger pictures its rise in a small canvas from the previous year, *Scaffolding – Festival of Britain*. It rose, in Frank Whitford's words, into a land that was 'grey, flat, joyless, cold, damp and constipated, yet somehow pleased with itself'.[6] The mix of pleasure, hope and dejection associated with mid-century, all overcast with the seductive

6. Frank Whitford, 'Mickey Mouse meets Norbert Wiener', *Art Monthly*, March 1990, p. 8.

shadow of American exuberant expansiveness feeds through to the present, albeit that it is now the subject of wry commentary. We can see it, for example, in Martin Boyce's sculpture, *Dark Unit and Mask*, that combines a dirtied version of Mondrian's Neo-Plasticism with a 'primitive' mask fashioned from a fragment of a Charles Eames field splint.

During the life of the Collection there has been independence for the Indian subcontinent, independence for many other former colonies, notably in Africa, the arrival of workers and families from the West Indies, the partition of Cyprus, the civil war in Pakistan and the independence of Bangladesh, the Common Market and its subsequent expansion into the EU, the expulsion of Asians from Uganda, the handing back of Hong Kong . . . All of these events and more have been factors in, and influences on, the work being made in this country. In speaking of them, however, we need to keep in mind the danger, described by Rasheed Araeen, of assuming this history to be a sufficient account of the work that might have come out of it:

> *It would be a mistake to emphasise only the socio-political determinants of mass emigration and not to fully understand the actual aims of individual artists who left their countries of origin simply to fulfil their artistic ambitions abroad. We should also recognise the peculiarity of these ambitions, which are not fulfilled merely by a success in the market-place but by the artist's entry into the history of art.*[7]

Time and again the distinction is made between, on the one hand, how and why one travelled to Britain, and on the other, what one did as an artist when here. Balraj Khanna, who came to England, his 'brave new world', in 1962, said: 'I had come here with a purpose – I could feel it resonating in me like a tuning fork held to the ear – to discover myself.' He admitted that he might well have done something similar at home in India, but the fact was that he had chosen to do so in England.[8] Zarina Bhimji was born in Uganda, but forced by Idi Amin to leave the country along with many other Asians. Asked about how important she felt the sense of difference engendered by this experience was, she replied that she would prefer to answer 'in terms of making the work, rather than in cultural terms'.[9] Mona Hatoum, who came to Britain from Lebanon and stayed when war broke out there preventing her return, likewise resists the reading of her work in biographical terms. Rather than looking for specific meanings related to her background, she finds it 'more exciting when a work reverberates with several meanings and paradoxes and contradictions'.[10]

The complication, of course, is that the very questioning of the singular account of art and the criteria of judgement that sustain it, while allowing attention to be paid to hitherto marginalised art practices, also dissolves the sense of a history of art within which those practices might otherwise hope to become more firmly situated. It is a curious situation that in general terms is favourable, but which in all specific instances demands dispute. The Arts Council Collection is a crucial forum for the stimulating of such disputation, and *How to Improve the World* is an opportunity to witness that process of

7. Rasheed Araeen, 'Introduction: when chickens come home to roost' in *The Other Story: Afro-Asian Artists in post-war Britain*, curated by Rasheed Araeen, Hayward Gallery, London, 1989, p. 9.

8. Balraj Khanna, 'England: my brave new world' in *The Other Story*, p. 109.

9. Interview between Zarina Bhimji and Sonya Boyce, in Zarina Bhimji, *I Will Always Be There*, Ikon Gallery, Birmingham, 1992, np

10. Mona Hatoum in conversation with Michael Archer in Catherine de Zegher et al., *Mona Hatoum*, Phaidon, London, 1997, p. 25.

disputation at work. It is an exhibition not of the line, but of the open field. It deliberately eschews the idea of a simple historical narrative in favour of multiple juxtapositions which may be complementary, contrasting, disjunctive, contrary, amusing, or otherwise. These rarely show explicit recognition of one artist by another, but instead propose relationships - very often across time - that both highlight individual preoccupations and reveal the persistence of more general artistic concerns.

The upward struggle of Kenneth Armitage's bronze *Figure Lying on its Side (No. 5)*, for example, is poles apart from the minatory lightness of the suspended frames that form Eva Rothschild's *Heavy Cloud*. Both, none the less, work through the sculptor's wish to escape what is inescapable: gravity. In *Dining Recess* Patrick Caulfield examines through a disarming economy of means the subtle expressiveness of design, form, placement and material. This resonates with the way in which Enrico David's work treads a fine line on the borders of art, design and craft, and also finds a strange echo in Richard Wentworth's ongoing series *Making do and getting by*, photographs of immediate small problems encountered in daily life whose solutions demonstrate our instinctive understanding of an object's material properties. Ian Breakwell's observations of apparently trivial incidents encountered on his travels through the city resonate with Oliver Payne and Nick Relph's *Mixtape*, a reference-rich celebration of youth culture. The glamorous punkishness of Andrew Logan's monumental, late 1970s safety pin *(Homage to the New Wave)* evokes a different kind of stylishness to the consumer culture, fashion consciousness observed by the latter-day *flâneur* in Mark Leckey's Parade. Logan's work pre-dates the impact of AIDS, something inescapable in Richard Hamilton's portrait of Derek Jarman, a poet of the visual whose eyesight failed in the latter stages of his fight with the disease. The deep blue paint covering the joined steel parts of Anthony Caro's *Slow Movement* serves to unify the sculpture's separate elements. Roger Hiorns, who at other times has made explicit reference to Caro in his work, allows the final form to build through a natural process from the metal surface of manufactured objects. In *Nunhead*, two BMW engines have been dipped in a copper sulphate solution until they become encrusted with blue crystals. Nigel Henderson's *Head of a Man* and Chris Ofili's *Popcorn Shells* each in their different manner wrest their images from media-saturated environments experienced 40 years apart. The perceptual disturbance caused by the pulsing globe lights of Angela Bulloch's *Pink Chance Corner* acknowledge the impact on the artist of Bridget Riley's *Movement in Squares*.

These are only a small number of the myriad possible connections within *How to Improve the World*. Some that will be found there are historically grounded, others imaginatively suggestive, speculative, more or less preposterous, startling, or intriguing. They will be made by visitors whose motivations and interests differ widely. They will support any given viewpoint and clash with it in equal measure. All of which is as it should be. Taken in sum they will confirm the propriety of that impulse to betterment that has driven the Collection over the past 60 years.

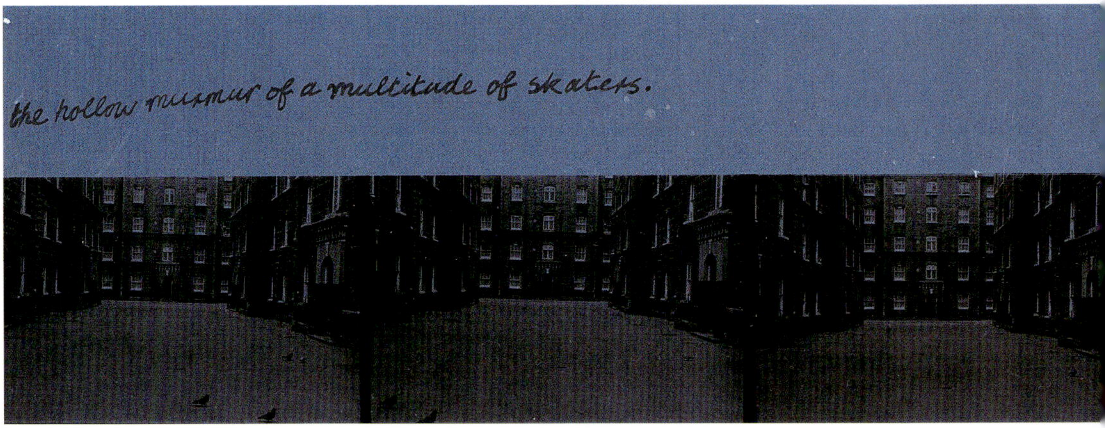
the hollow murmur of a multitude of skaters.

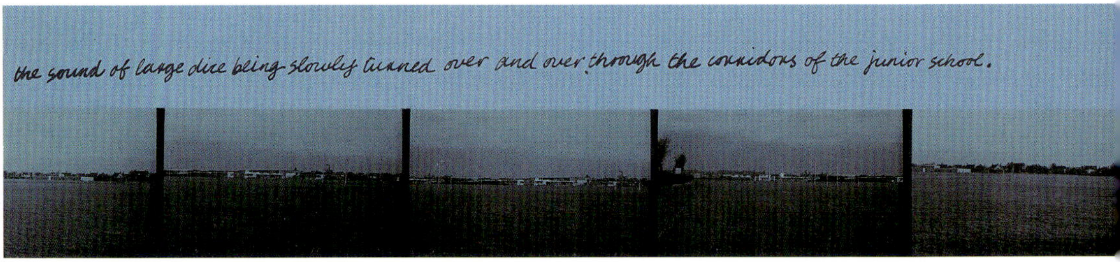
the sound of large dice being slowly turned over and over through the corridors of the junior school.

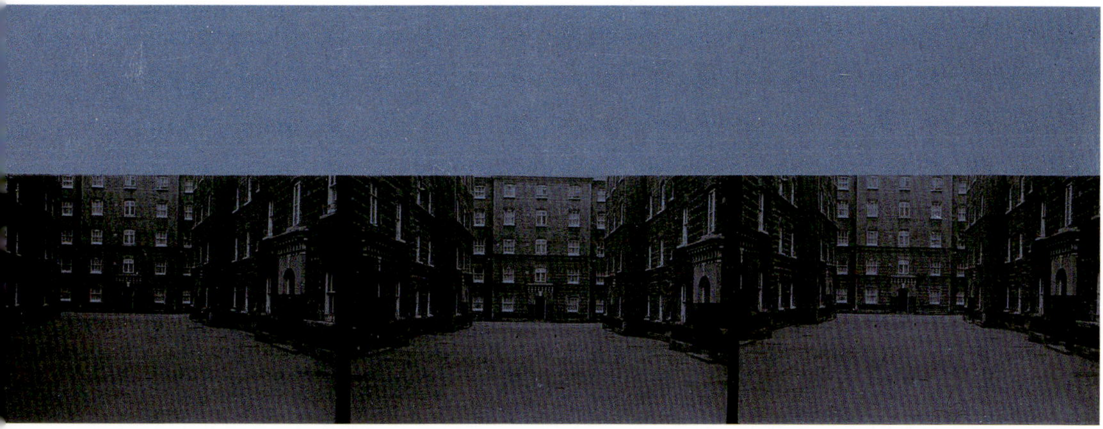

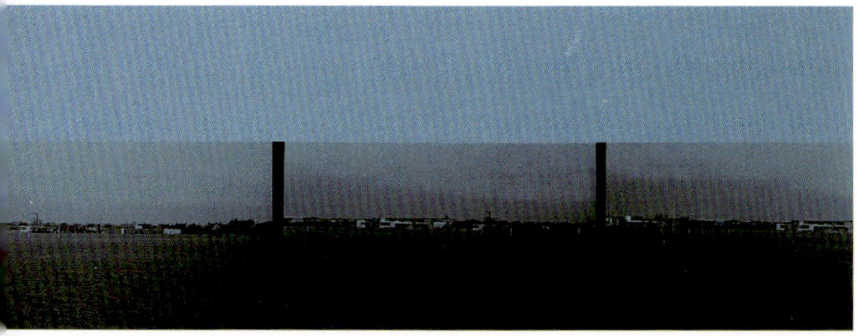

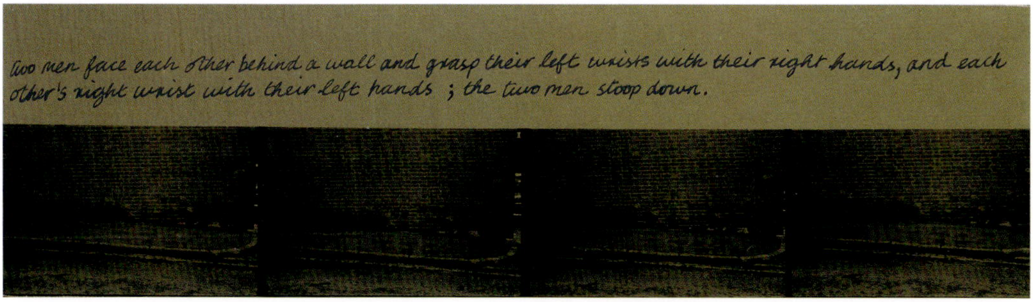
two men face each other behind a wall and grasp their left wrists with their right hands, and each other's right wrist with their left hands ; the two men stoop down.

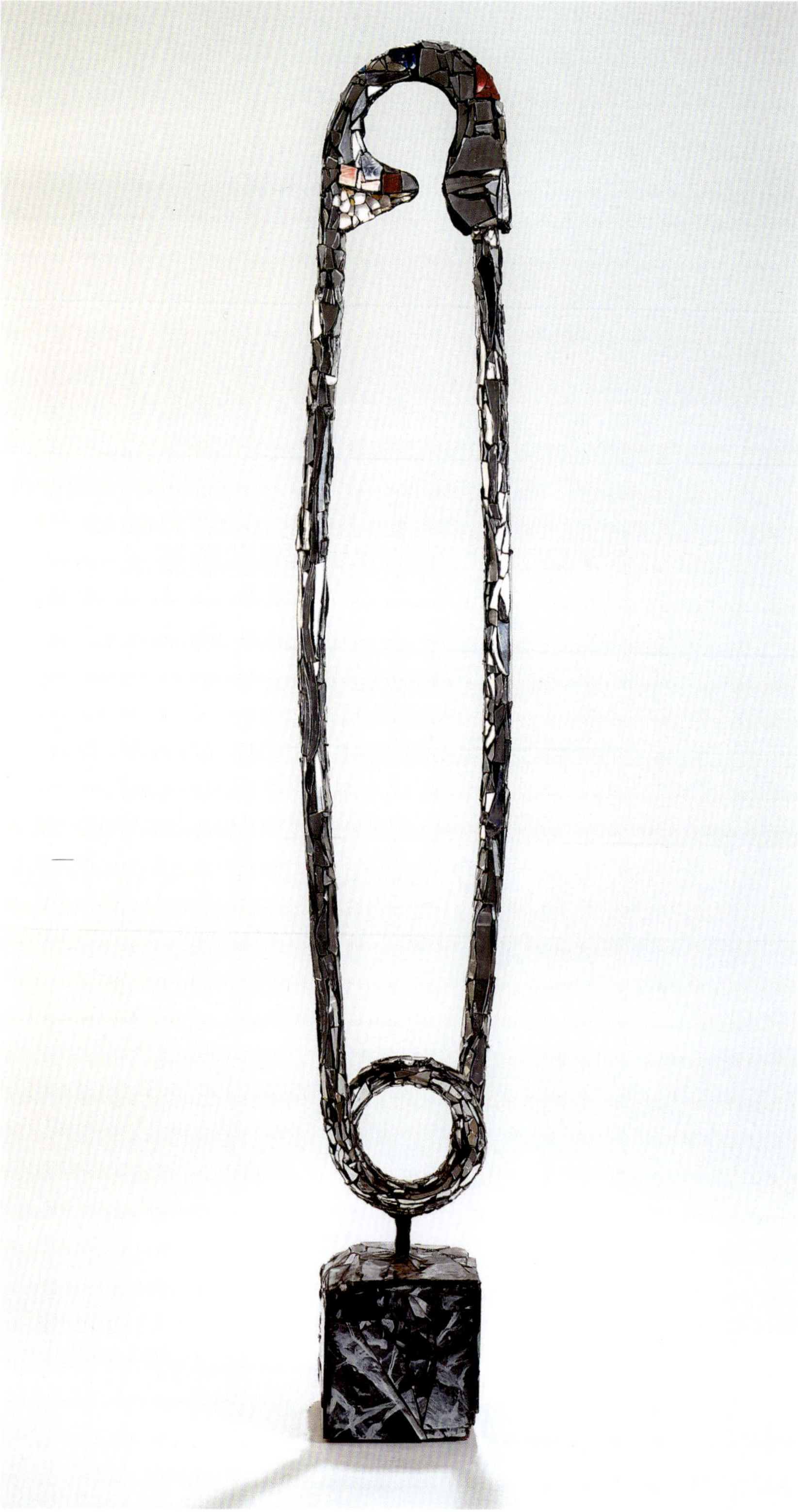

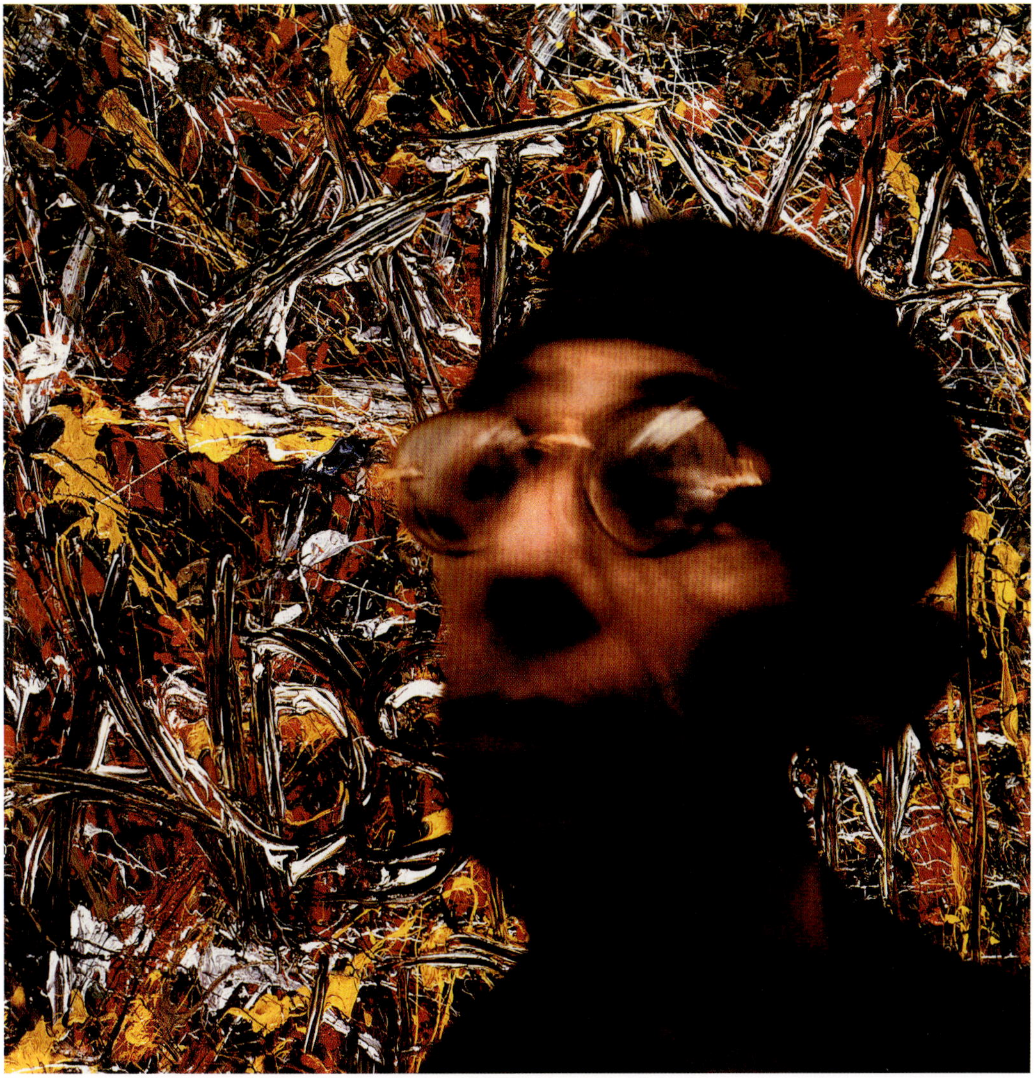

opposite **Andrew Logan** Homage to the New Wave, 1977
above **Richard Hamilton** Portrait of Derek Jarman, 1996–1997

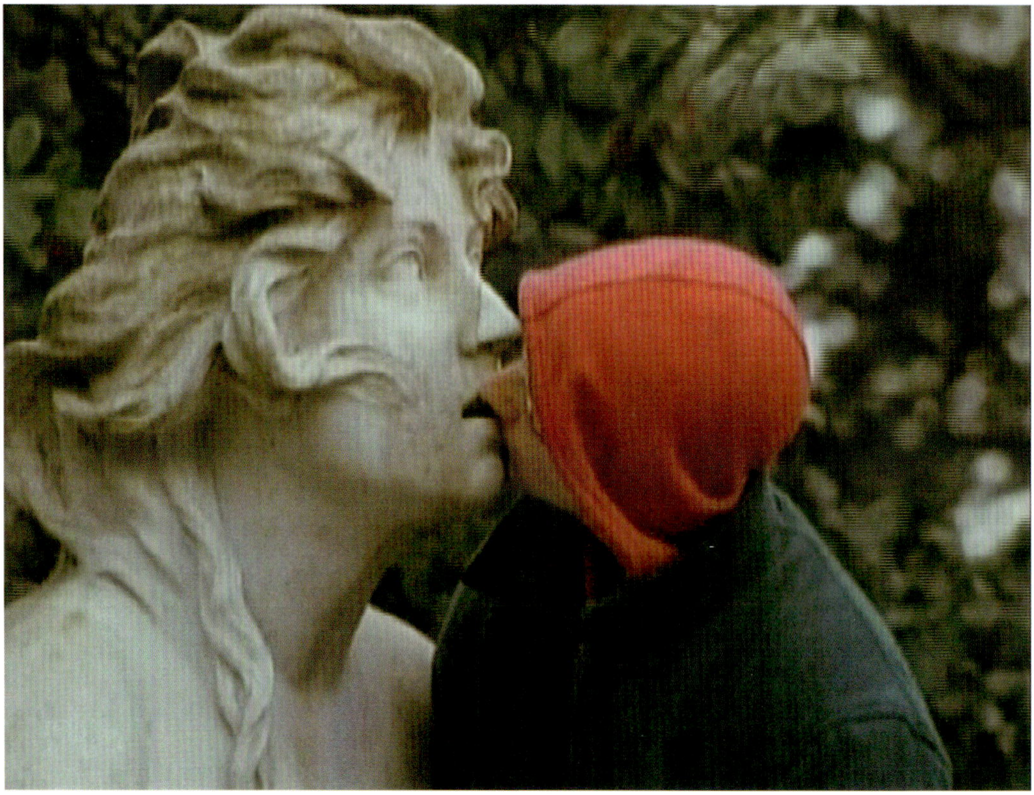

Oliver Payne and Nick Relph Mixtape, 2002

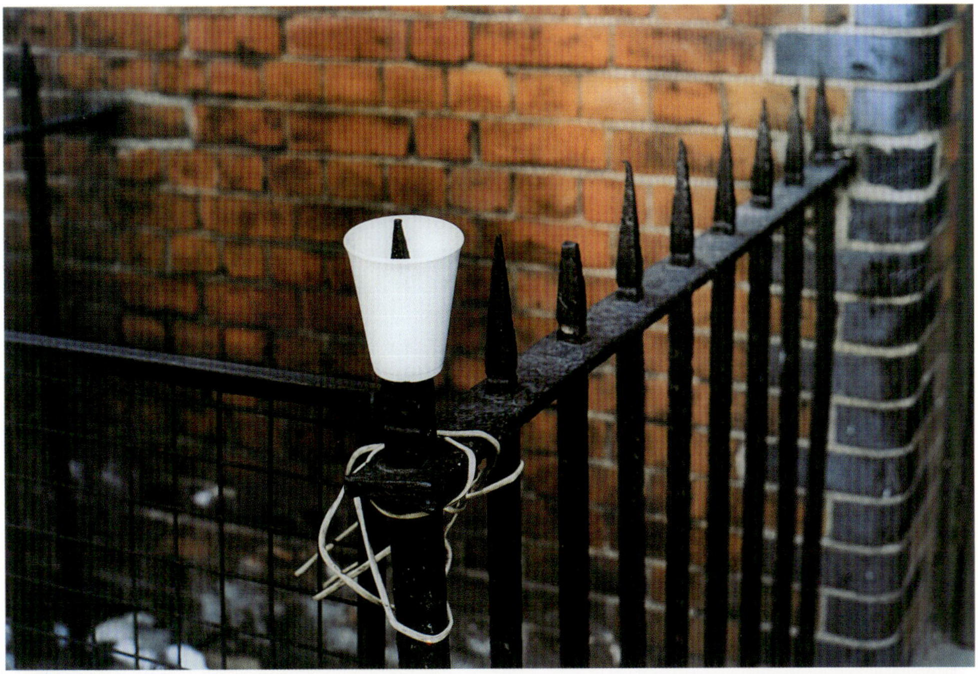

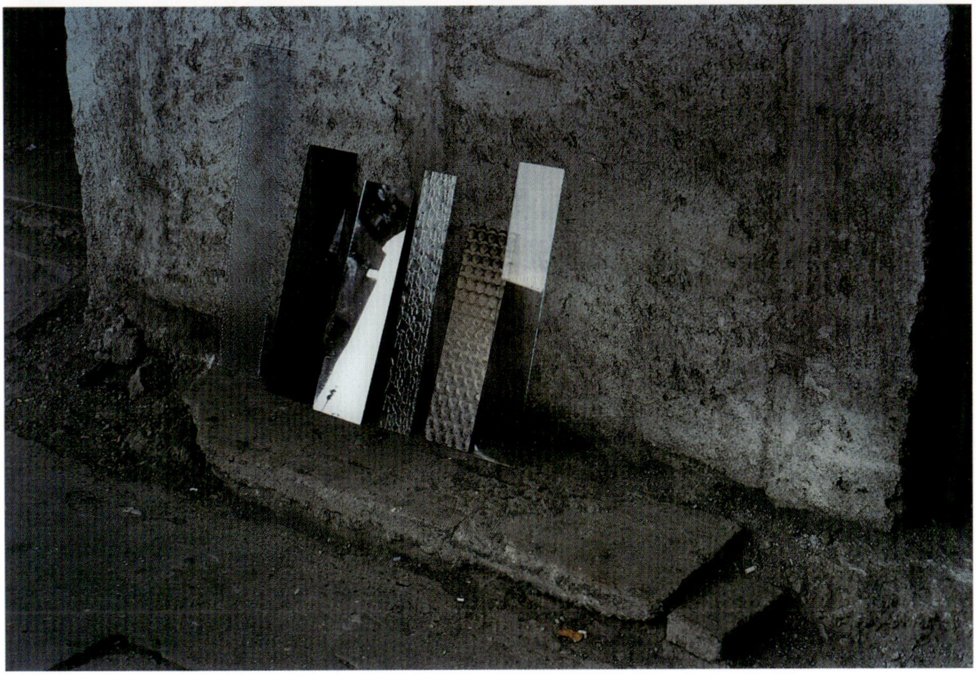

Richard Wentworth London, 1999. Making do and getting by., 2000

Richard Wentworth Tirana, 1983

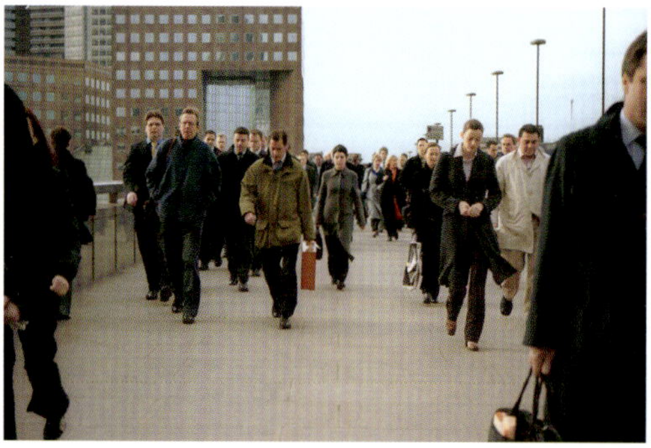 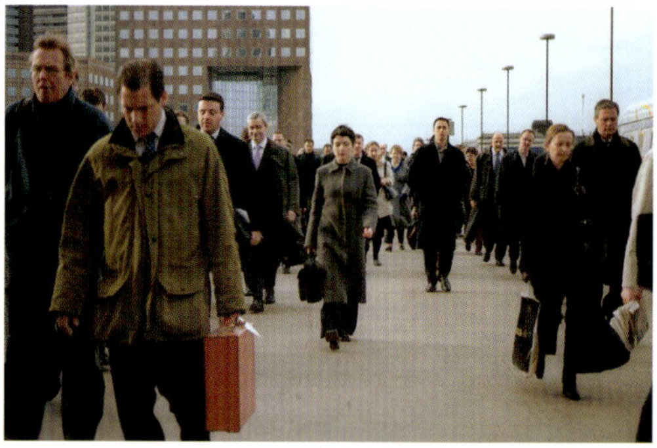

Carey Young Lines Made by Walking (after Richard Long), 2003 (details)

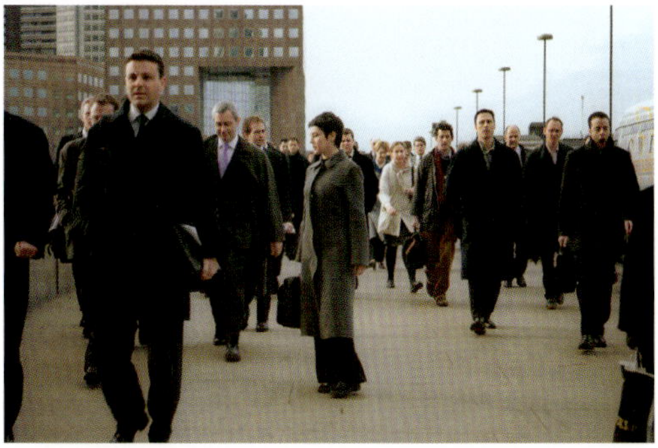

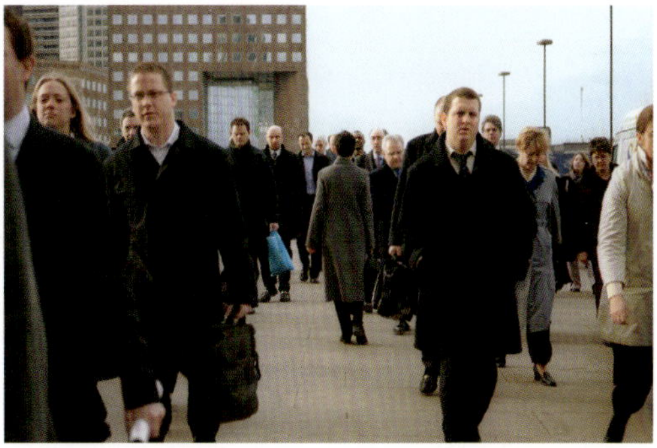

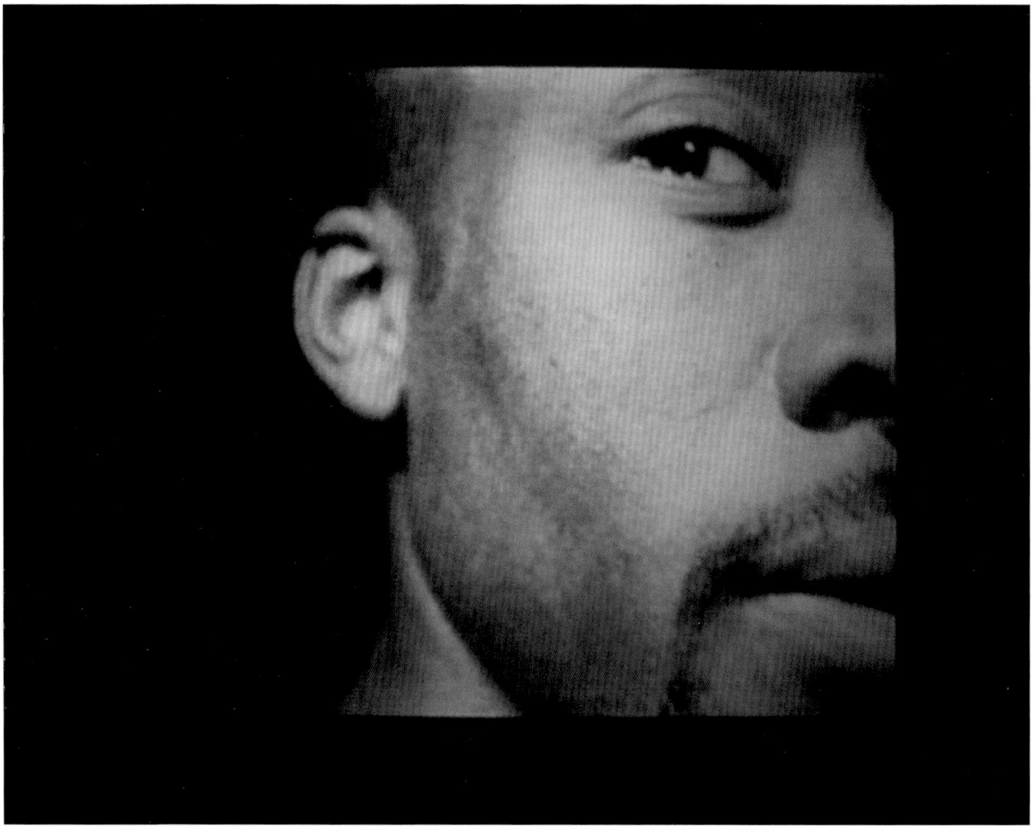

Steve McQueen Bear, 1993

Many Lives, Many Conversations

by Marjorie Allthorpe-Guyton

There is no collection like it, in character or in use, in the world. The Arts Council Collection is a precious cultural asset for Britain: a public collection built adventurously and lent widely to a range of organisations across the country for many purposes, often to remote and non-gallery venues where the works reach new audiences of all ages. The contemporary art collector Dakis Joannou says that for him collecting is 'engaging in conversation' and that very much describes the organic process by which the Arts Council Collection is grown. The Collection shares some of the characteristics of a private collection, in as much that it includes a wide range of artists, most of whom are not represented in particular depth. Unlike a personal collection, the work is not selected by any one discerning eye, but rather through the collective subjectivities – and the conversations – of those who have been invited to be temporary purchasers over the last 60 years.

Independent critics, curators and artists guide the acquisitions for the Collection. These passionate and authoritative individuals (some 150 or more) include many of the best-informed and influential art-world figures of their time – from Adrian Stokes, David Sylvester and Bryan Robertson to Lynne Cooke, Adrian Searle, Sonia Boyce and Susan Hiller. (A list of external purchasers, excluding Arts Council staff, can be found on page 176.) The quality and breadth of the Collection is due to their judgement, prescient or otherwise. Over six decades, and with famously modest funds, they have built a collection in which most of the leading British artists of the past half-century are represented. Above all else, the Collection is an ongoing record of emergent art, and recent purchases indicate that it continues to be closely attuned to new developments.

Bypassing the usual long and cumbersome process of institutional acquisition, especially over the last ten years, has won the Collection many timely purchases, often at very low cost. The inevitable element of risk has for the most part been justified by the fine discrimination of the purchasers, who have targeted the work of an artist at the right moment in his or her career, and have chosen the right work , before prices have gone beyond the reach of the budget (now £150,000 per year). Damien Hirst's dark and mortuary *He Tried to Internalise Everything* was acquired in 1996, when the artist was, arguably, at the height of his powers and when prices were at their lowest. This major piece was acquired with the help of a grant from The Henry Moore Foundation. Steve McQueen's magisterial *Bear*, 1993, was also acquired early in the artist's stellar career, and its beauty and power make it one of the most important video works in the Collection. The radar has again detected the work of mid-generation and older artists, who may already be represented in the Collection, when a new intensity or pertinence is evident, as is the case with Susan Hiller's *Wild Talents*, 1997, and Gustav Metzger's *Historic Photographs: To Crawl Into – Anschluss, Vienna, March*

1938, 1996–98. Some artists have remarked that particular works of theirs in the Collection represent defining moments in their careers.

Contemporary art often demands curatorial courage and stamina. While mindful that the Collection's core role is to be seen as widely as possible, the Collection's curators have not baulked from acquiring significant works that are challenging to conserve or install. Dr Isobel Johnstone, who retired in 2004 after more than two decades as Curator of the Collection, assumed responsibility in 1994 for the 40,000 clay figures of Antony Gormley's celebrated *Field for the British Isles*, which has now been shown in over 20 venues in the UK, from the British Museum to Salisbury Cathedral, and has been seen by almost two million people. The recent addition to the Collection of Roger Hiorns' *Nunhead*, 2004, where the blue luminescence of copper sulphate crystals will require regular re-immersion to re-form, is another test for the curatorial nerve. These adventures in fearless acquisition give the Collection strength of character and attract borrowers who are also keen to rise to the challenge of tricky installation. This is a good test for the ambitious young curator who wants to stretch the imagination of an institution's management and audiences.

The Hayward Gallery runs the Collection as a national resource for borrowers and is developing its powerful and still under-exploited educational role as a training opportunity for regional curators and gallery education, especially in showing new work in the context of art from the past. This role is growing with the opportunities offered by the new Collection facilities at the Longside Gallery and sculpture facility at Yorkshire Sculpture Park and the new London store for two-dimensional works, both of which provide greater access and study resources. The rate of loans is increasing year by year. In 2005, 42 venues in the UK showed Arts Council Collection exhibitions and this year works will be shown in 26 exhibitions in 49 venues across the UK.

The Collection also offers many opportunities for professional development. Curators can borrow works to support their own collecting agendas and exhibitions through the *Select* programme. Since 1997 over 50 *Select* shows have been presented by regional museums across the country. With an inherently flexible approach to collaboration, *Select* offers multiple possibilities for partnership and involvement with the curatorial and technical teams at the Arts Council Collection. Curators may have a free hand in choosing works to form a show, while others may seek advice from staff with extensive knowledge of the Collection. The initiative is part of the Collection's continuing commitment to providing nationwide access to its resources, and is the area of activity with the greatest potential for expansion. Mobility being the Collection's *raison d'être*, a single work from the Collection can have many lives, over time serving many audiences through the programmes of curators across the UK.

When there is deepening concern about the lack of strong regional collections of contemporary art, the role and purpose of existing national collections comes into focus, especially the need to strengthen partnerships

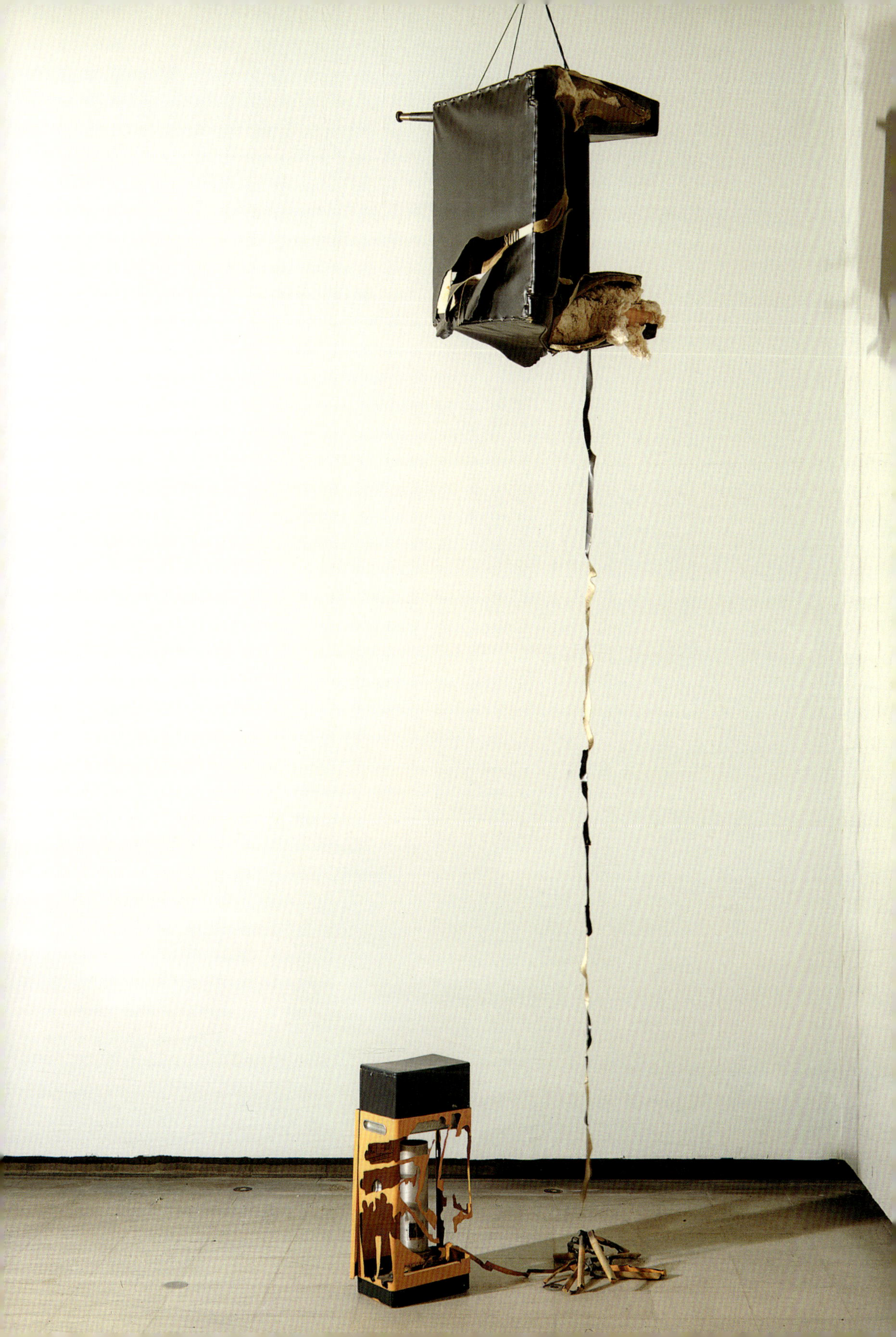

previous **Bill Woodrow** Armchair and Paraffin Heater with Campfire, 1981
above **Angela Bulloch** Pink Chance Corner, 1990

to share works, resources and expertise. While museums in the Netherlands, France and Germany have a longstanding commitment to contemporary collections and exhibition, in England our major regional museums may suffer a lack of staff expertise and public funds, not only for acquisitions but for commissions and programmes of contemporary art. This means that opportunities to benefit from the significant support of charitable foundations, such as the Art Fund, are either lost or not maximised.

Arts Council England recently launched *Turning Point*, a ten-year strategy for the contemporary visual arts. This outlines plans to work with the Tate and with the Museums, Libraries and Archive Council's 'Renaissance in the Regions' programme to assess the feasibility of regional consortia of visual arts organisations. The aim is to share expertise and resources so that new collections can be developed through joint programmes of both acquisition and commissions. To enable strategic collecting, an online database of existing regional public collections of modern and contemporary art is planned. This would build on the new investment in collections and professional development that was begun by the Contemporary Art Society's Special Collections Scheme funded by the Lottery, through Arts Council England during the period 1997–2006. The momentum of this initiative must be sustained by new national and regional partnerships.

The current Hayward Gallery touring exhibition *British Art Show 6* includes many new works from the Arts Council Collection, and illustrates how partnerships between local authority museums, independent galleries and artist-run spaces can take most benefit from regional expertise and resources. The Arts Council Collection is also working with the British Council Collection to provide new training resources for regional curators. New collections need to be built with regionally distinct histories and context. The nomadic nature, range and quality of the Arts Council Collection is a key to that process. With common cause and commitment, and some new public investment that will also unlock private support, there can be a new future for both national and regional collections.

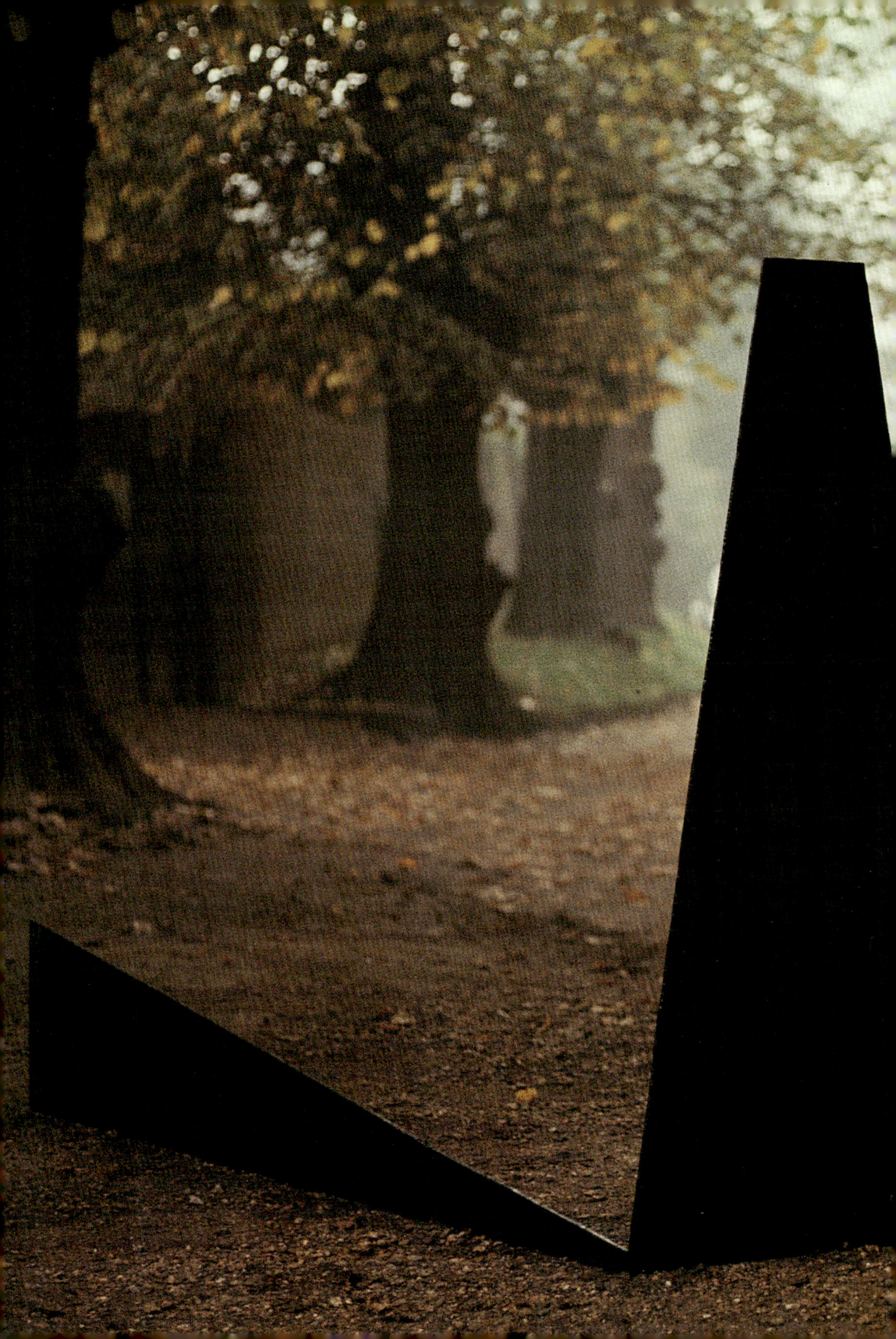

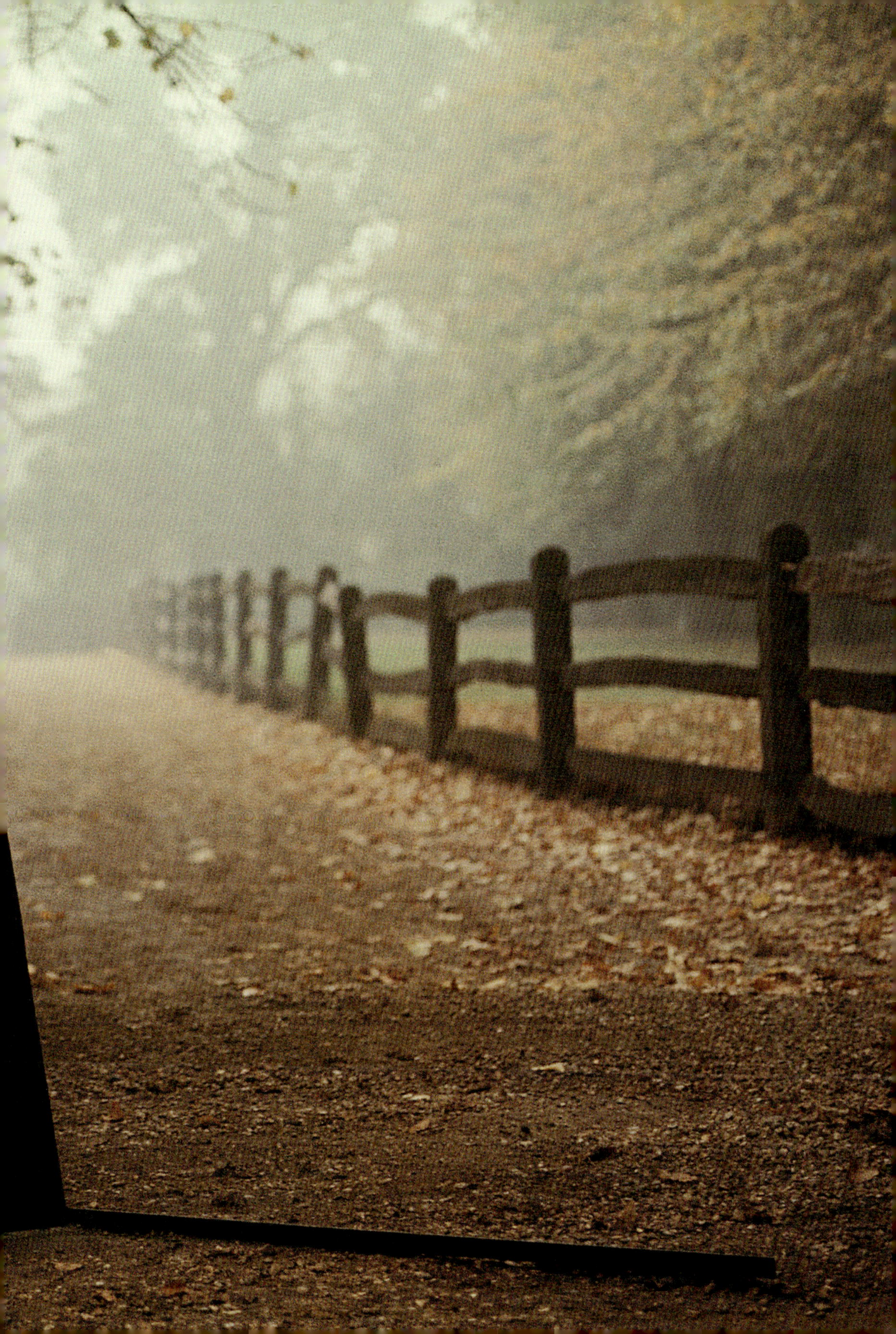

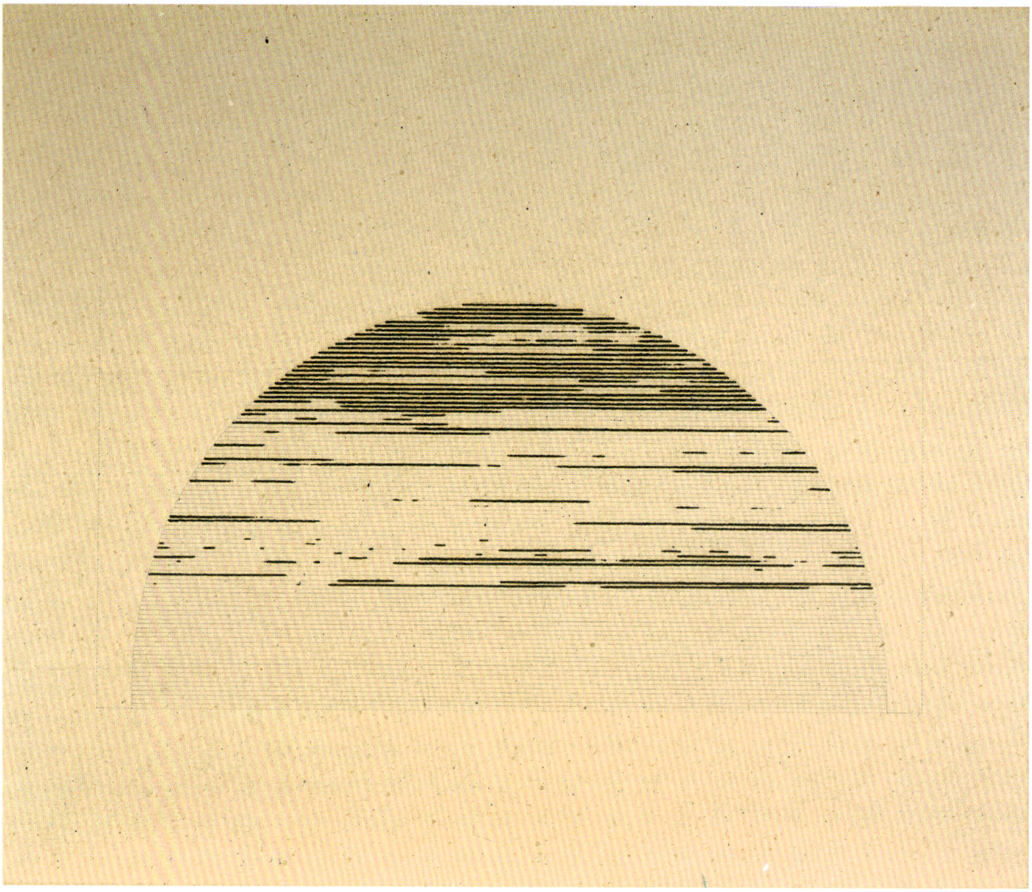

previous **Anthony Caro** Slow Movement, 1965
above **Roger Ackling** Five hour cloud drawing, 1980

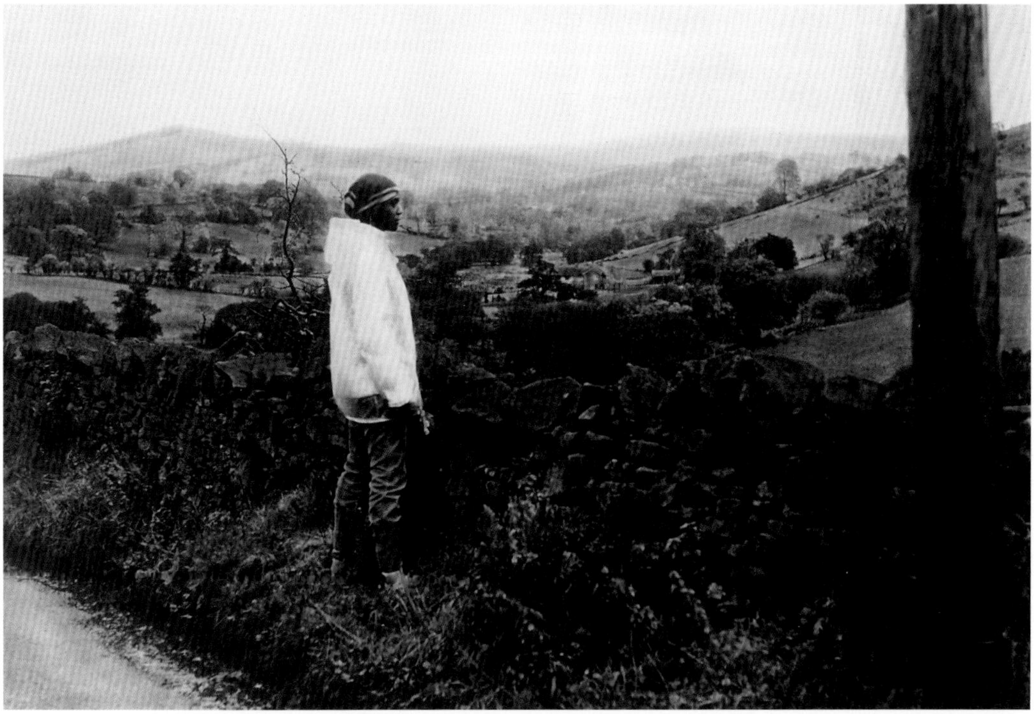

Ingrid Pollard Pastoral Interlude, No.4, (detail) 1988

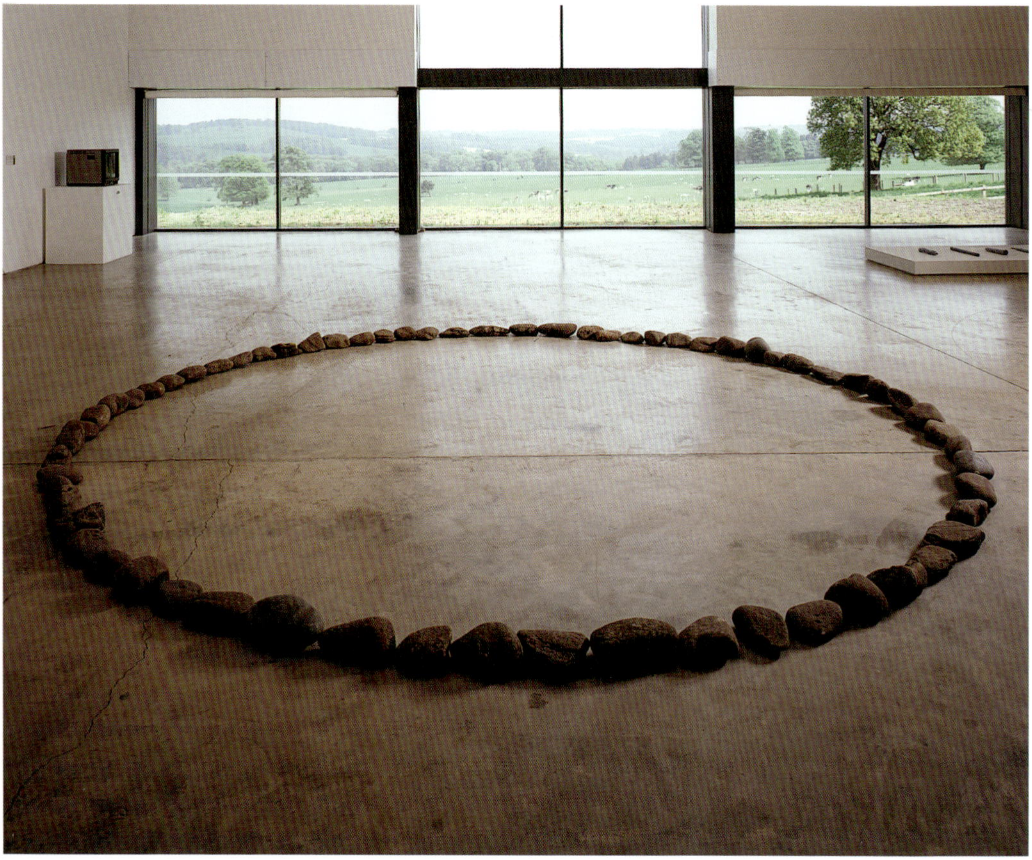

Richard Long Stone Circle, 1972

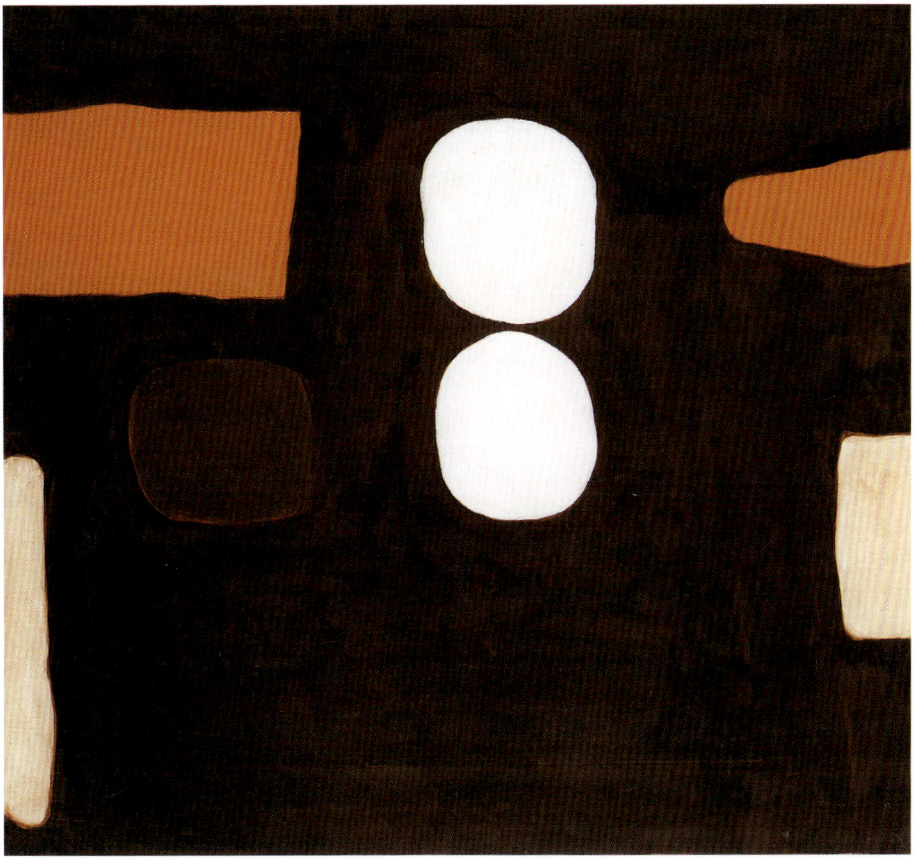

William Scott Dark Brown, Orange and White, 1963

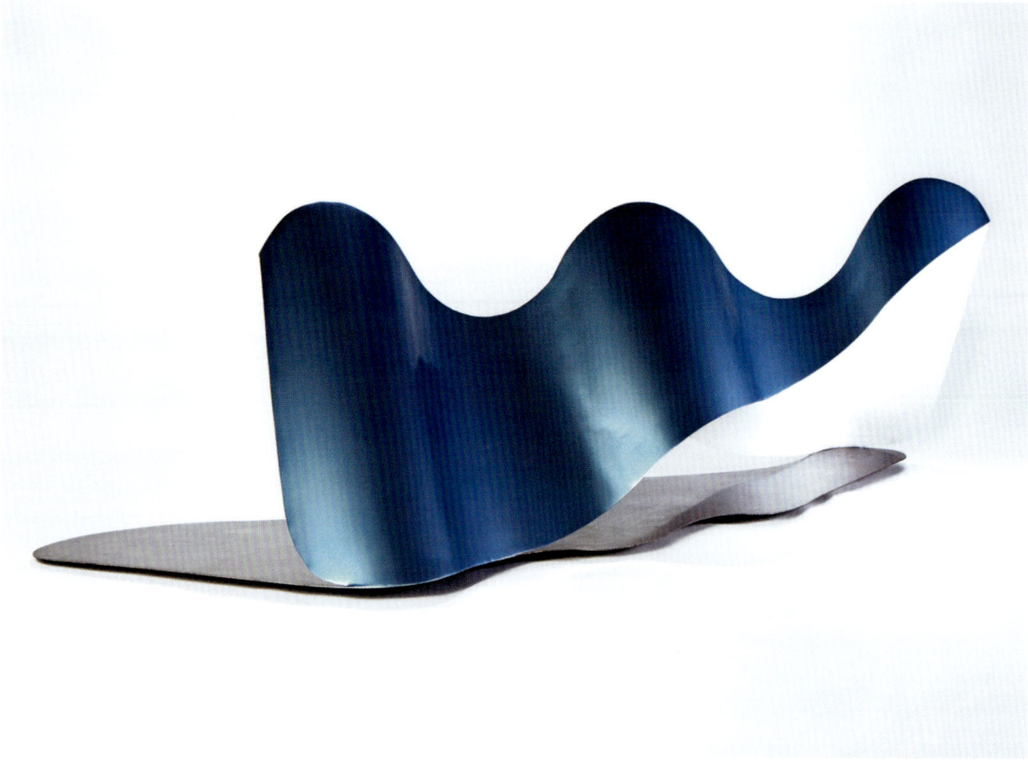

Isaac Witkin Vermont III, 1964–1965

John Hoyland 20.5.68, 1968

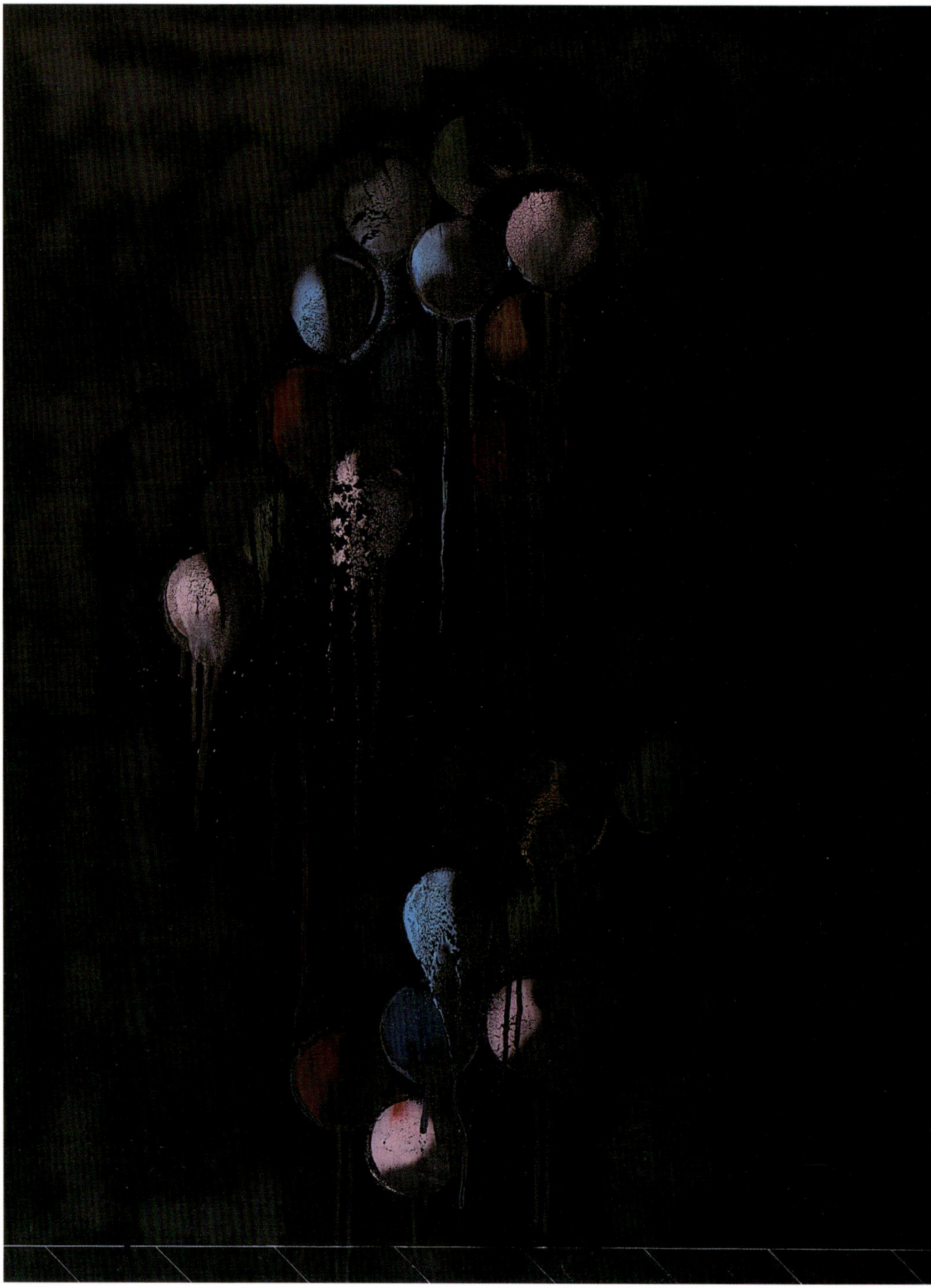

Peter Peri Pageant, 2005

New and Improved! Exhibiting Collections

by Roger Malbert

Exhibitions are ephemeral events and their lasting impact is hard to gauge. A young artist may encounter work in a temporary show that turns out to be a decisive influence, or someone unfamiliar with contemporary art may be introduced to it by an exhibition and continue to visit galleries and museums for years to come. Historically, many of the seminal moments in modern art have first been signalled in exhibitions that resonate long after all immediate recollection of them has passed. They enter the mythology, immortalised in a few grainy black and white photographs, a smattering of recorded first-hand descriptions and some – often vituperative – reviews. Many of those ground-breaking exhibitions were artists' initiatives, but a few were organised by 'official' art institutions, with prescience and even daring.

The relationship between the temporary exhibition and the permanent collection, in galleries where both have their place, is complex and begs much closer attention, especially in the context of regional museums. To begin with, at the most basic level, the temporary exhibition is a sign of institutional life, a reason to visit a museum now rather than later. And in a pluralistic and internationalised visual culture, where many competing and perhaps antagonistic artistic tendencies are in play, exhibitions allow a far greater diversity of attitudes and practices to be represented than could possibly be found in any medium-sized collection.

To state the case for temporary exhibitions is not to diminish the importance or urgency of the campaign for proper funding for regional galleries to build their own collections of contemporary art. Nor is it to suggest that exhibitions are a substitute for the long-term benefits to museums of actually acquiring new works. In theory, the two should be complementary; in practice, most of Britain's municipal museums are without the resources for new acquisitions, whether of contemporary or historical work, and few have sufficient funds for ambitious exhibitions either.

In these dire circumstances, critics sometimes dismiss the Arts Council Collection as an anachronism, a remnant of another age – of paternalism, centralism and regional quiescence. But this is to underestimate the extent to which the Collection is an actively deployed resource with multiple uses. It is the most versatile of the national collections, the most accessible and widely used by galleries across the country (the *Select* programme being perhaps its most progressive recent initiative and one with the greatest potential for expansion). As a pool of works that can be drawn on with relative ease, it offers curators the opportunity to experiment with different models of exhibition-making, from historical surveys to thematic and issue-based or media-specific shows. Around 300 exhibitions have been formed from the Collection over the past 60 years. They demonstrate its range and provide fascinating examples of different approaches to art and curatorial practice.

From its inception, exhibitions have been one of the principal purposes of the Collection. The Arts Council of Great Britain's wartime precursor,

CEMA (Council for the Encouragement of Music and the Arts) bought 50 oil paintings and 25 watercolours in 1942 and toured them around Britain under the banner 'Art for the People'. These and a variety of loan exhibitions were accompanied by guide-lecturers trained in art history, 'village explainers', who interpreted the works for the public. This modest effort to enlighten and divert a people under daily threat of destruction seems innocuous enough, but it was not always perceived to be so at the time.

In the midst of war, in 1944, an irate question in the House of Commons about the 'poor quality and debasing effect' of the art being toured by CEMA prompted a furious controversy in the letters columns of *The Times*. The first letter from a group of Royal Academicians – including the President, Sir Alfred Munnings – supports the questioner: 'For the most part the exhibitions comprise paintings devised to carry on the baleful influence of what is known as "modernistic" art. This is a subversive movement which, with its several "isms", has been for many years endeavouring to undermine the traditional glories of painting and sculpture.' The letter ends with a call to 'amend the evil by the double means of reducing national expenditure and openly opposing the aforesaid organised activities for a lowering of art standards'.[1]

1. *The Times*, 11 March 1944. (thanks to Robin Footitt for uncovering this correspondence.)

In a lengthy and scathing reply, John Maynard Keynes, Chairman of CEMA and subsequently founder of the Arts Council, remarks that 'so far, our three major efforts have been the circulation through the provinces of the Sickert Exhibition, the Wilson Steer Exhibition, and the Tate Gallery's wartime acquisitions. Your correspondents do not particularise which of these exhibitions was more especially responsible in their judgement for degrading the public taste'. Among the other 22 exhibitions toured that year, he points out ironically, two were 'selections from the summer exhibitions of the Royal Academy, chosen on the responsibility of the Council of the Academy (two of the signatories of the letter of complaint were represented in these)'. Perhaps the protesters had forgotten this for, as another correspondent points out, 'the average age of the signatories . . . must be the biblical three score years and ten, but years do not seem to have added wisdom'. Other letters compare the Academicians' attitude to 'the childish mentality of Dr Goebbels' and to Nazi principles. The heated exchanges continue over 3 weeks, with 11 letters in all. The argument is referred to triumphantly in CEMA's annual report later that year: 'In the result the Council was able to prove clearly its claims to catholicity. At the same time, the Art Panel is not ashamed, but very much the contrary, to show itself the patron of contemporary and – if it so happens – controversial work.'

In the history of controversies associated with the Arts Council and the visual arts over the next 60 years, the tone of these exchanges is often repeated, with the plain man's outrage at the folly and pretentiousness of modern art harnessed to a political demand – for its eradication from the sphere of public funding. Whether or not the Arts Council has always been so robust in countering such criticisms, the Collection has not shied away from exhibitions that push the parameters of institutional presentations

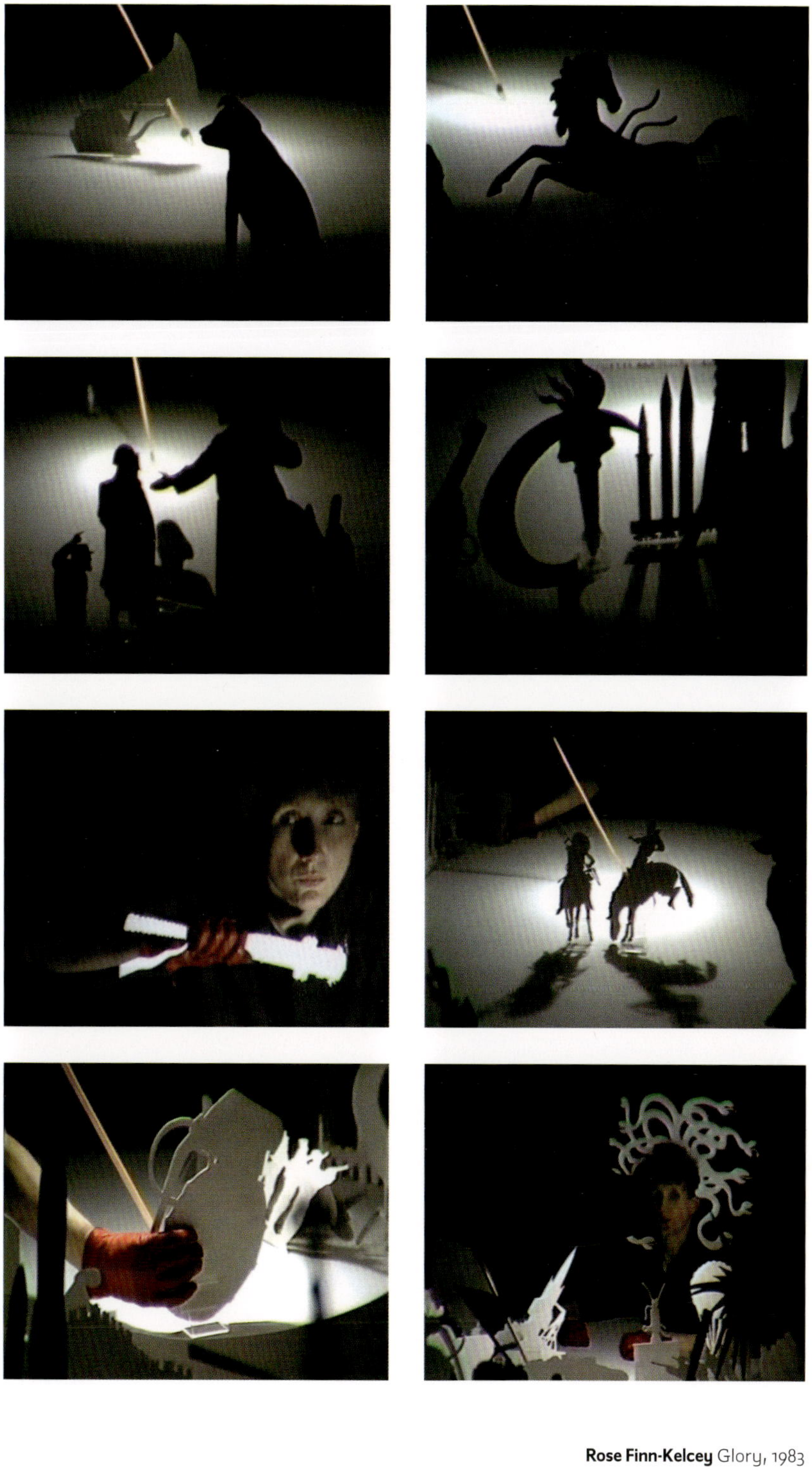

Rose Finn-Kelcey Glory, 1983

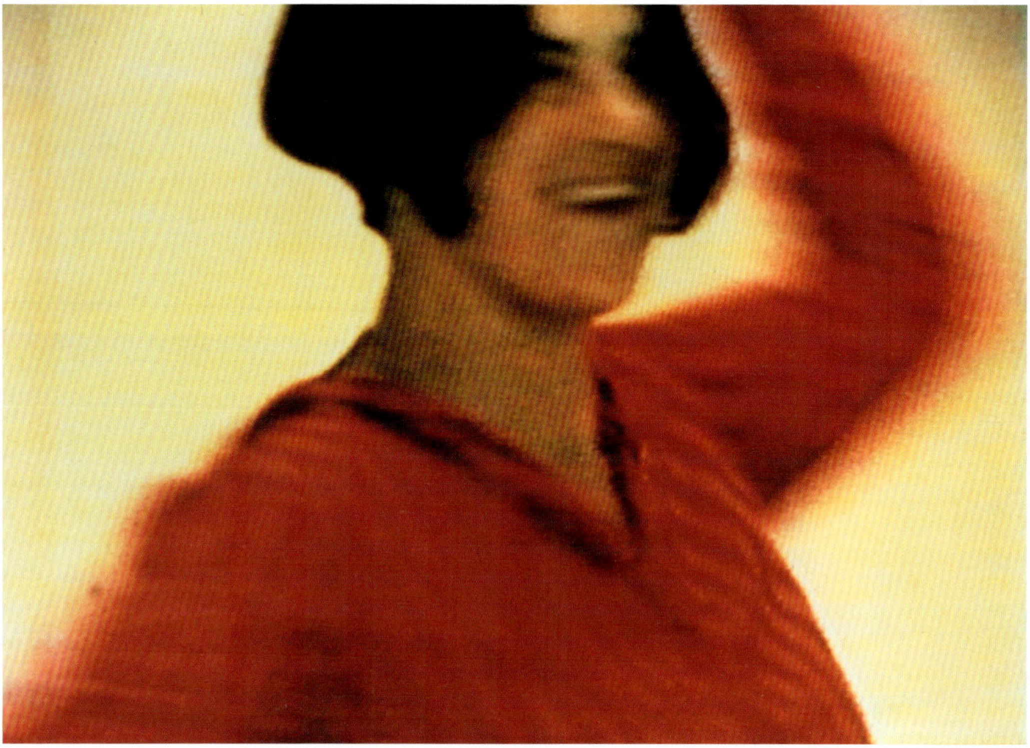

Tracey Emin Why I Never Became a Dancer, 1995

of contemporary art. It has done this largely through the appointment of independent critics, artists and curators to buy works and to make exhibitions.

Among past Arts Council Collection exhibitions, several were the result of invitations to purchasers to buy specifically for a show. This practice may be questionable, in so far as the works will continue to belong to the Collection long after the show has run its course and may not be particularly appropriate for other uses. It has not happened since the mid-1980s. But in earlier decades the Collection was enhanced by excellent, sometimes seminal, purchases made in this way, and its history enriched by argumentative, closely focused and timely shows. The act of buying, as everyone knows from daily experience, demands decisiveness and commitment. The power to buy works especially for an exhibition can give a show a special vigour and immediacy. In the two examples described here, the Arts Council's adherence to the principle of catholicity is evident in the contrary positions of its guest curators.

In 1973, the 24-year-old critic Richard Cork was invited to spend 'several thousand pounds of public money', as he put it, on new acquisitions, resulting in the touring exhibition *Beyond Painting and Sculpture*. Following Anne Seymour's pioneering exhibition, *The New Art*, at the Hayward in the previous year, Cork bought videos (the first to be purchased for the Collection) by Gilbert & George, 16 mm films by David Dye, an audio-tape by Gerald Newman, text pieces by John Stezaker and Keith Arnatt, and a photo-text series by Victor Burgin. In her essay for *The New Art*, Seymour had remarked on 'the somewhat uneasy bed' such work 'has made for itself in art schools in this country', and 'its lack of representation in its more radical forms in public museums and art galleries'. Cork recognised the challenges his purchases would present for the Collection: virtually everything he wanted to acquire was 'riddled with fundamental questions about status and function', he wrote, and the works resisted 'attempts to package them into a neat array of rapidly digestible gallery fodder'. Reflecting on this exhibition now, Cork recalls the liberating effect of a Marcel Duchamp retrospective exhibition organised for the Arts Council by the artist Richard Hamilton at the Tate Gallery in 1966. This was a turning point in the British art world; before that, Duchamp was rarely mentioned.

A different 'moral landscape' was perceived by the painter R.B. Kitaj, invited by the Arts Council three years later to buy works for an exhibition to be shown at the Hayward and then to tour the country. *The Human Clay* (the title was from a line of Auden's that Kitaj's friend David Hockney liked to quote) consisted of figurative paintings and drawings, pictures of people, the kind of art that Kitaj believed was very much 'against the grain' of the prevailing conceptualist aesthetic. His introductory essay opens with a magisterially languid disavowal: 'I hardly know why I agreed to buy pictures for the Arts Council. I should have stayed in bed like Oblomov.' This is followed by an apology for the inadequacy of the works he has chosen: compared to Goya, whose 'Sanlúcar Sketchbooks' he is looking at as he writes, '. . . it should be clear enough when all the pictures are brought together for this showing that revelations of that burning order have not found their moment. But I grow to love the way we fail.' Such humility is found in sincere artists who set themselves unattainable goals. So this was an exhibition of art that had failed – at least, when judged by the standards of Goya, it fell short. Of course. But even by less exalted criteria the purchases alone would not, apparently, have made a show: 'The group of things you see here came together in diverse ways. Many things were bought for the nation. They are not always the best things I could find. That would have been too expensive, so most often pictures are small or they are drawings or prints or not the most ambitious works of the painters. Some much finer pictures have been borrowed so that the thing could be more substantial.' In fact, Kitaj bought some impressive works – among them, drawings by Lucian Freud, Frank Auerbach and Richard Hamilton – and the exhibition made a considerable impact, promoting what could be described as an aesthetically conservative – though socialist-humanist – position, in support of his claims for a School of London, a fellowship of artists whose work was grounded in the experience of living and observing in this particular city.

The polarisation between post-Duchampian conceptualism and traditional studio-based practice was overcome in British art in the 1980s with the 'Freeze generation' (named after the exhibition *Freeze* curated by Damien Hirst in 1988) of 'young British artists', who launched a strategic assault on the old gallery structures and conventions. Artists can now make anything – figurative painting, film, installation, books – with conceptualist awareness and panache. The whole spectrum of modernist experiment, with its lines of demarcation and contradictory dogmas, has collapsed into an eternal present where everything is possible. The artist's new role as interventionist and conscious manipulator of live situations throws up questions for the collection-based exhibition, which draws on art that has already passed out of the artist's hands and into those of institutions. So much art today cannot be bought: for the work to be realised, the artist needs to be present. At the same time the market for that which can be bought and sold has grown with unprecedented speed and this presents another problem for all public collections with their tightly limited funds. The Arts Council Collection's traditional rationale of patronage and support is hardly relevant here: we are far from the days when impecunious artists were each provided with a piece of canvas of uniform size and commissioned to paint a picture to celebrate the 1951 Festival of Britain. Now, public collections must make decisive judgements to buy works by young artists who will soon be out of range. And imaginative, high quality art is being produced in this country in abundance, which means that the race is against time as well as a competitive market, for this is an especially vital creative moment to capture.

To compose a picture of art's evolution over a period of 60 years and to show how very recent work sits with that of preceding generations is one of the possibilities offered by a broad-based and expanding collection. Didactic, thematic and historically focused shows have their place, but sometimes the wayward interruption of predictable stories is more effective in bringing old art to life. If the past is to be made to serve the present rather than vice versa, if curators are to be more than merely custodians of the past, they should take their cues from artists' own wilfulness, borrowing what they need and discarding – temporarily – the rest. When an artist intervenes in a collection, mixing historical periods and categories and introducing new elements, we are liberated from habitual readings: the familiar becomes strange, new meanings are revealed. A generation of talented curators has emerged in Britain who are more than equal to this challenge. The resources are needed now to put their ideas into action.

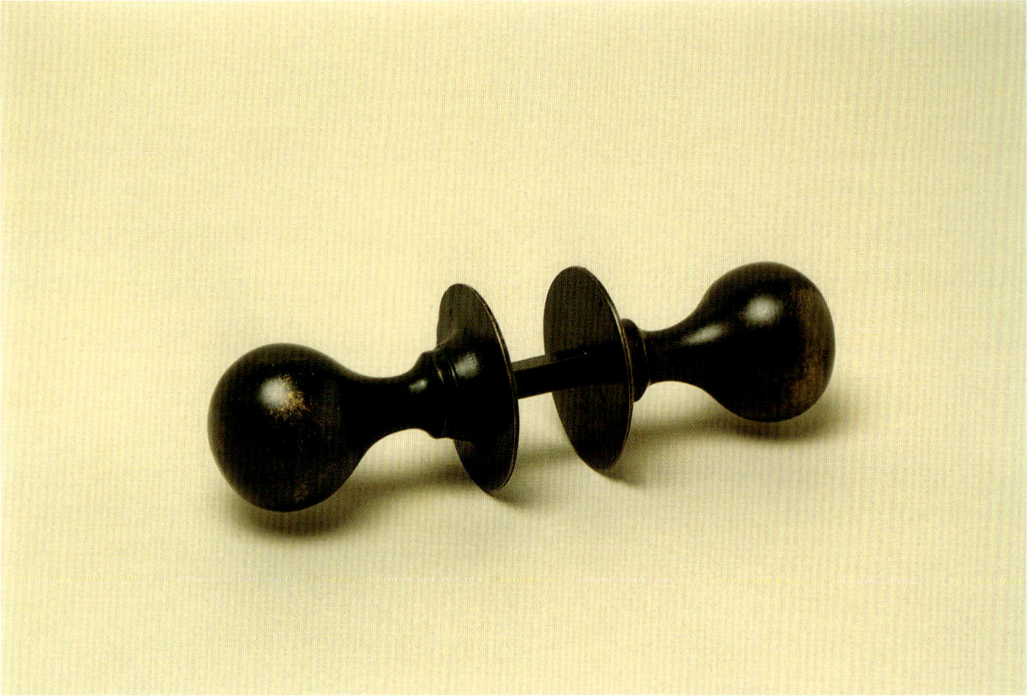

Rachel Whiteread Untitled, 1993

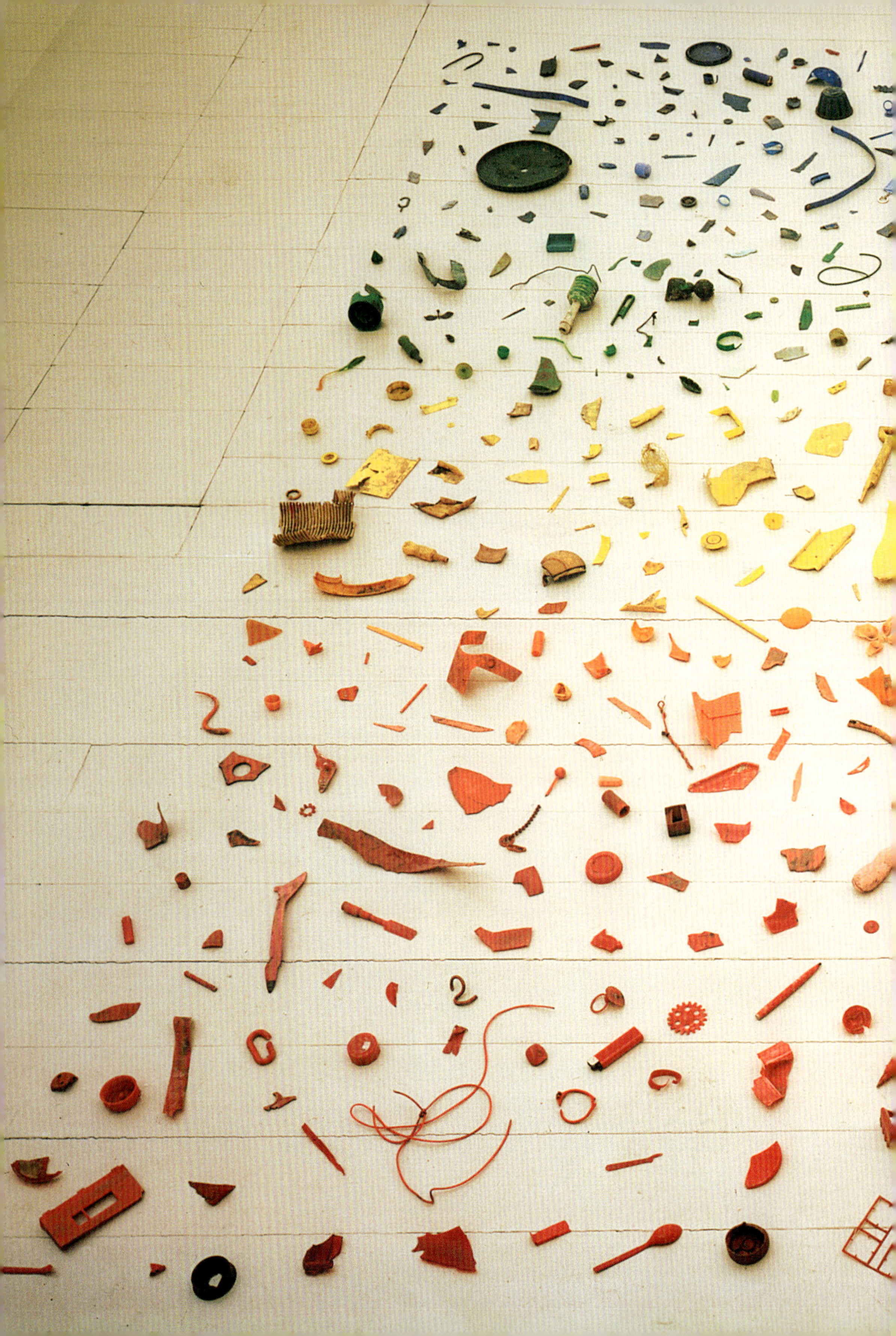

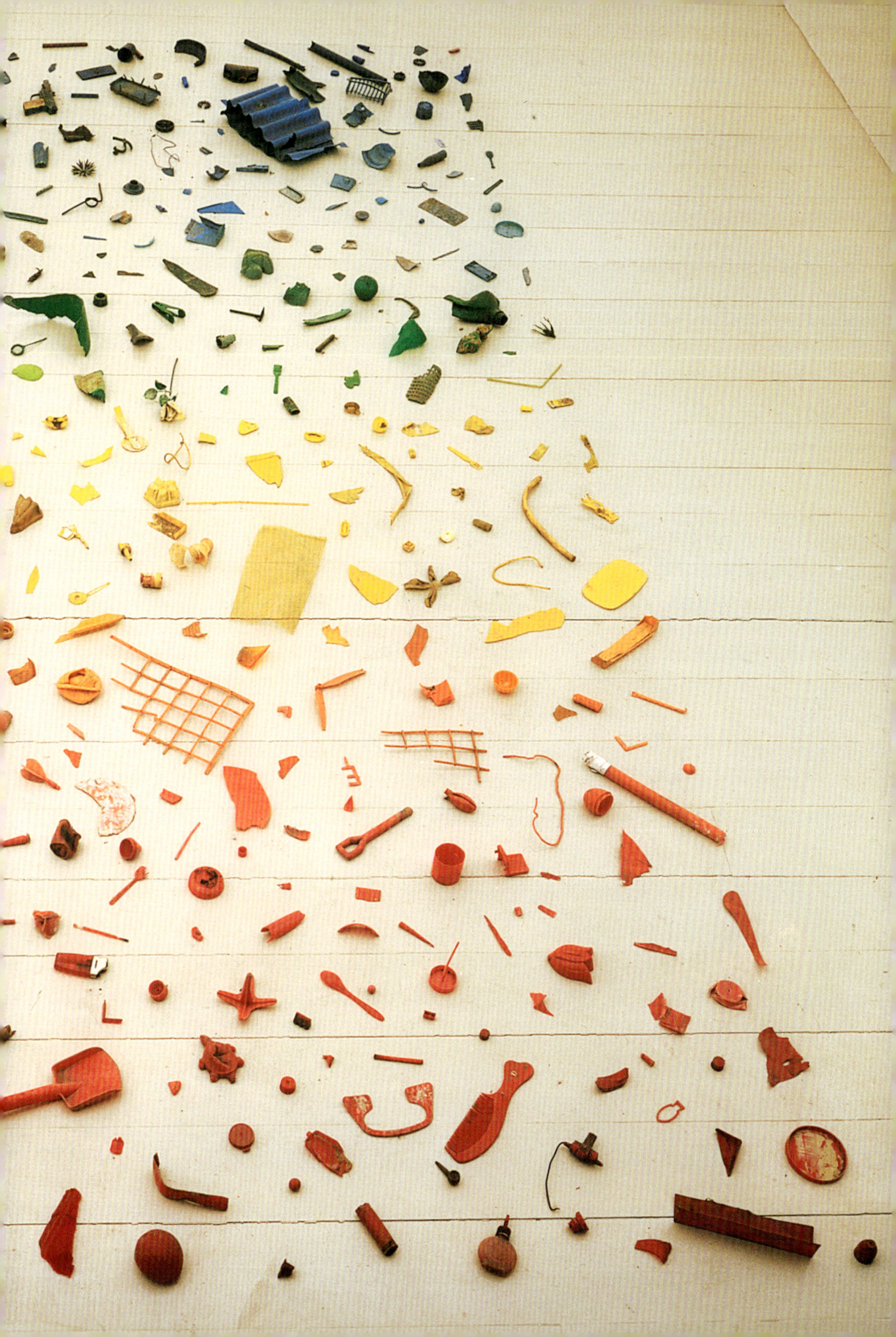

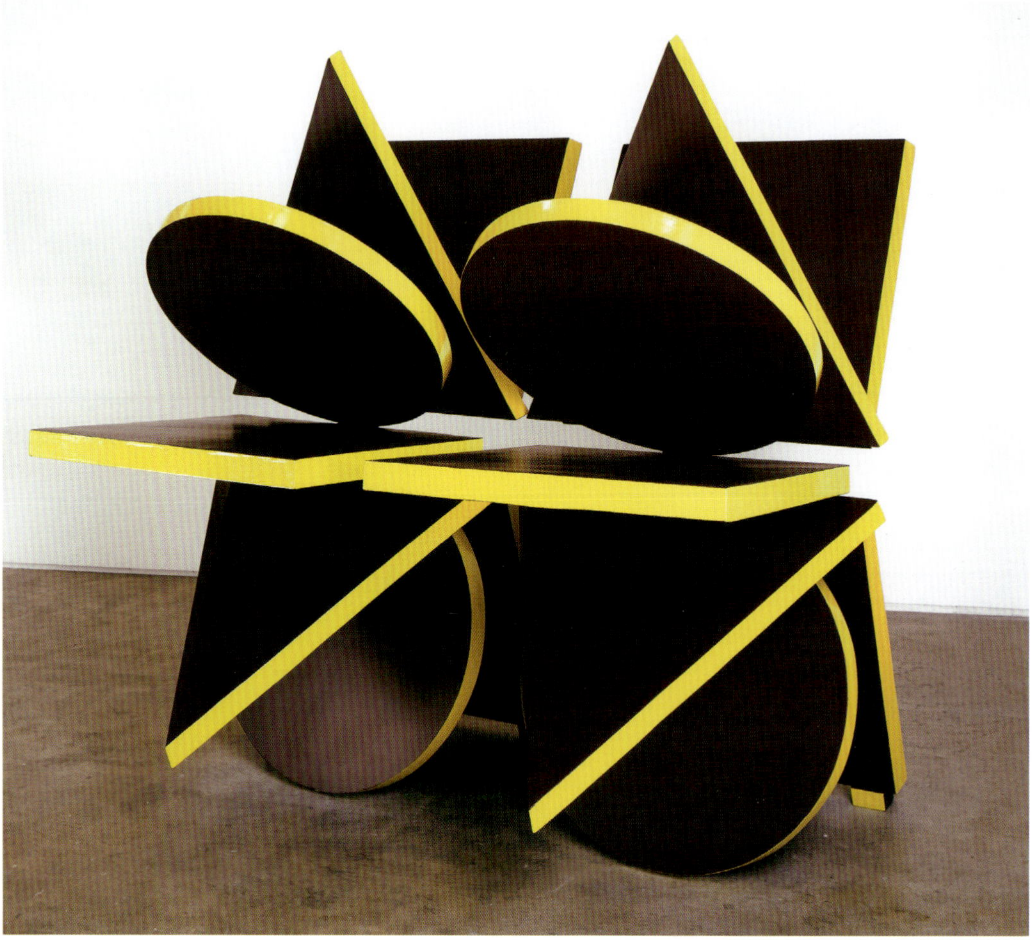

previous **Tony Cragg** New Stones – Newton's Tones, 1978
above **Phillip King** Point X, 1965

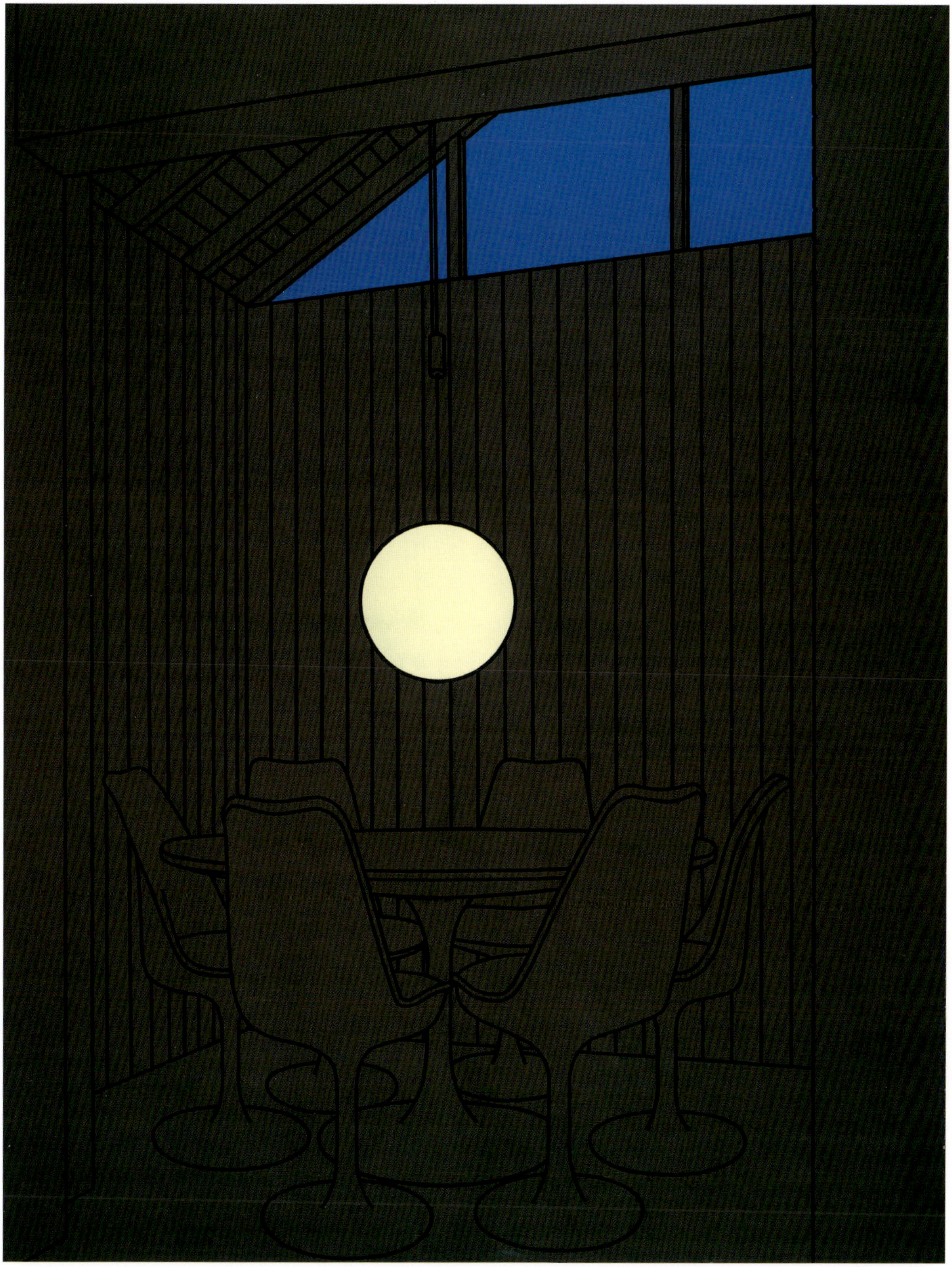

Patrick Caulfield Dining Recess, 1972

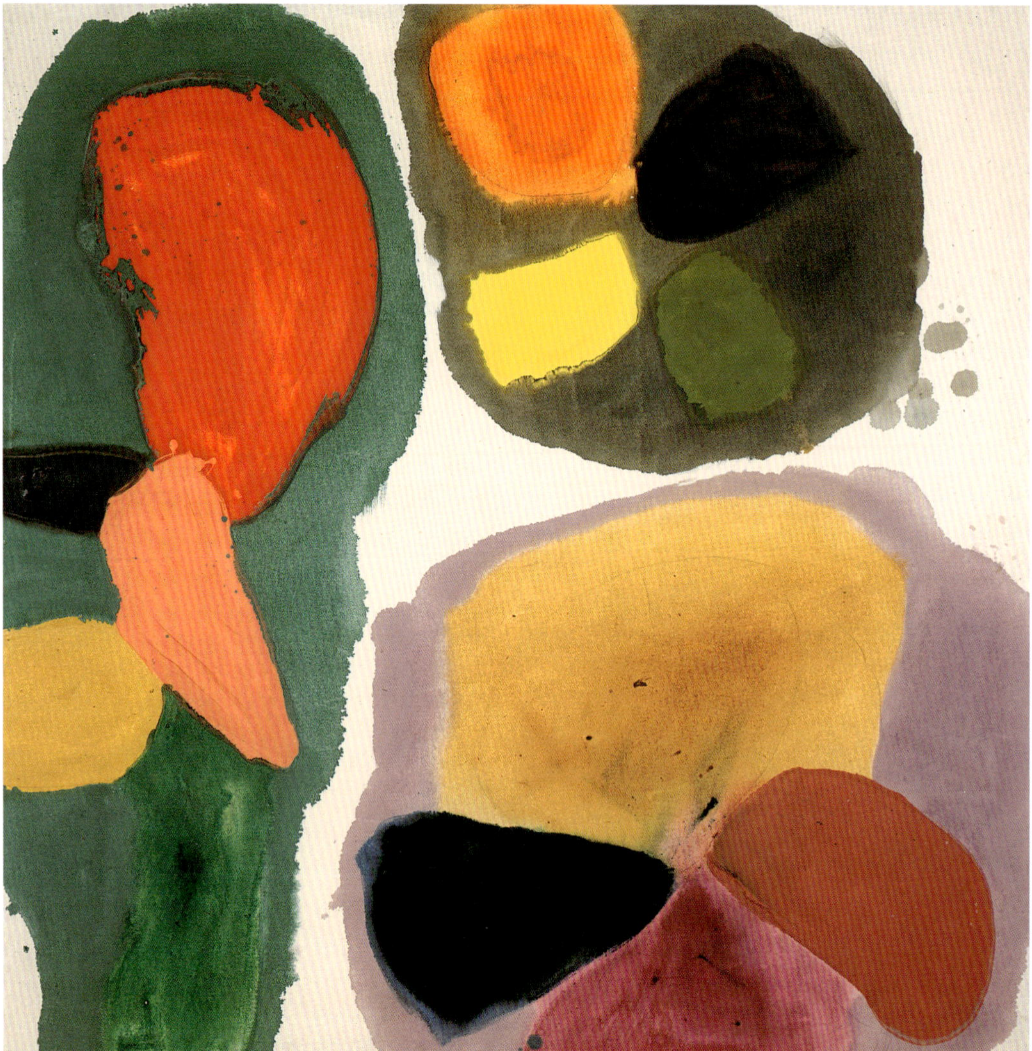

Gillian Ayres Lure, 1963

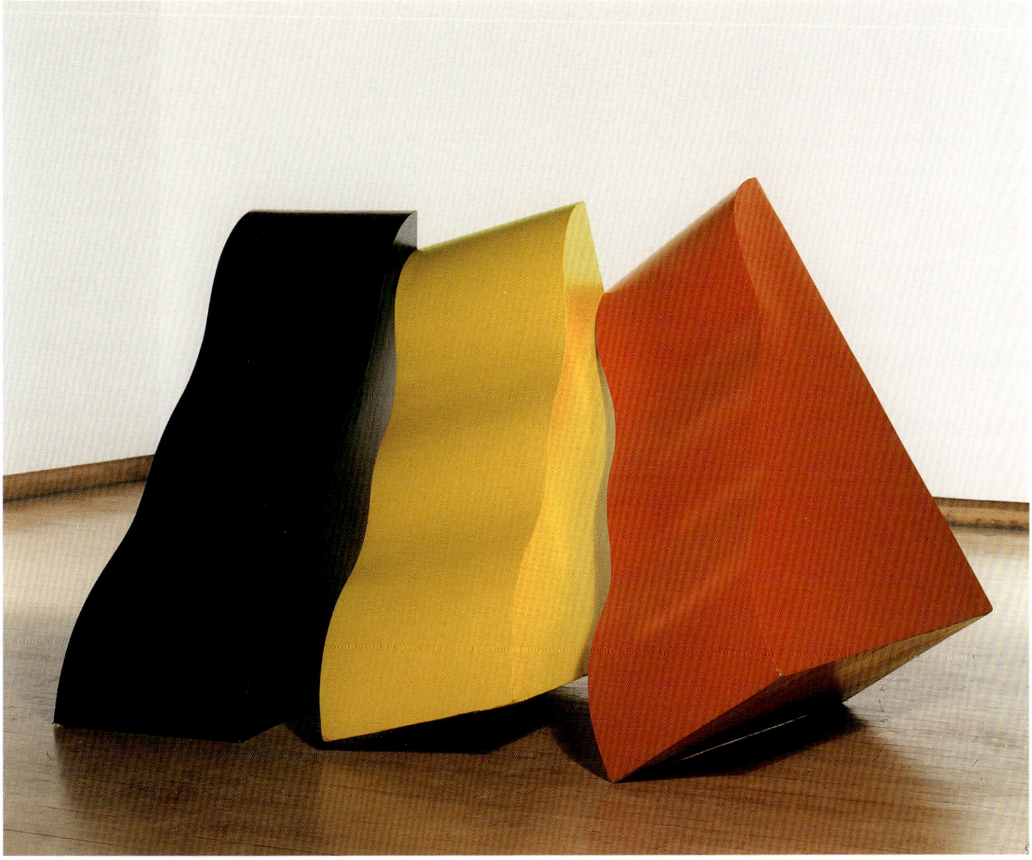

William Tucker Thebes, 1966

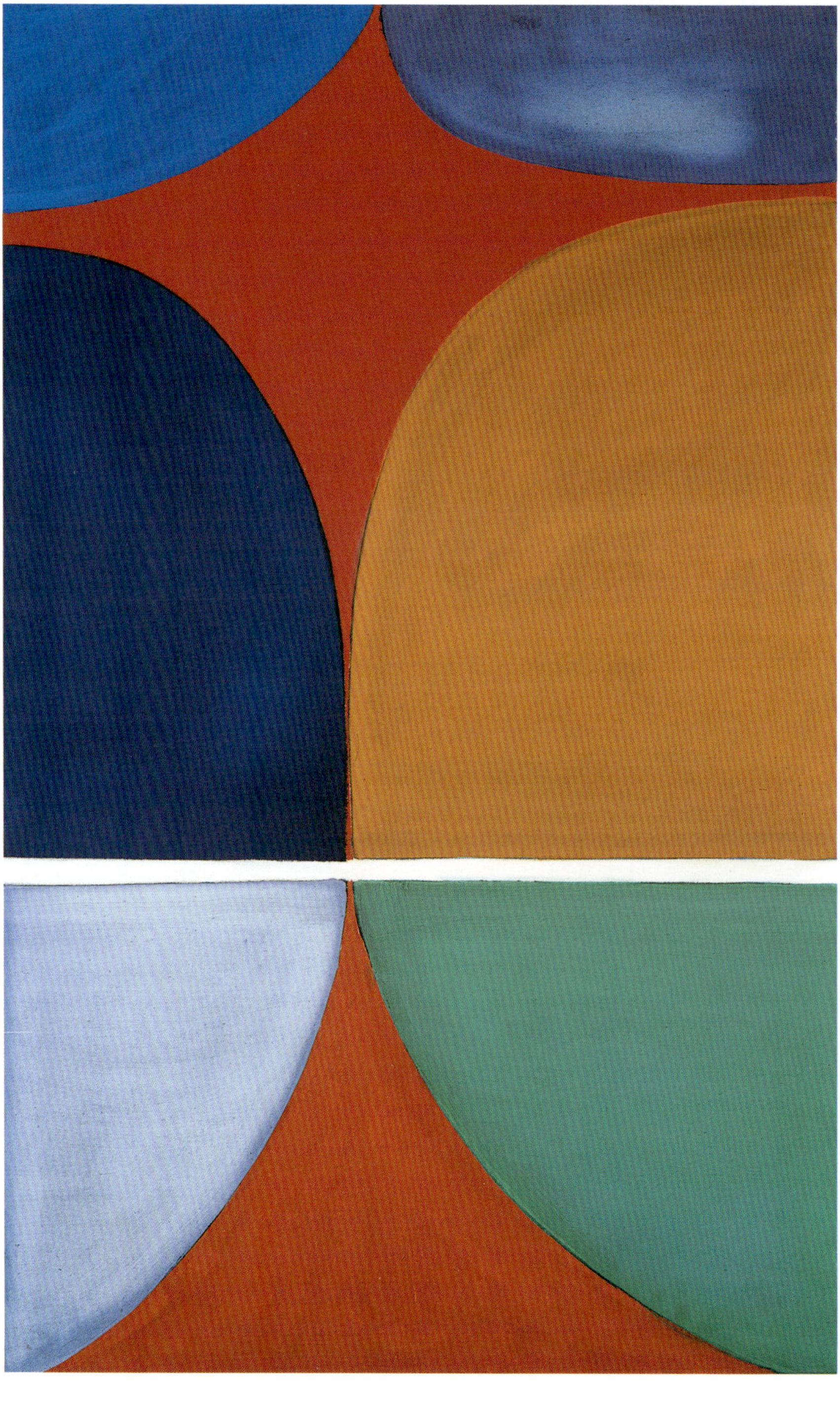

above **Terry Frost** Ginger and Purple 'Chirpy', 1966
opposite **Barbara Hepworth** Spring, 1966

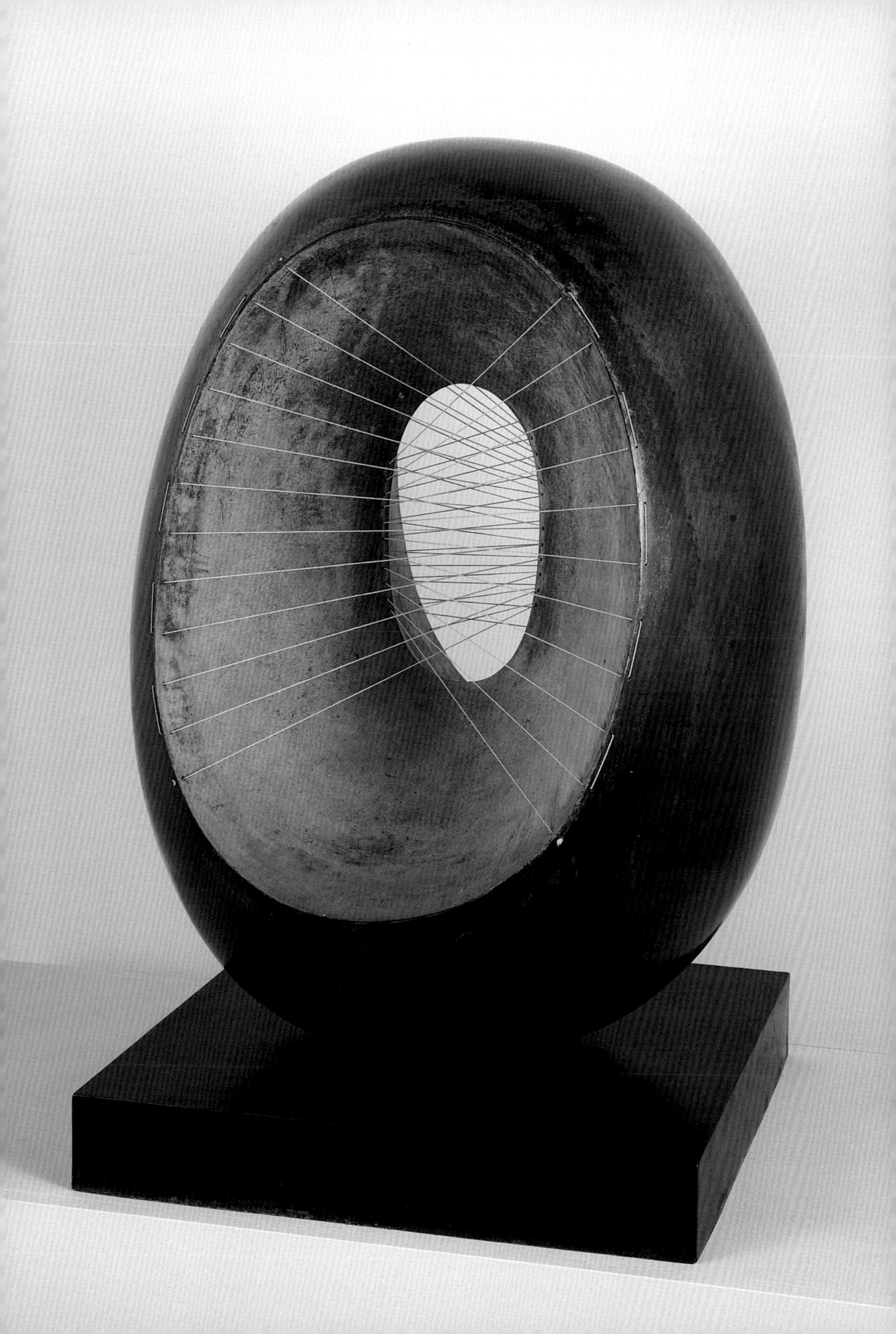

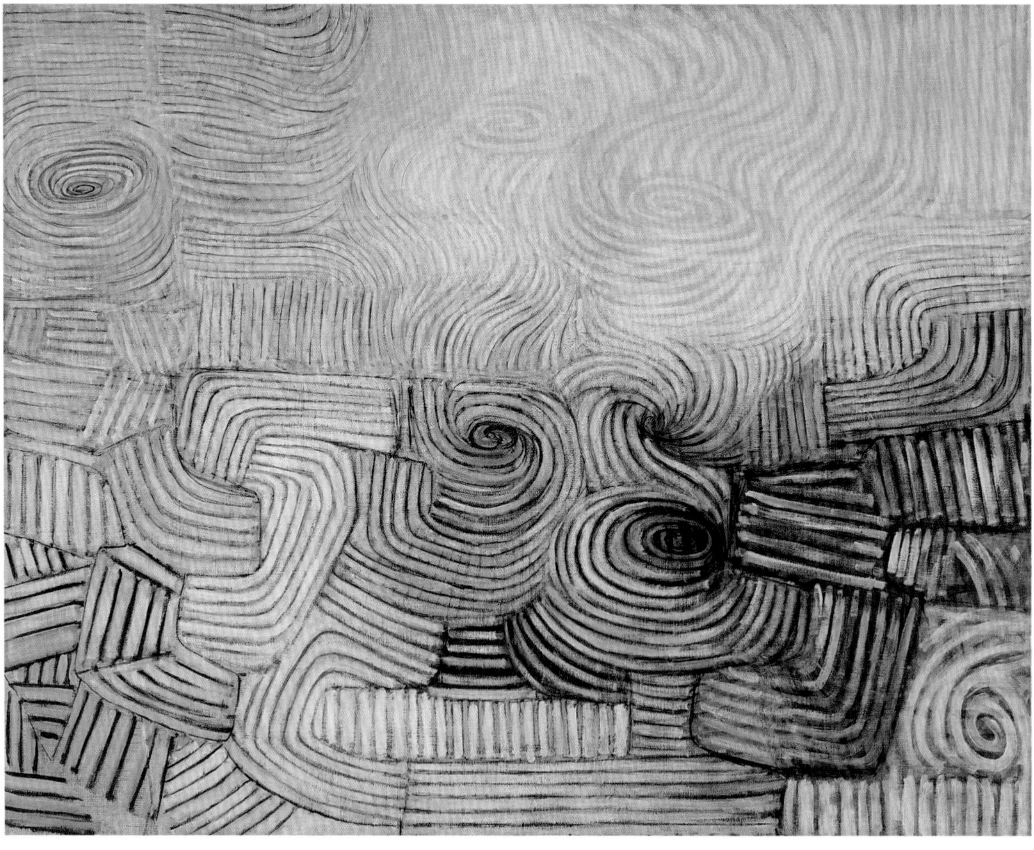

Victor Pasmore The Snowstorm: Spiral Motif in Black and White, 1950–1951

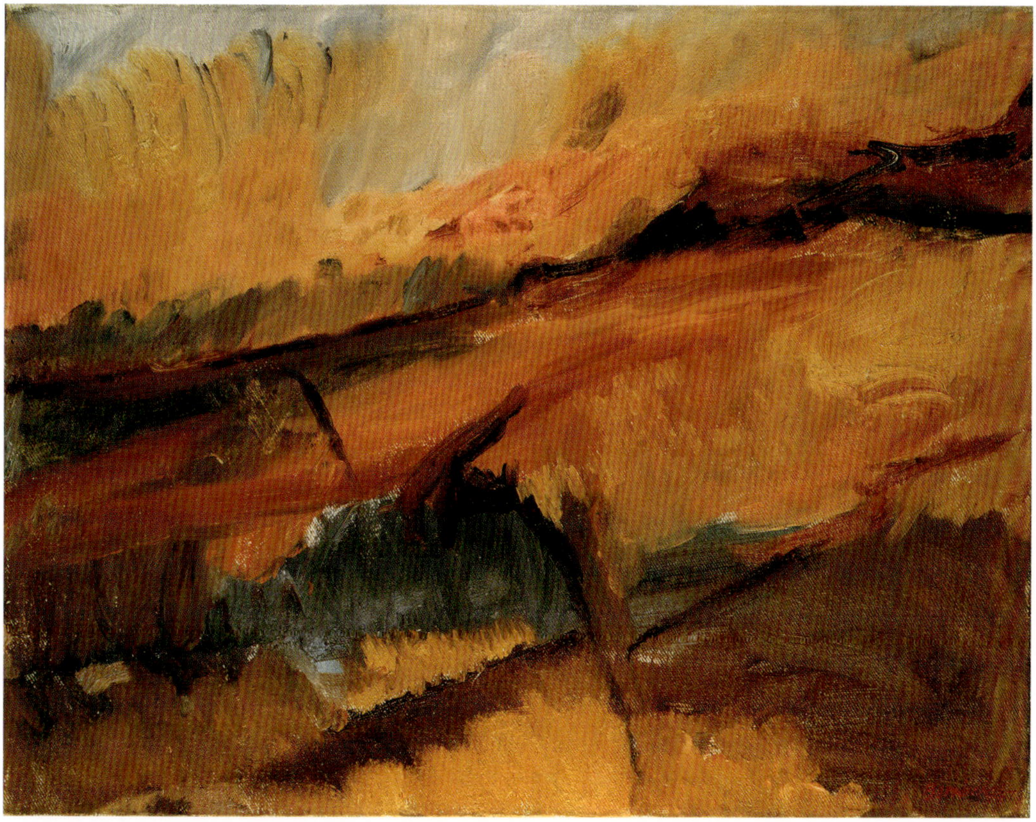

David Bomberg Trendrine, Cornwall, 1947

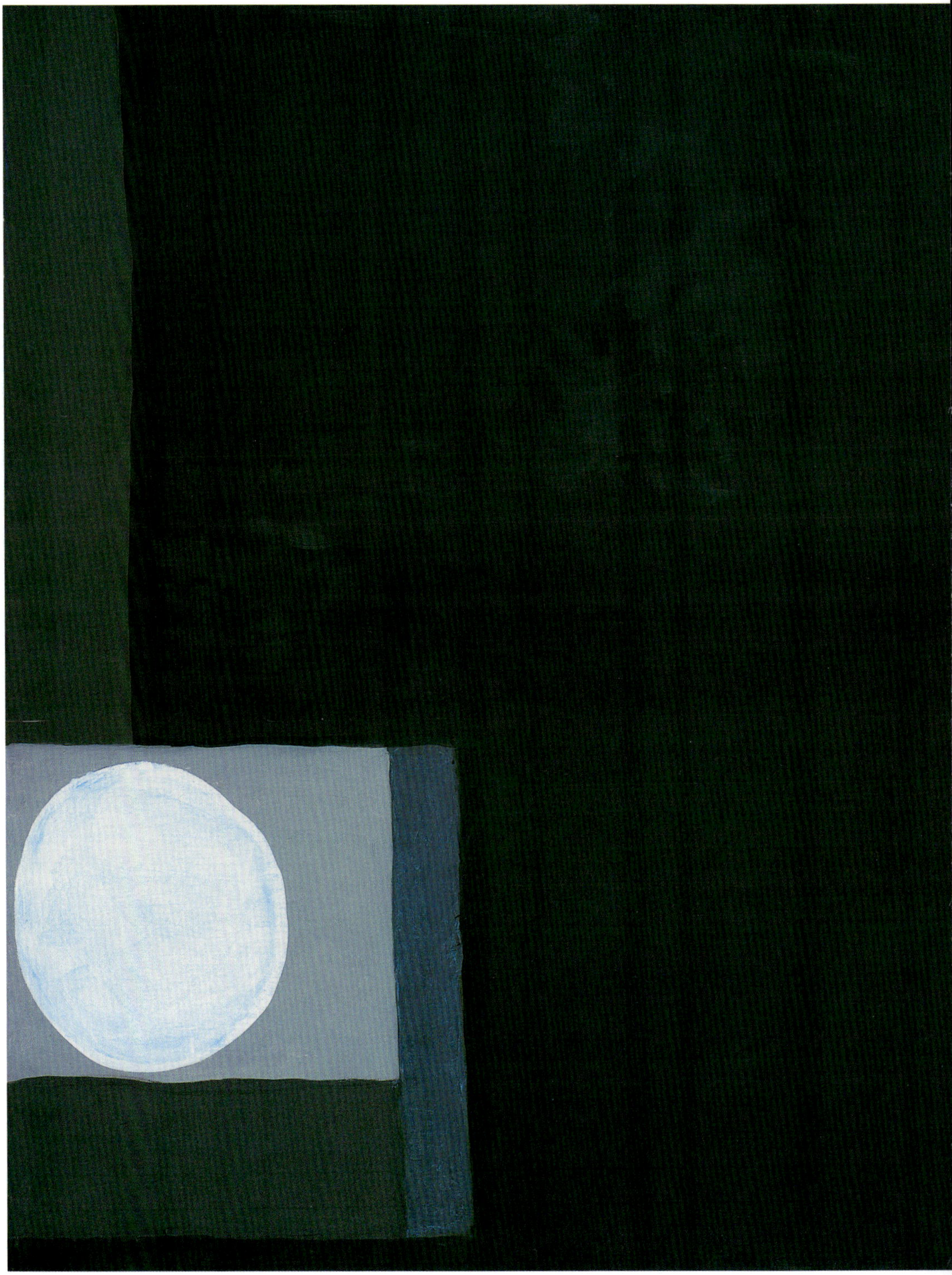

Patrick Heron Green Painting with White Disc, 1964

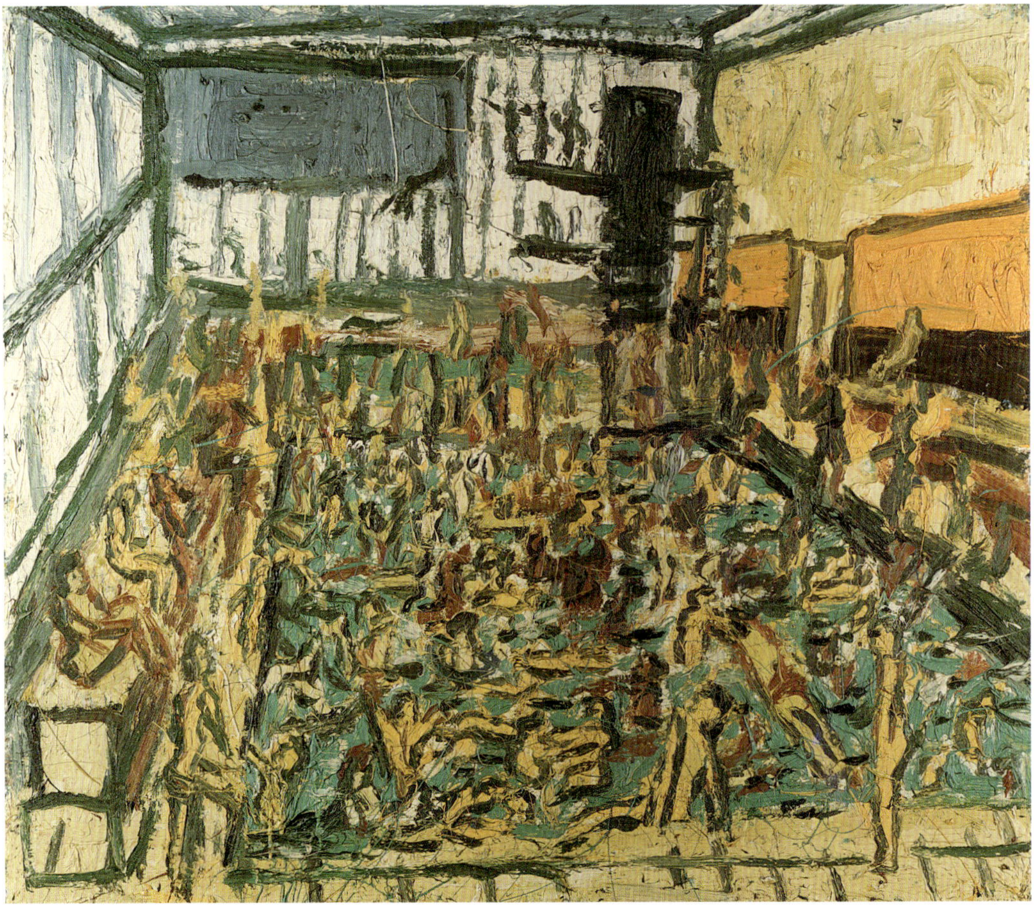

Leon Kossoff Children's Swimming Pool, Autumn 1972, 1972

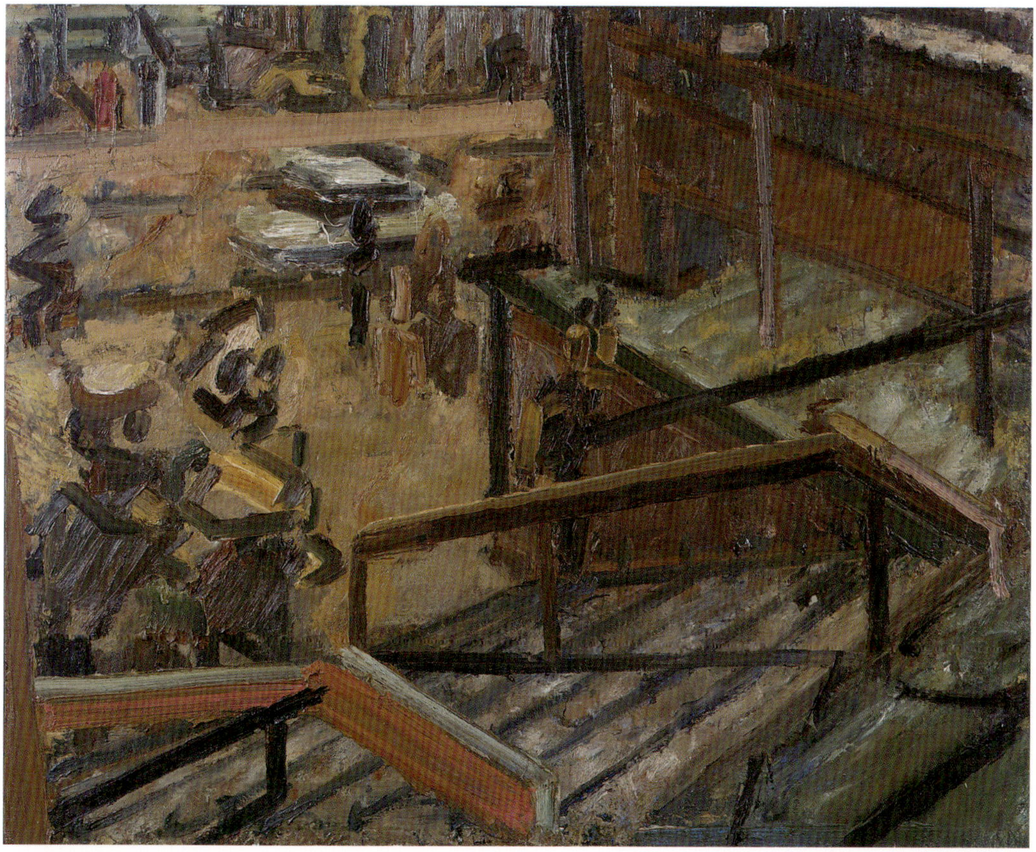

Frank Auerbach Euston Steps - Study, 1980–1981

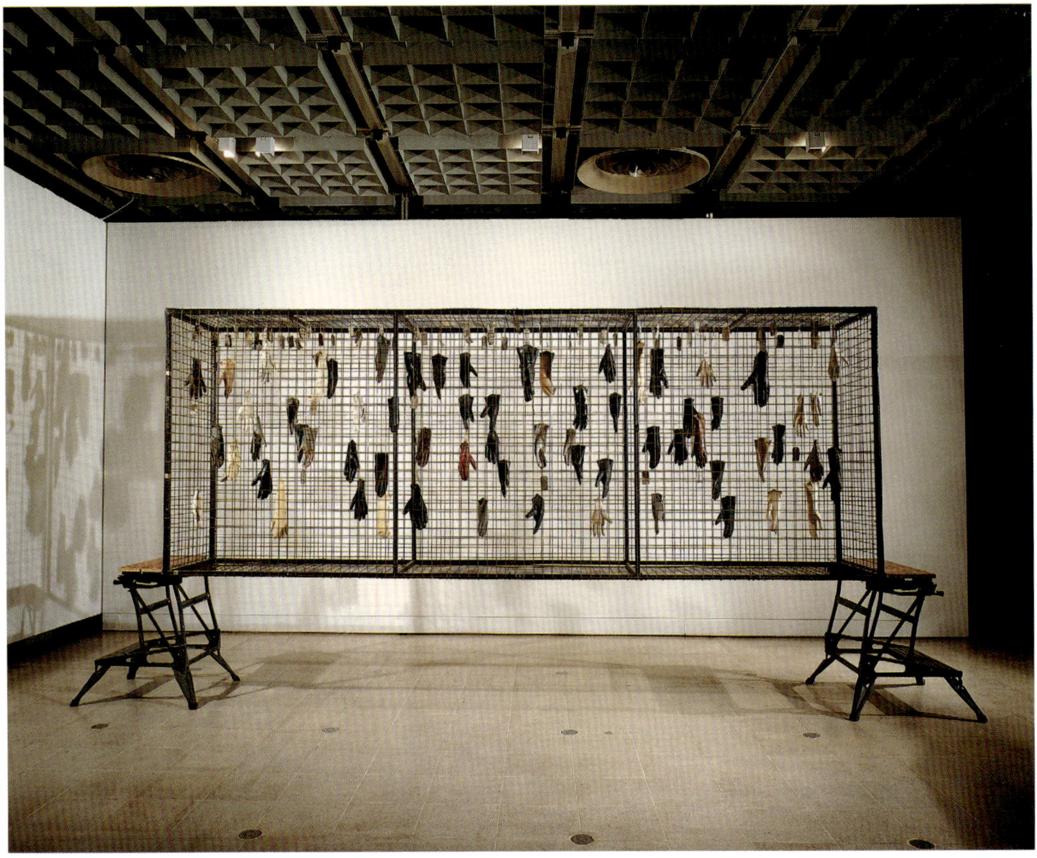

Stuart Brisley 1=66,666 (March 1983 – Georgiana Collection VI), 1983

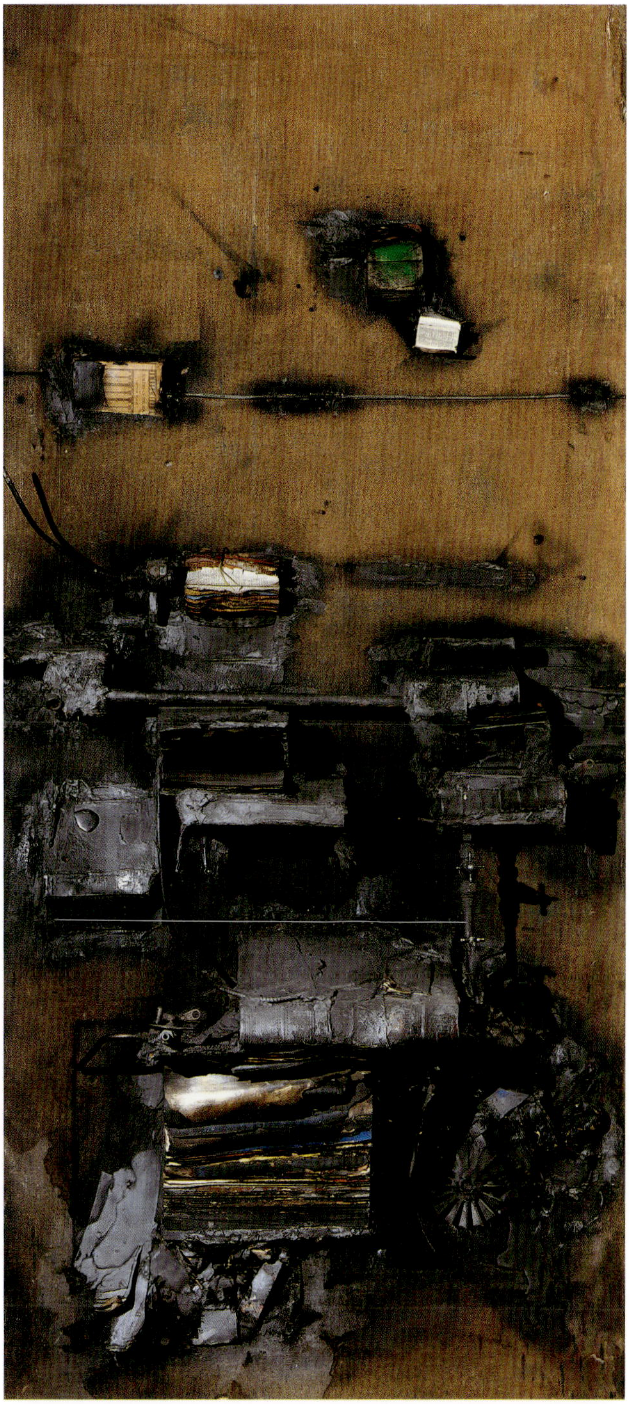

John Latham Shaun II, 1958

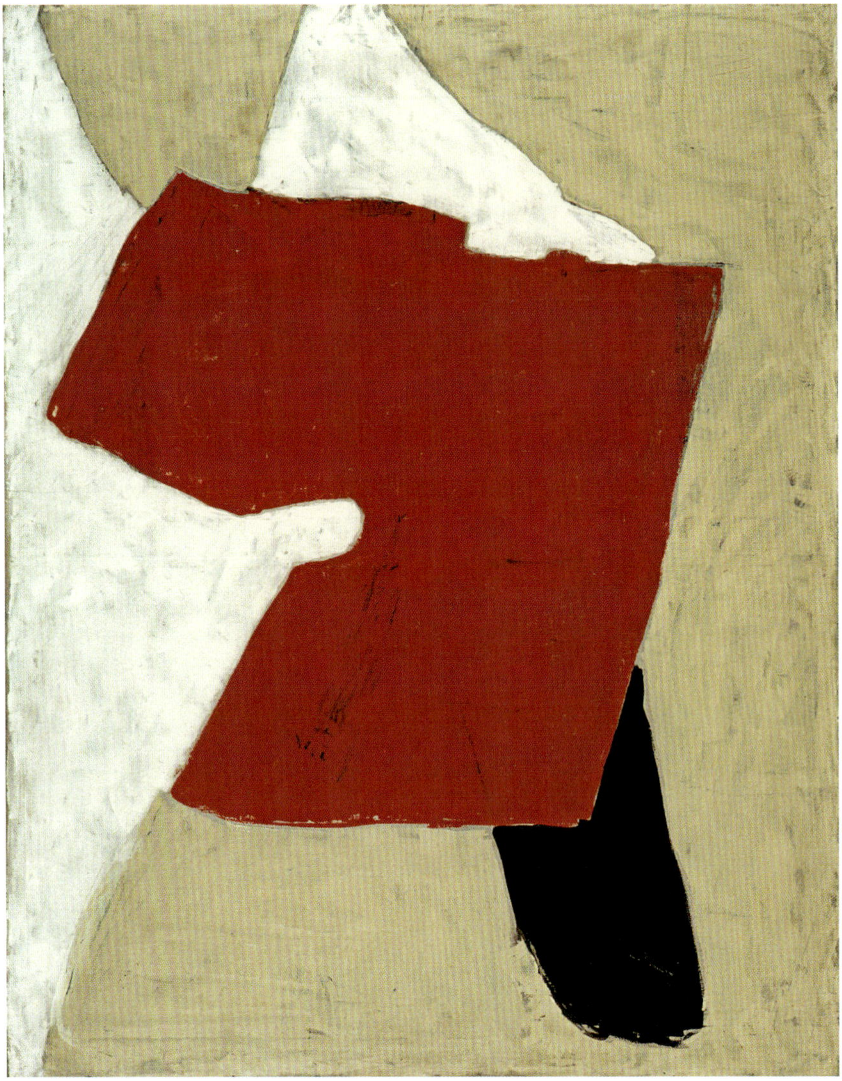

above **Roger Hilton** February–March 1954, 1954
opposite **Lynn Chadwick** The Seasons, 1955

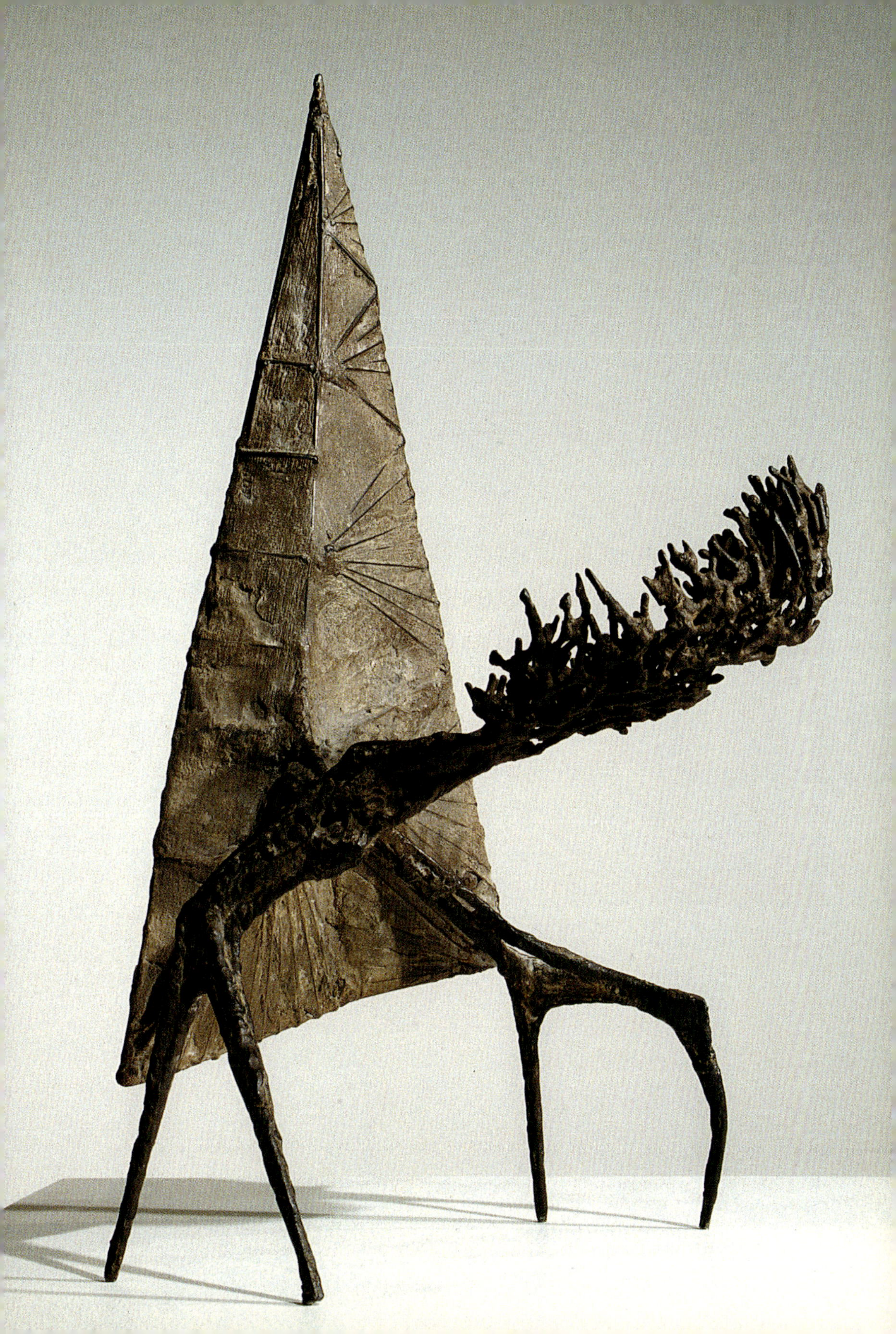

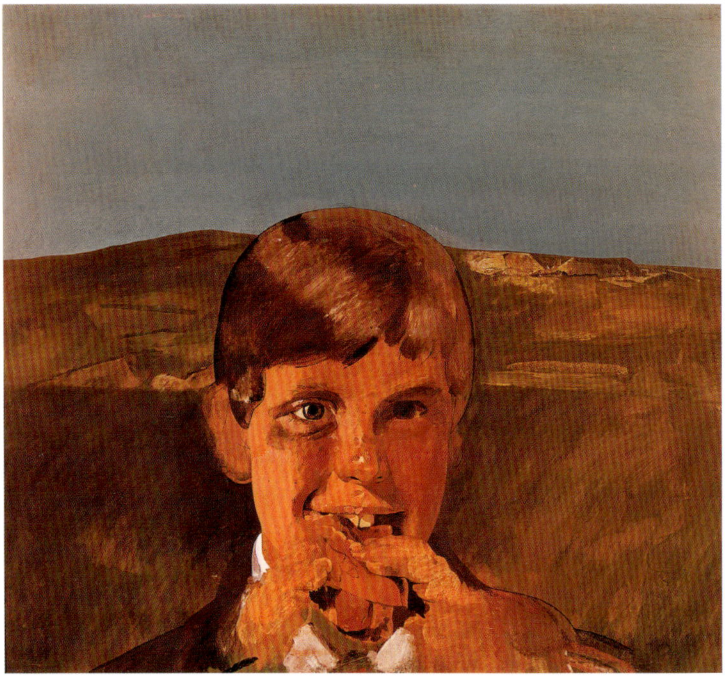

Peter Blake Boy Eating a Hot Dog, 1960–1965

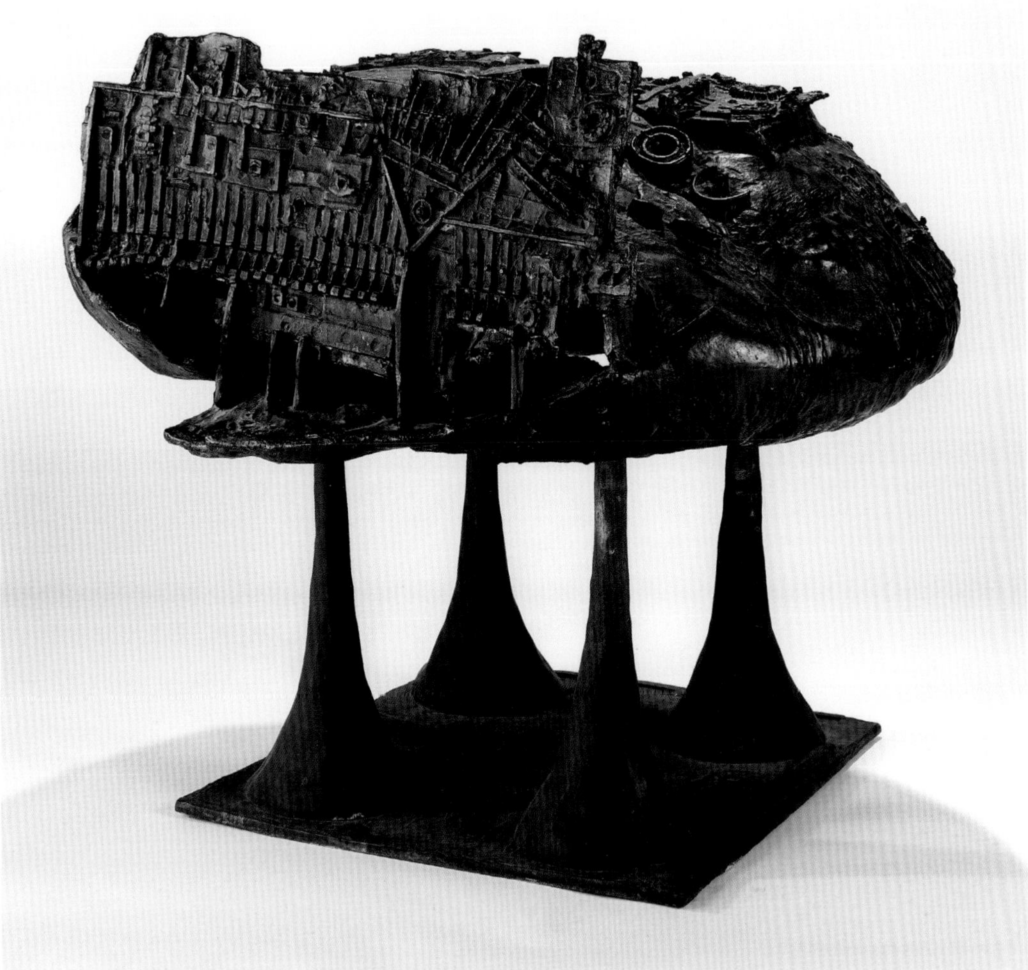

Eduardo Paolozzi The Frog, 1958

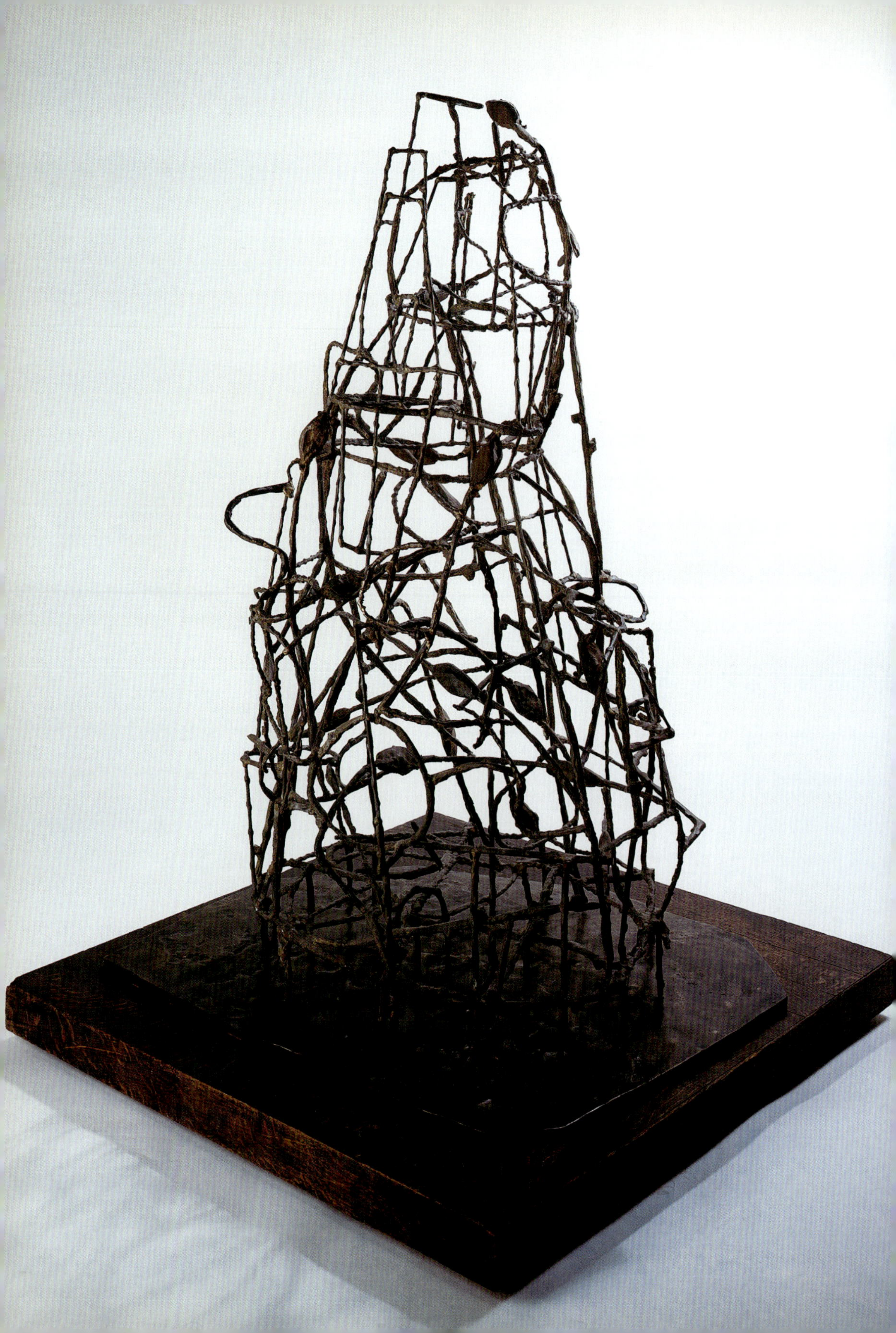

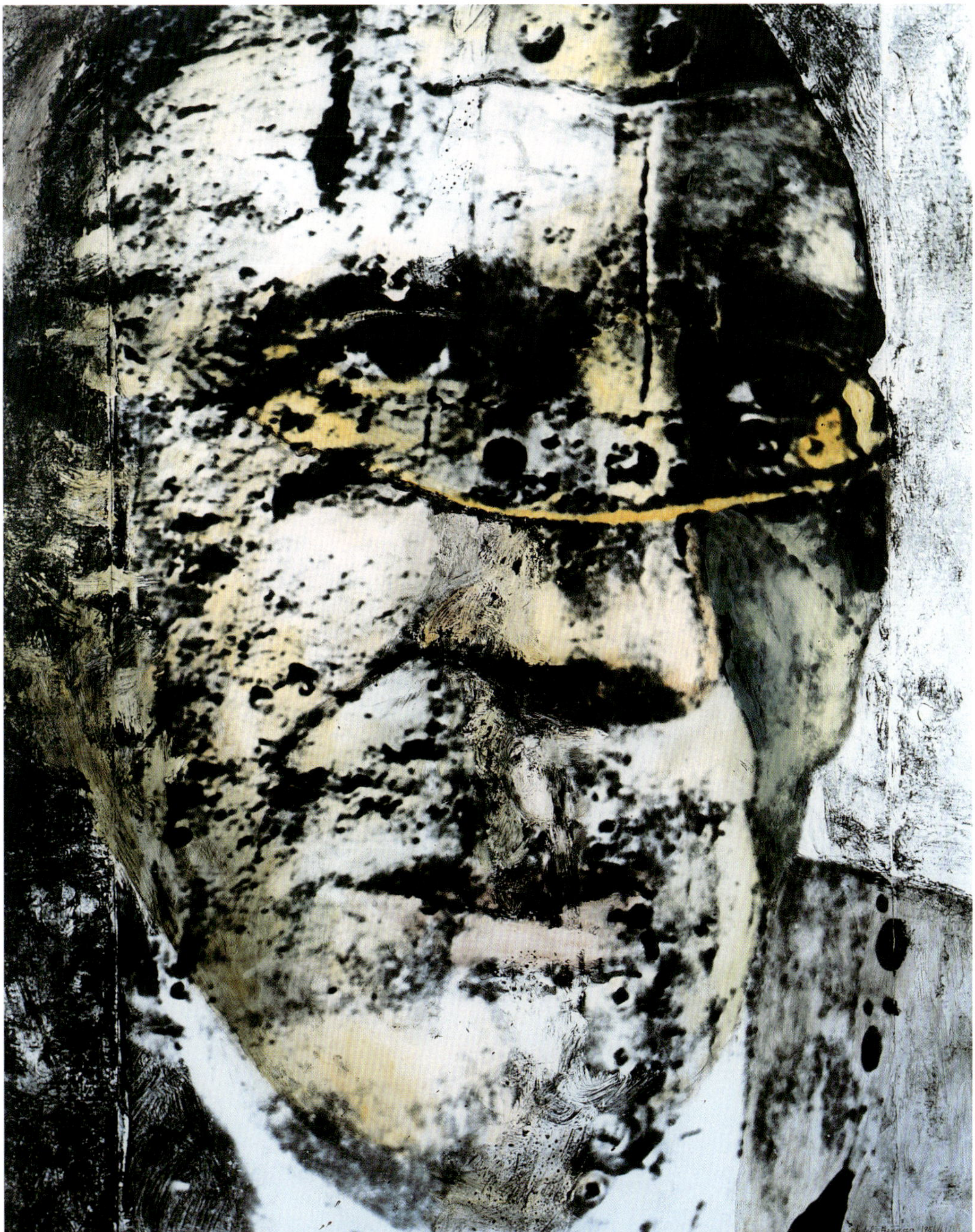

Nigel Henderson Head of a Man, 1956–1961

opposite **Eduardo Paolozzi** The Cage, 1951

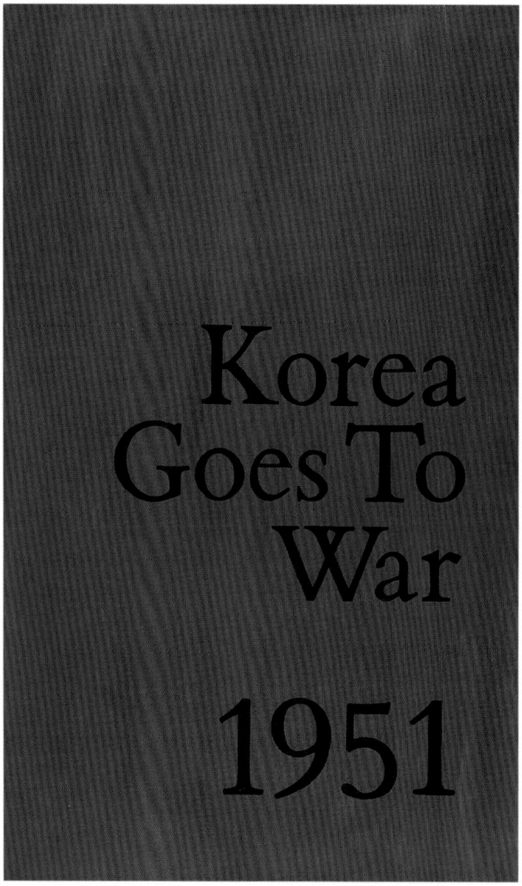

Douglas Gordon Painting No. 19: Mark Rothko / Betty Parsons, 1992

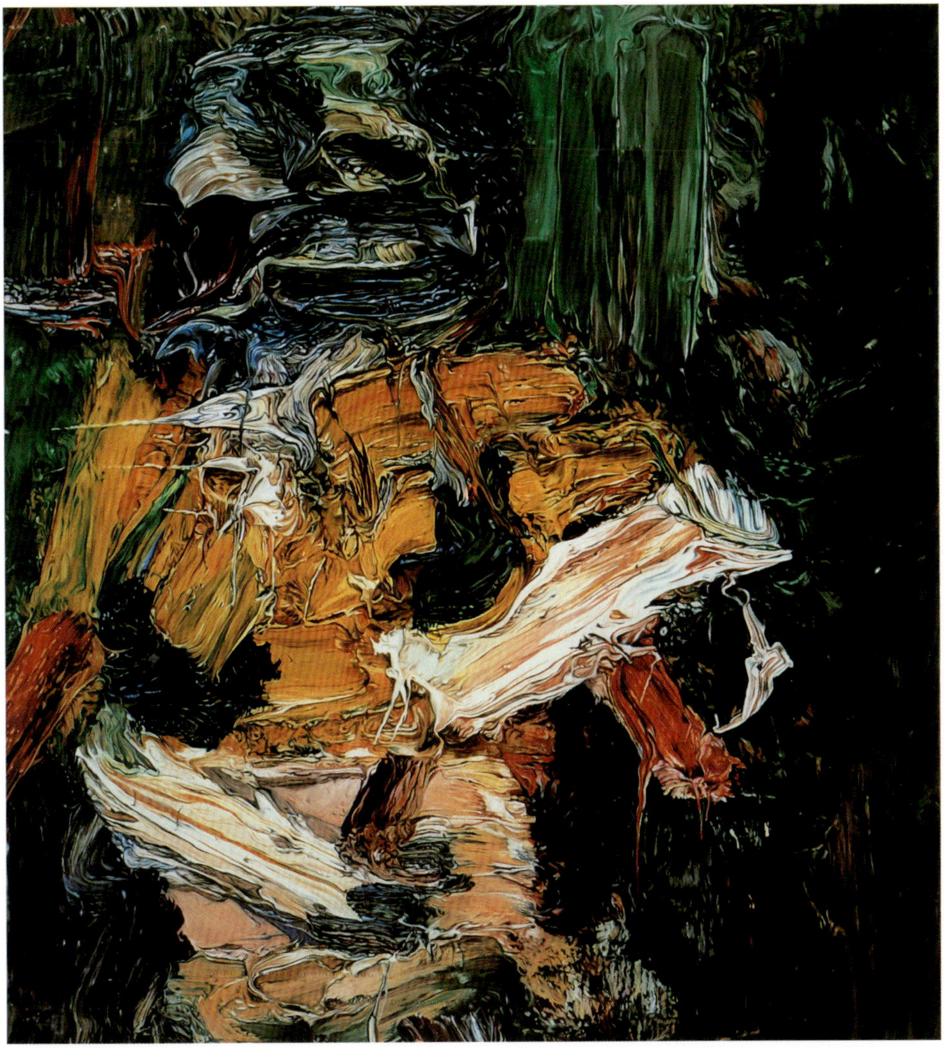

Glenn Brown Decline and Fall, 1995

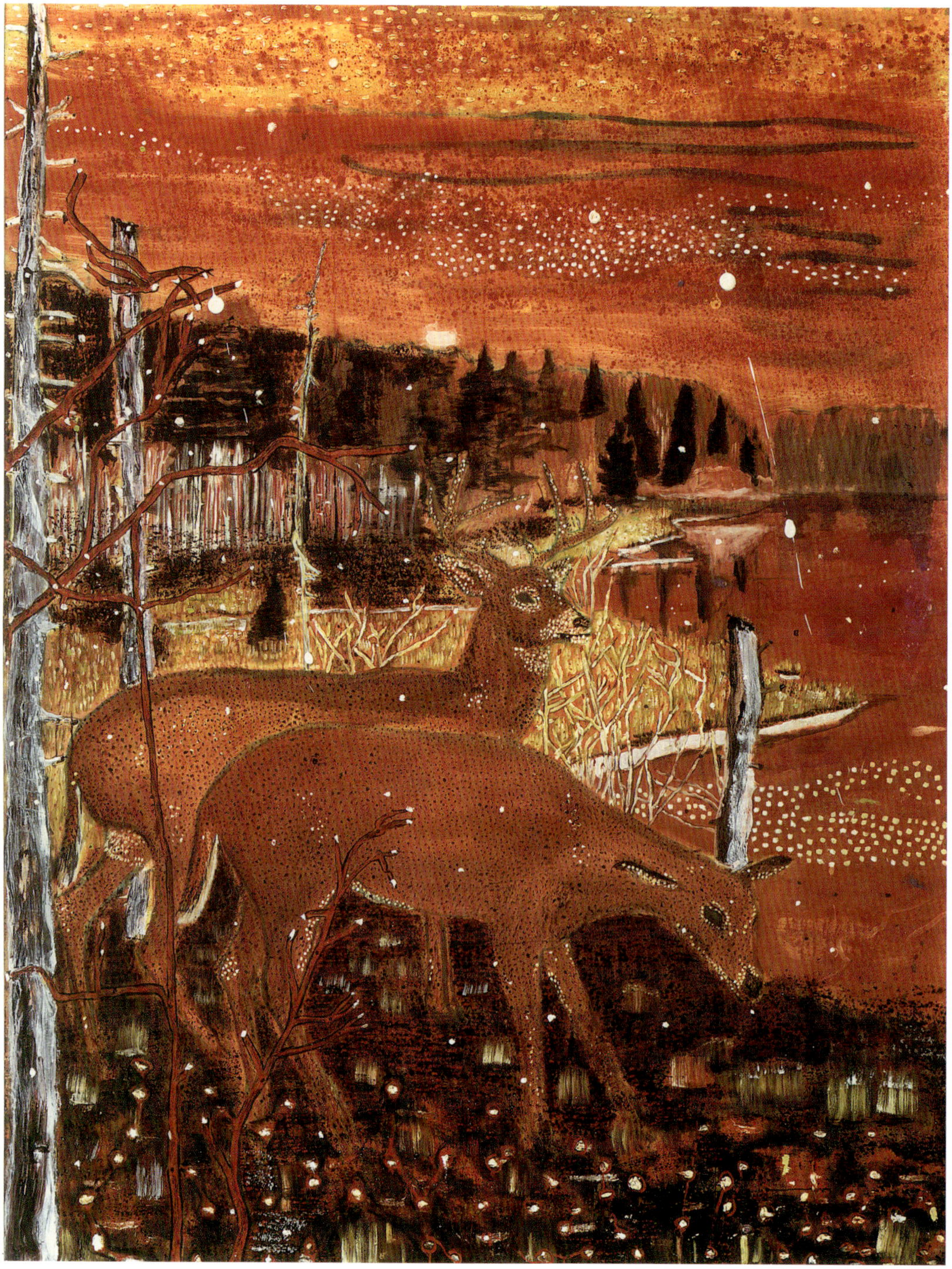

Peter Doig Red Deer, 1990

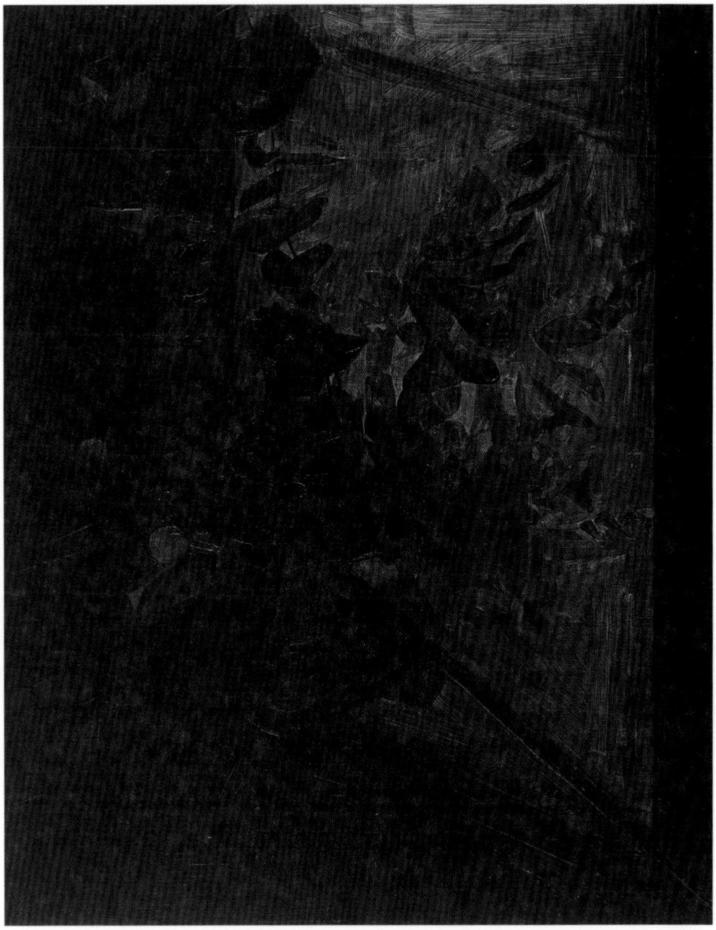

Gillian Carnegie Mono, 2005

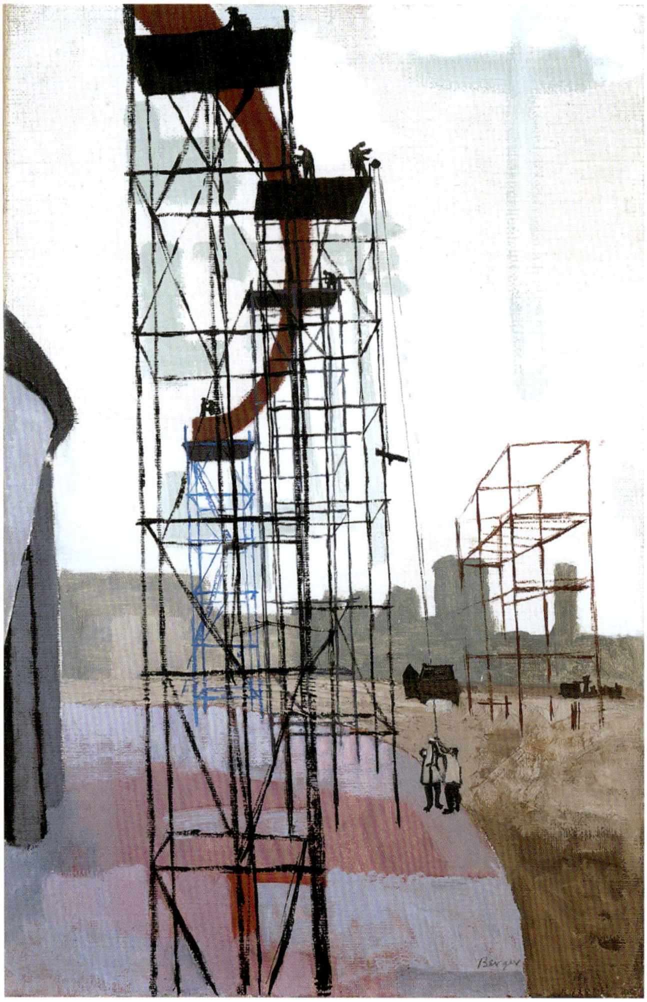

John Berger Scaffolding – Festival of Britain, 1950

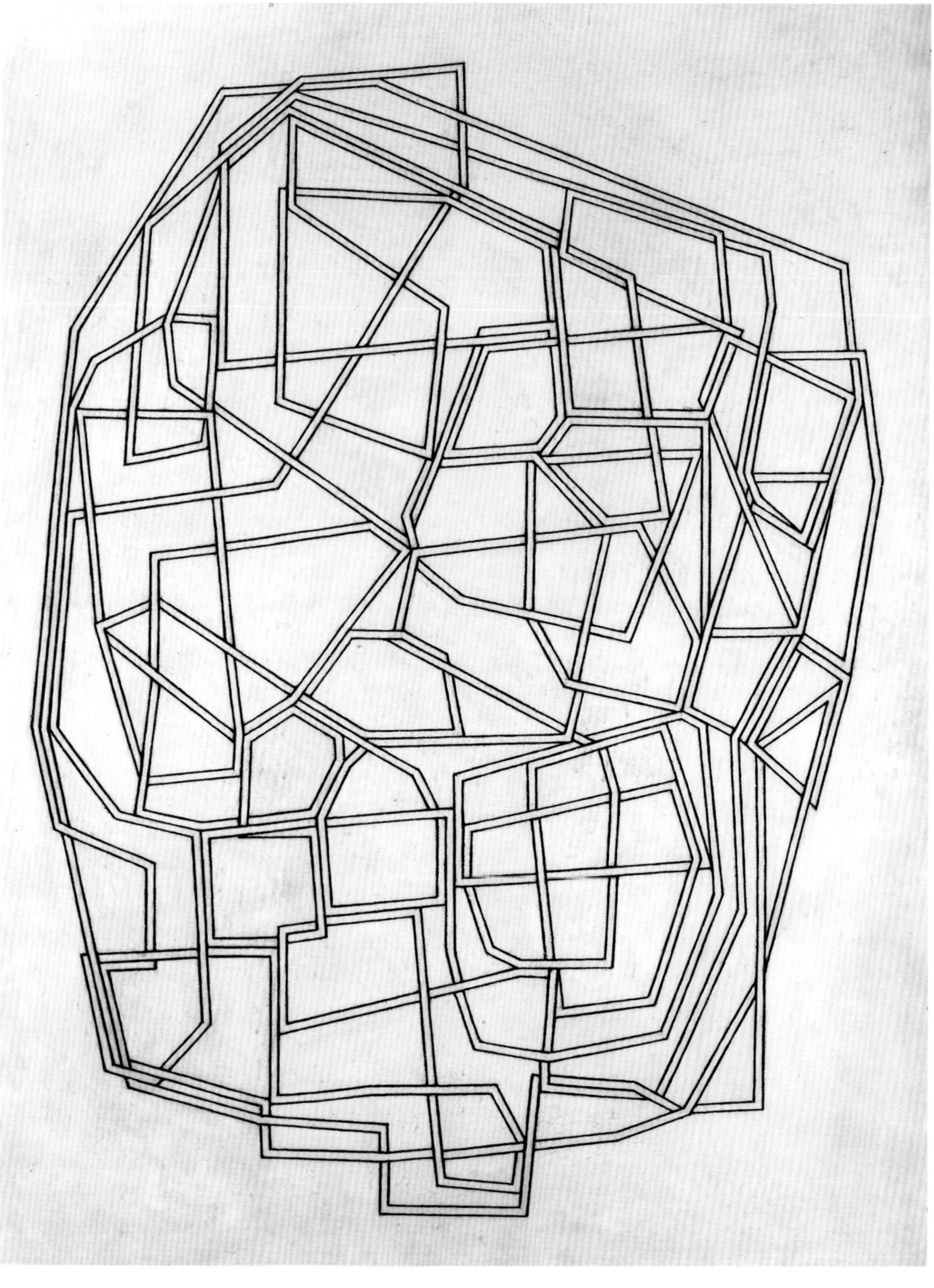

Kenneth Martin Endless Configuration, 1964

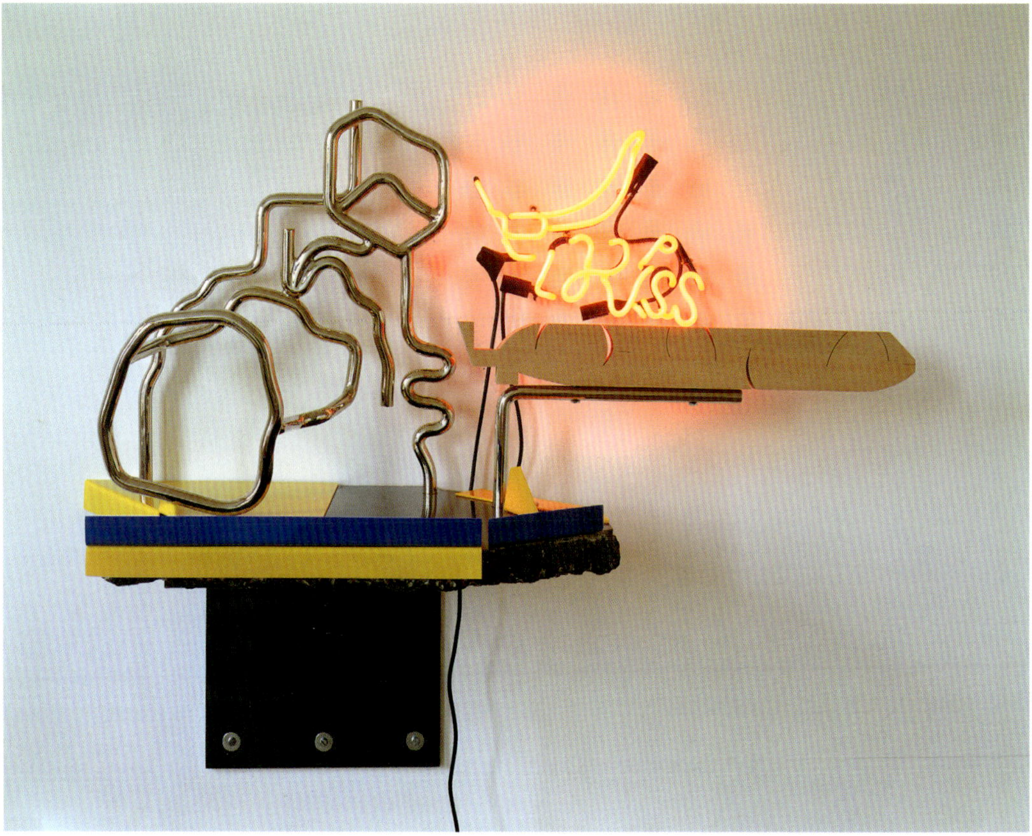

above **Gary Webb** Mirage of Loose Change, 2001

opposite **Camilla Løw** 7, 2004

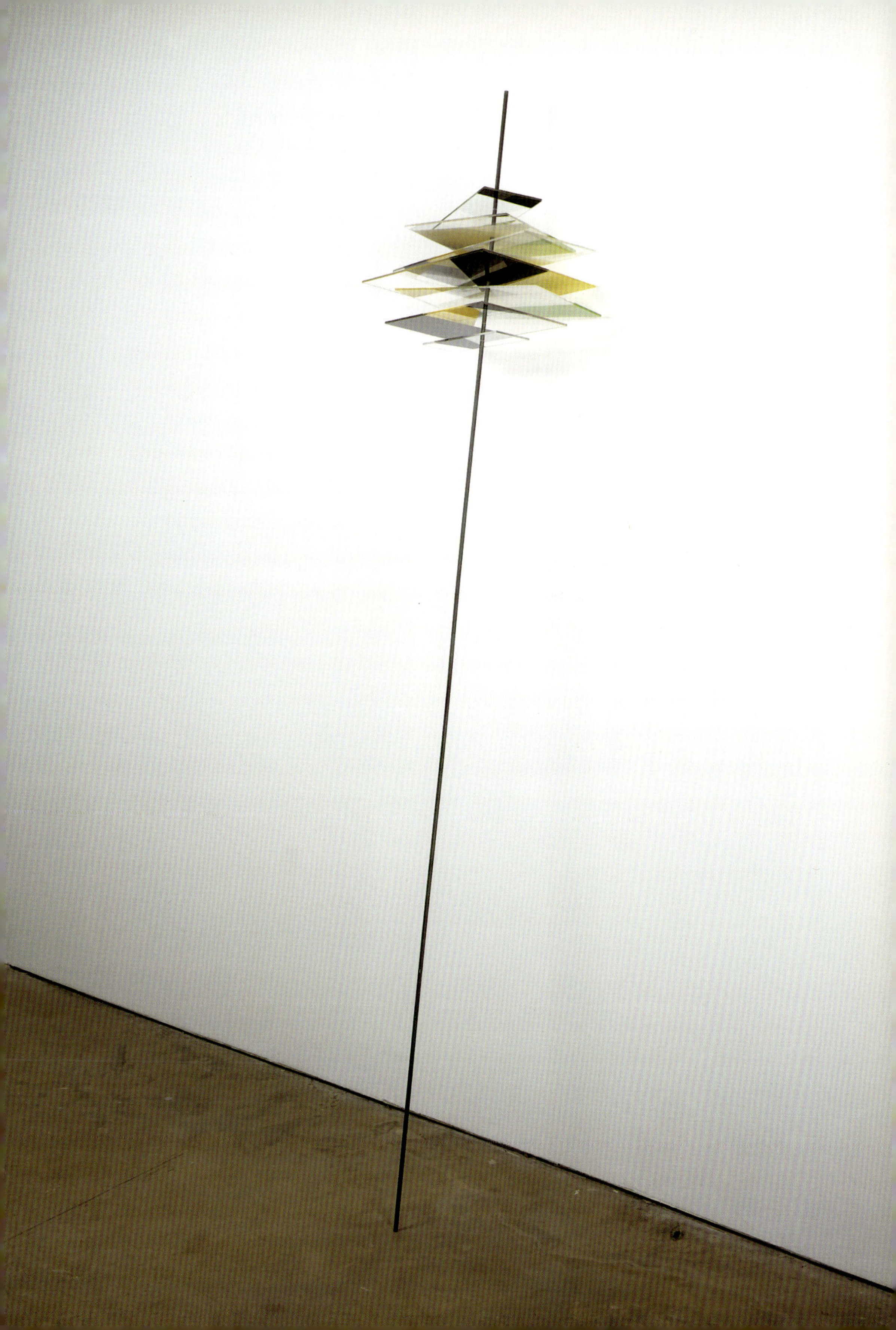

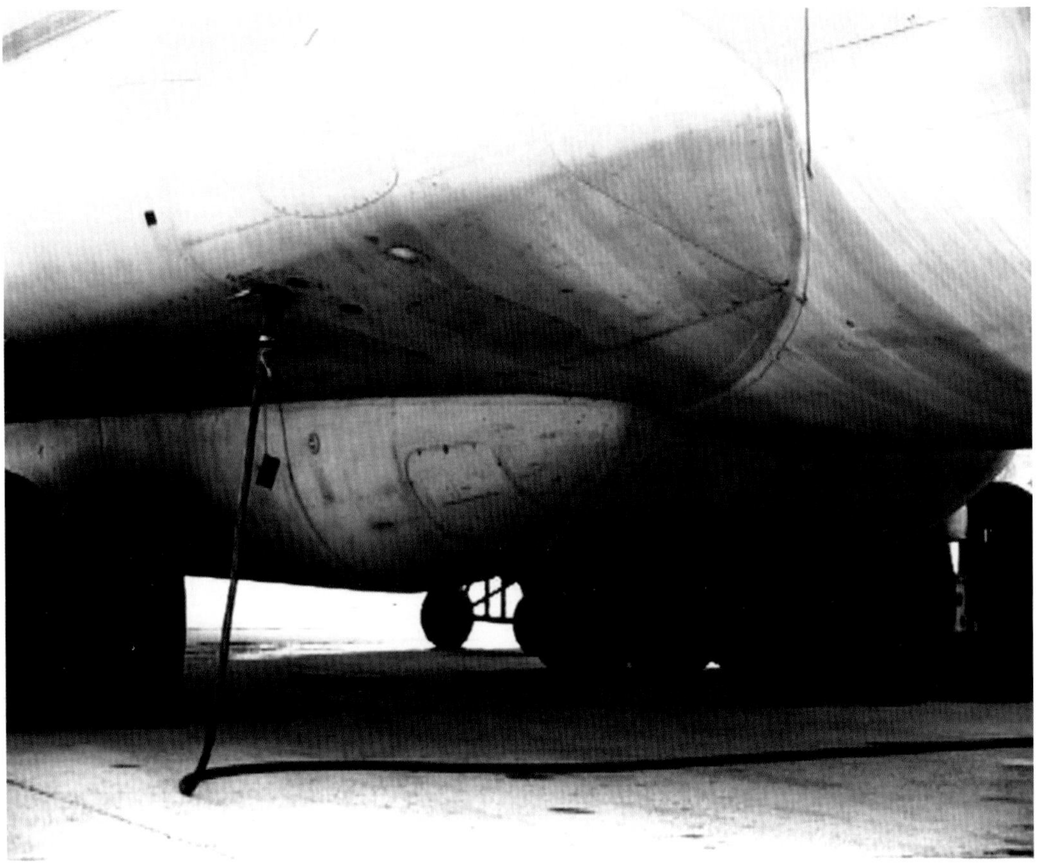

The Otolith Group (Anjalika Sagar, Kodwo Eshun and Richard Couzins) Otolith, 2006

opposite **Reg Butler** Girl and Boy, 1950–1951

overleaf **Bruce Bernard** Leigh Bowery and Nicola Bateman posing for 'And for the Bridegroom', 1993

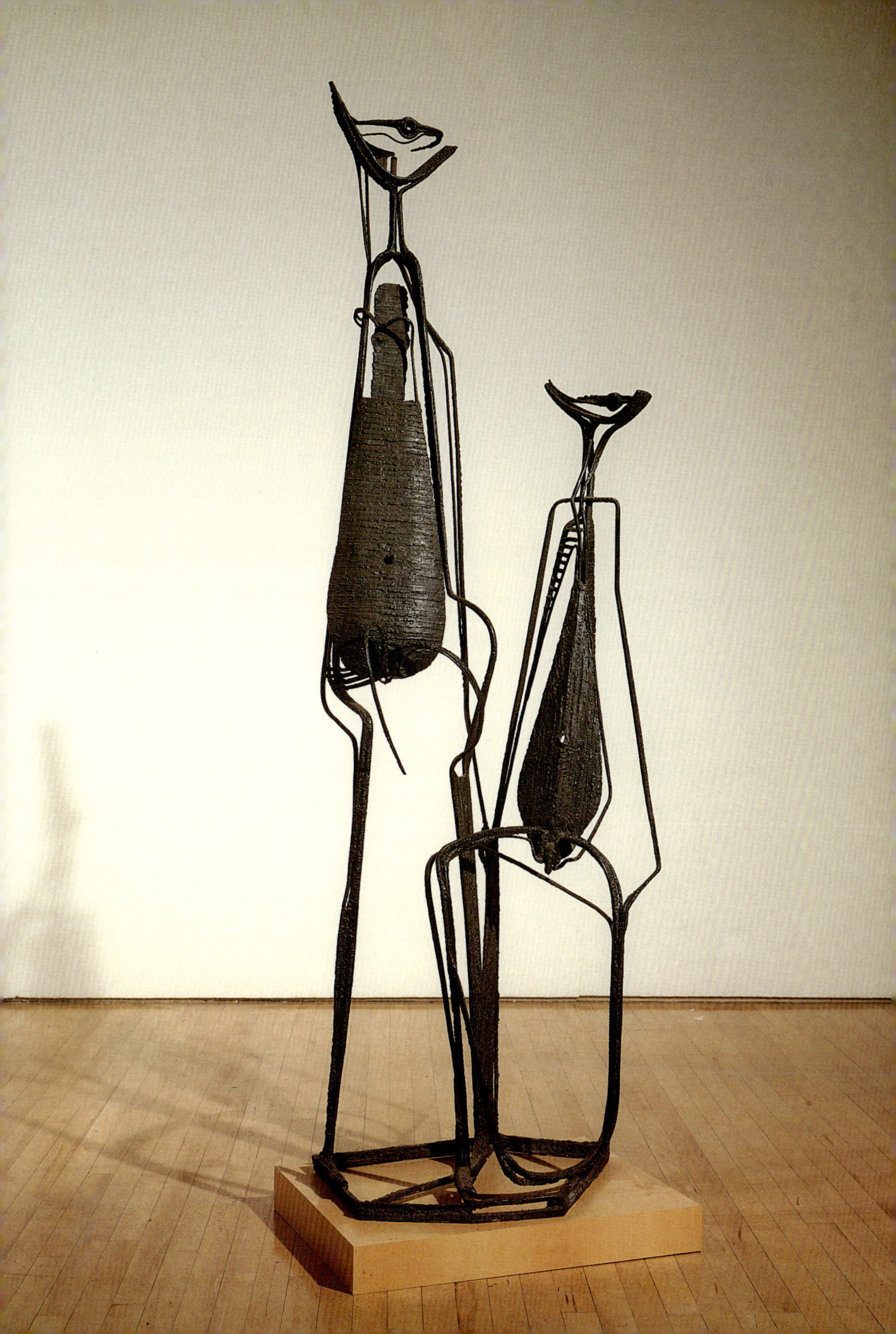

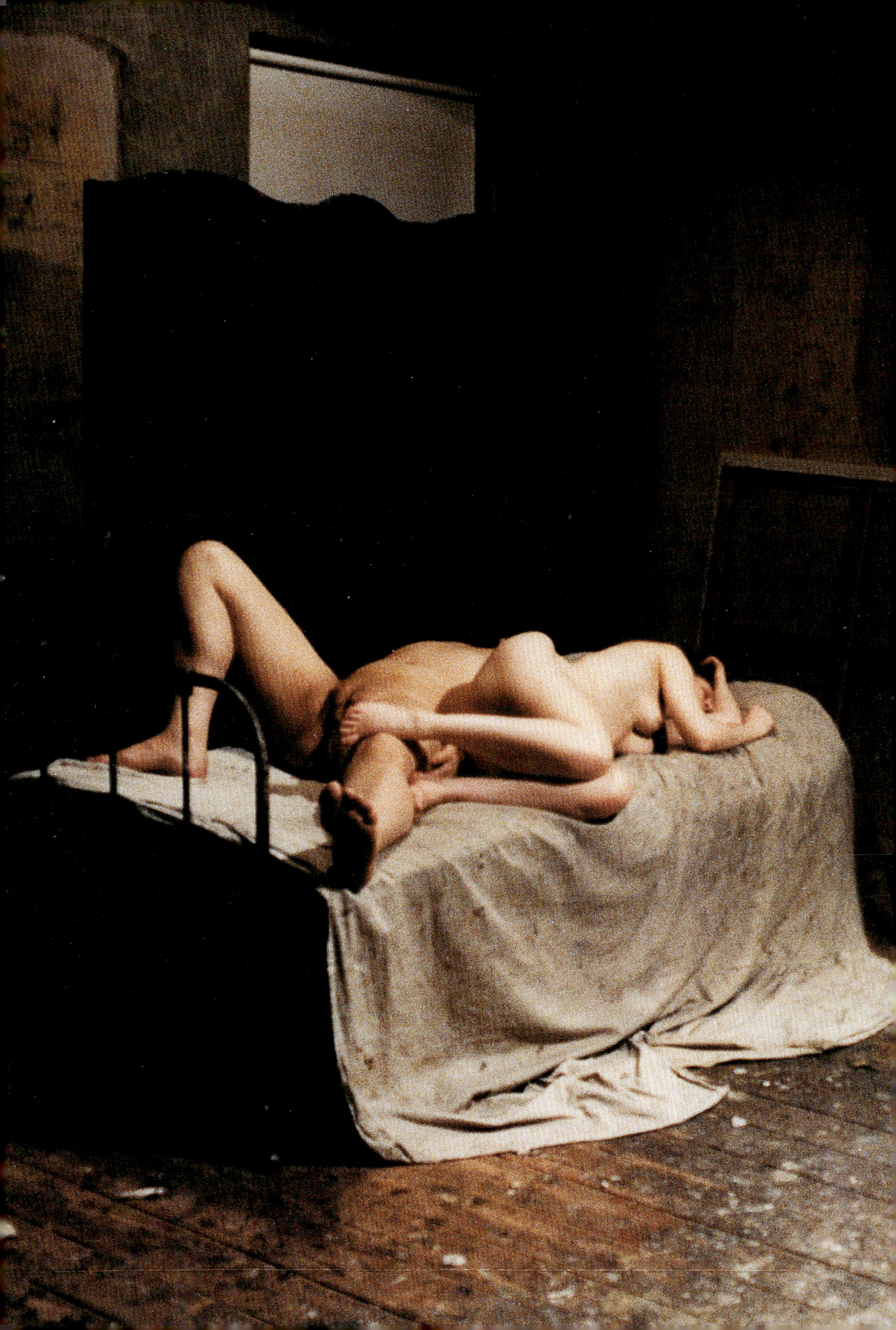

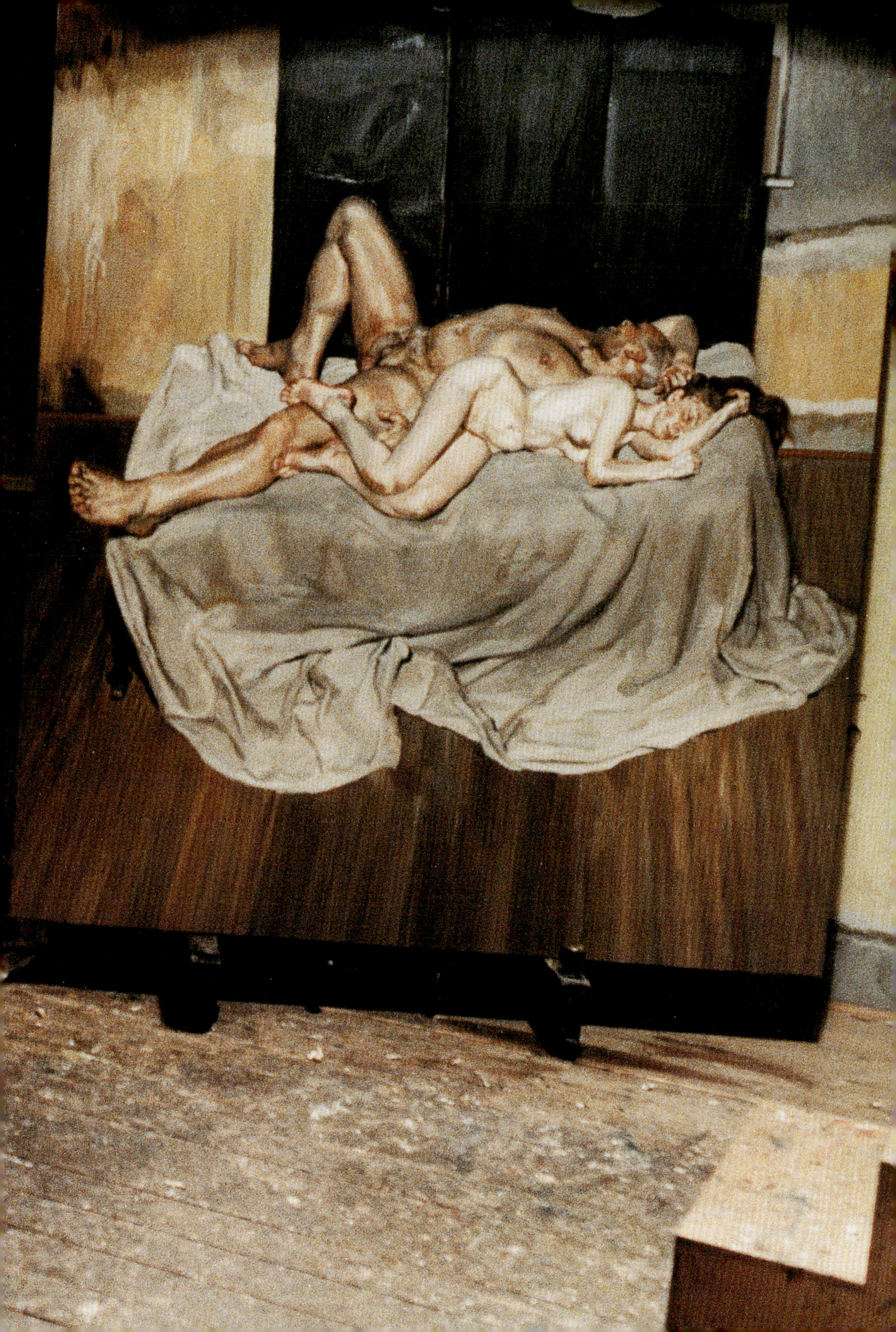

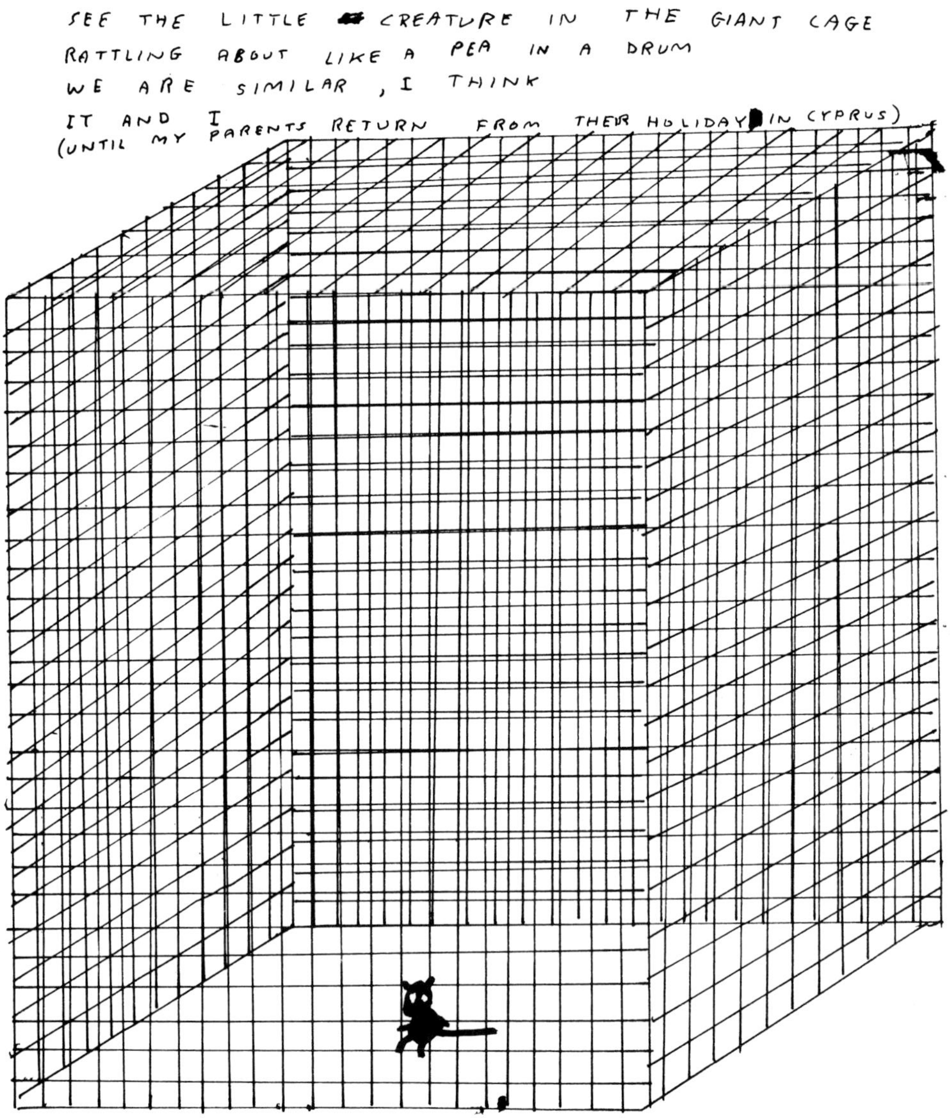

David Shrigley See the little creature in the giant cage..., 1998

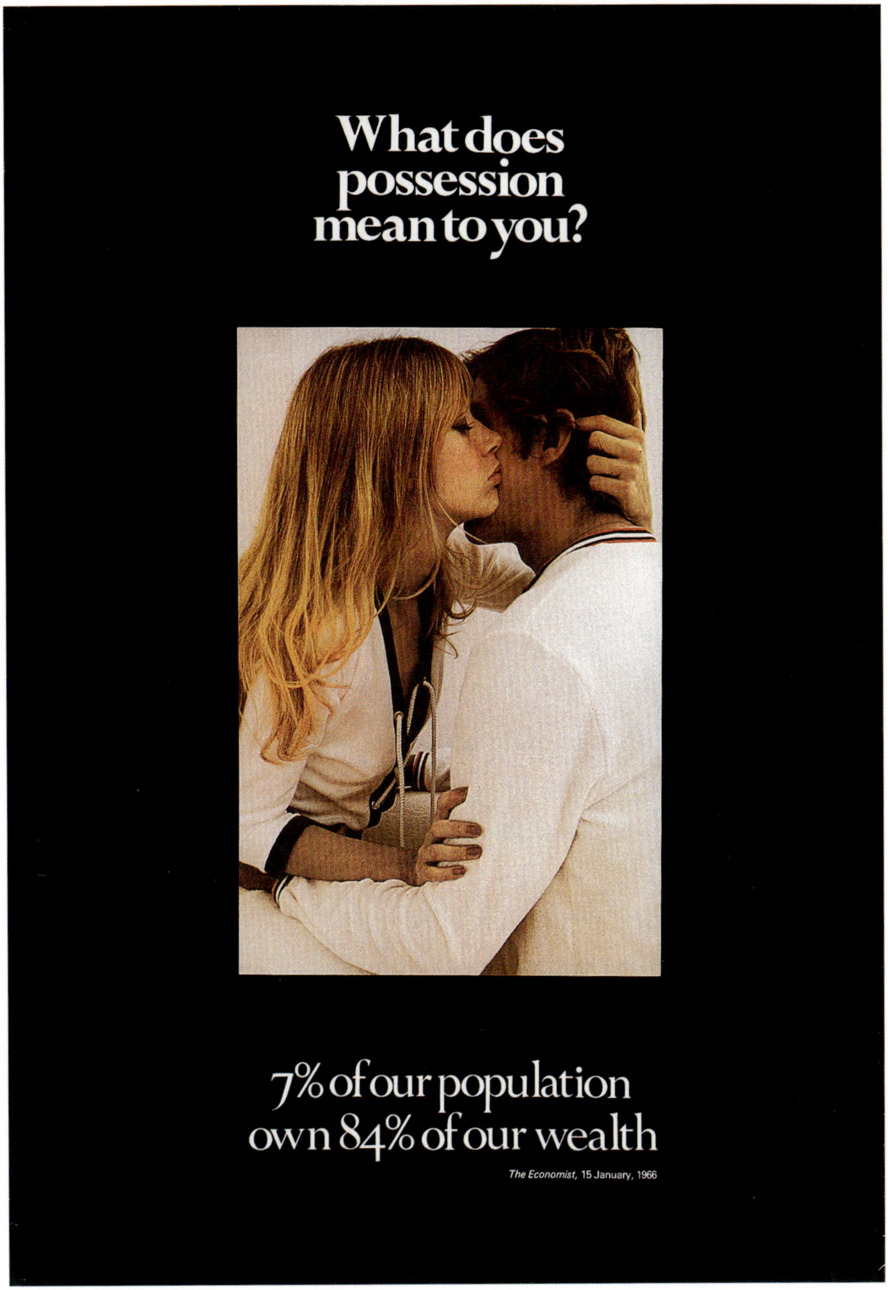

Victor Burgin Possession, 1976

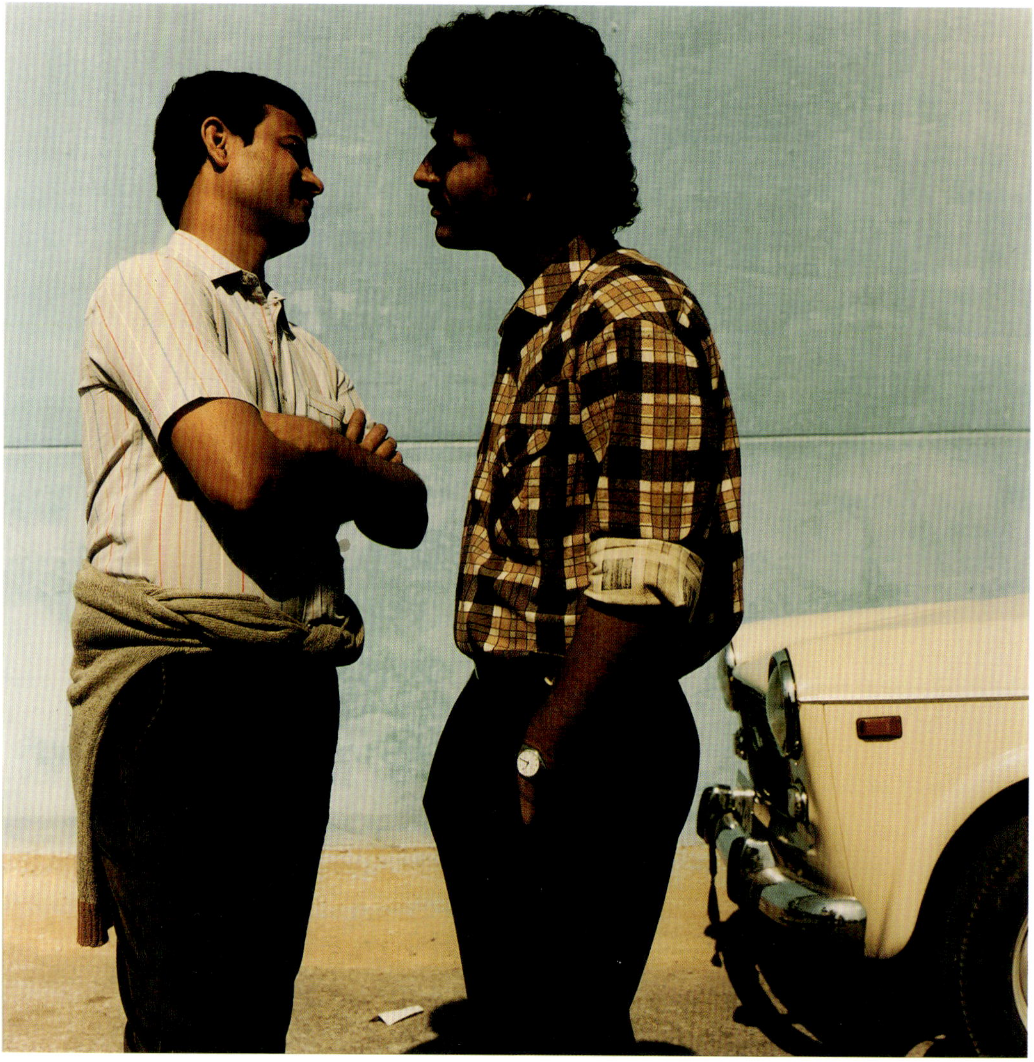

Sunil Gupta Pragati Maidan II from the series 'Exiles', 1987

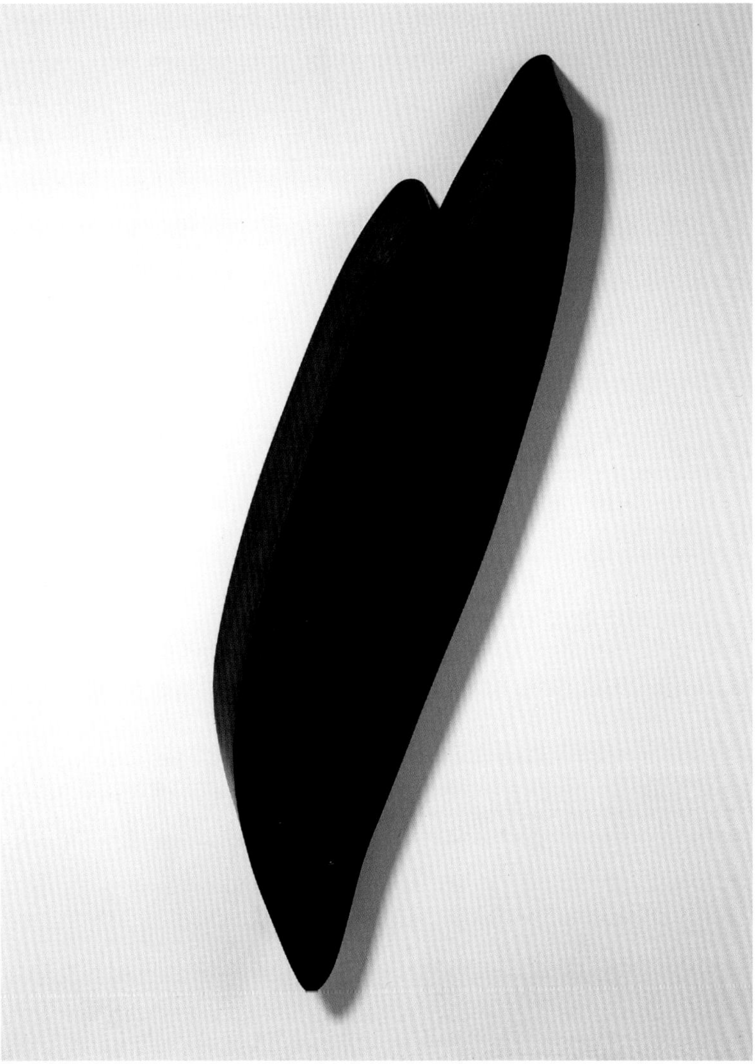

Siobhan Hapaska Heart, 1995

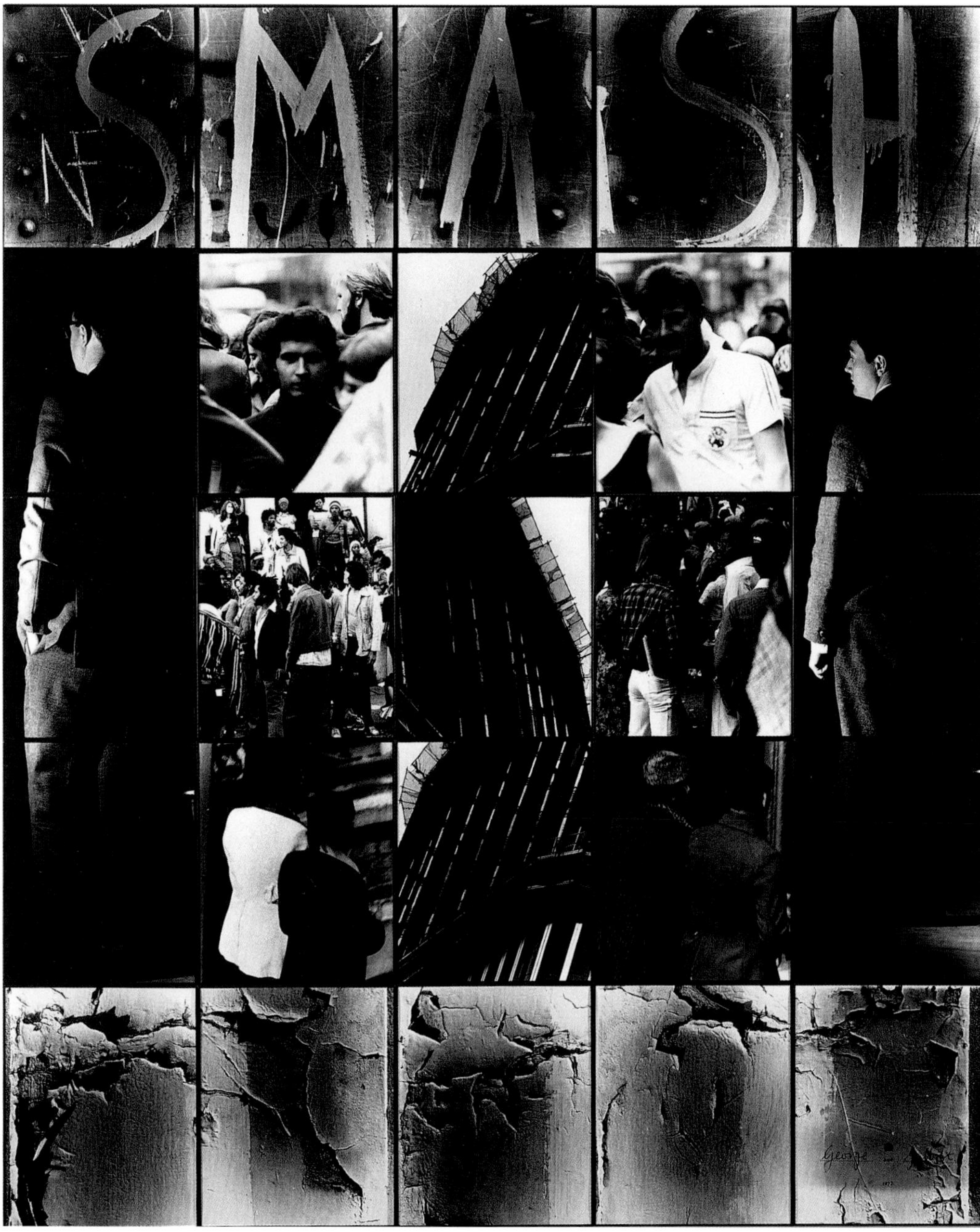

Gilbert & George Smash, 1977

“ A PORTRAIT OF THE ARTISTS AS YOUNG MEN ”

Summer 1972

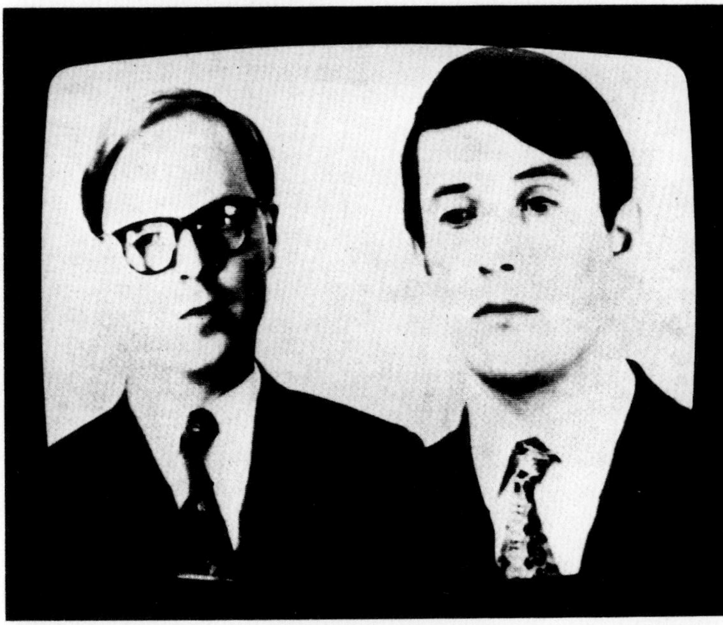

Sculpture on Video Tape

NO. 7 OF 25

This tape should be viewed with
‘high contrast’ as in this photograph

George and Gilbert

the sculptors

‘ART FOR ALL’ 12 Fournier Street London E1
01-247 0161

Gilbert & George A Portrait of the Artists as Young Men, 1972

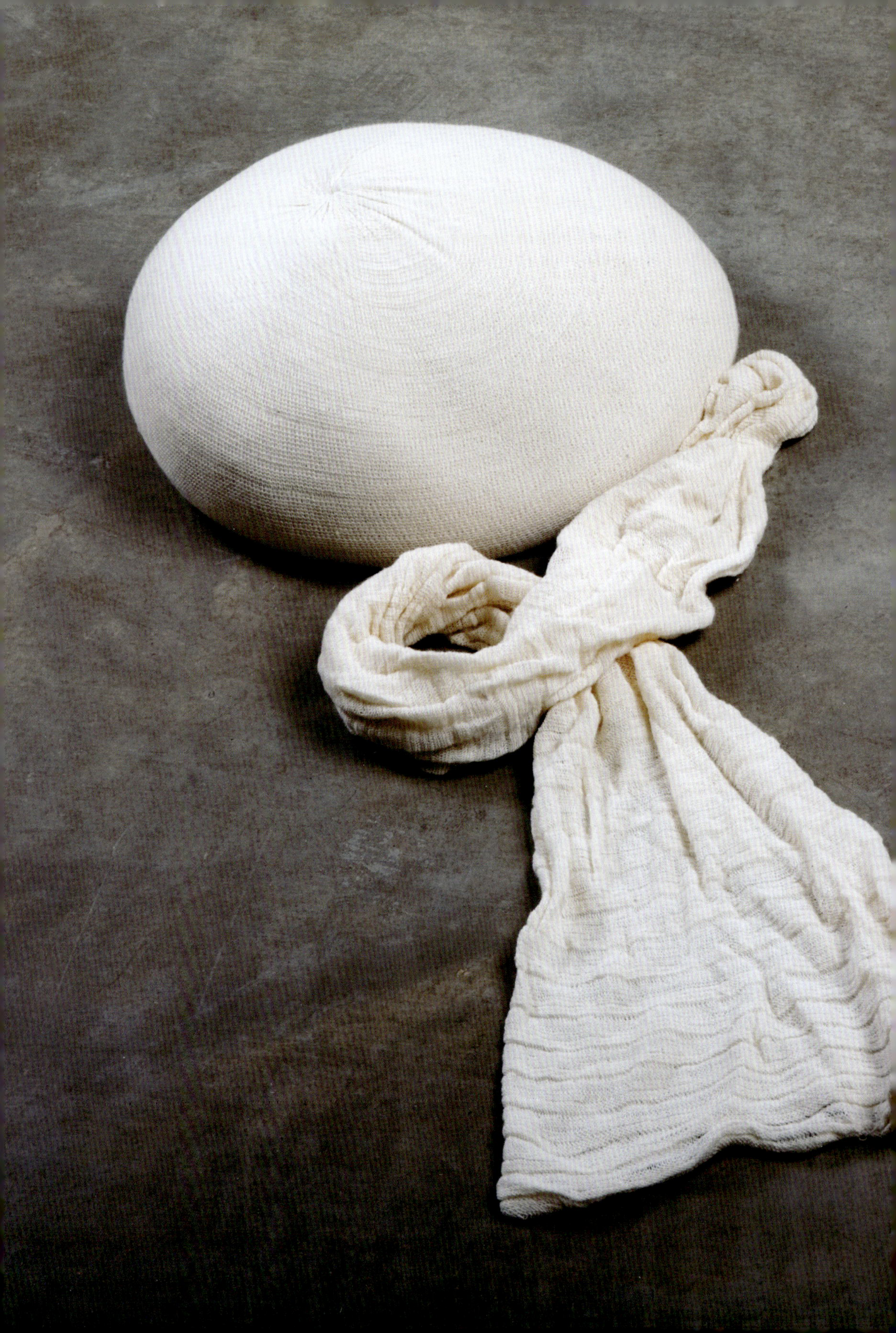

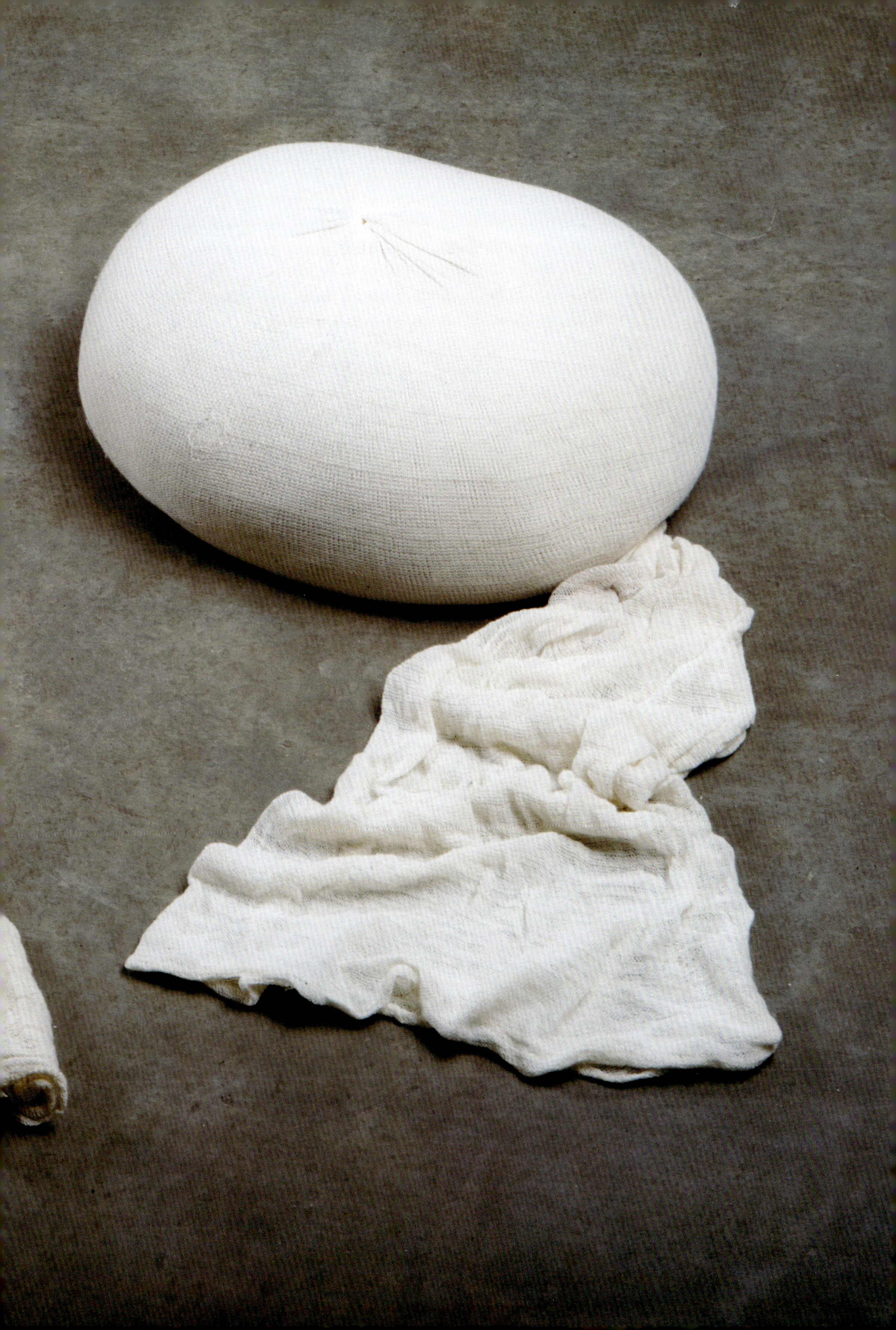

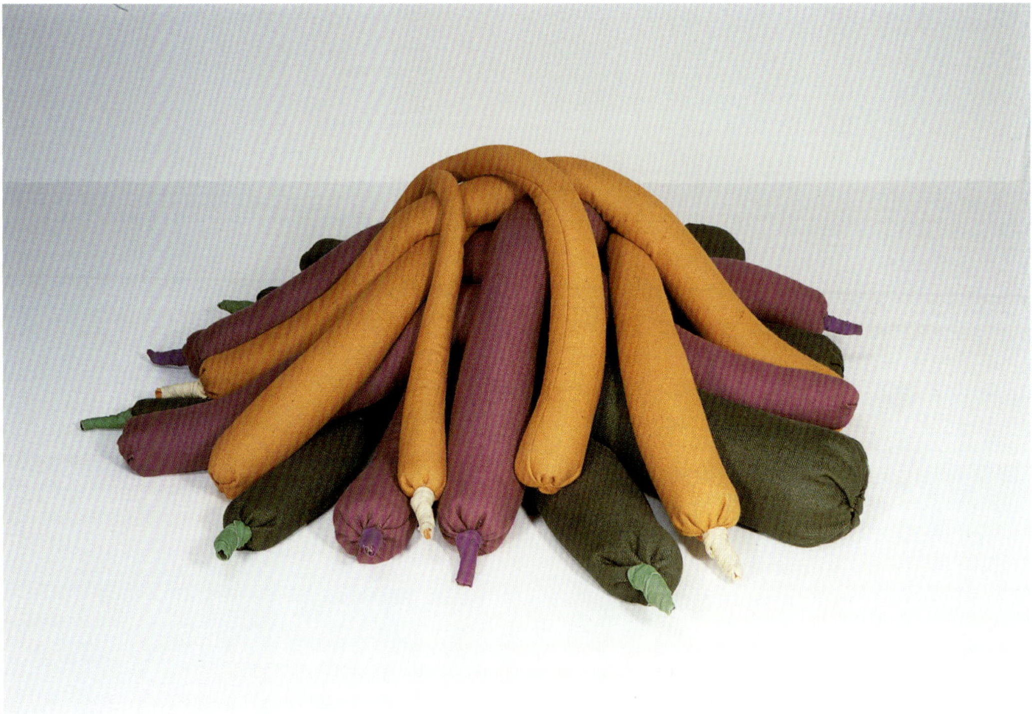

previous **Barry Flanagan** Sand/Muslin, 1966
above **Barry Flanagan** Heap 4, 1967

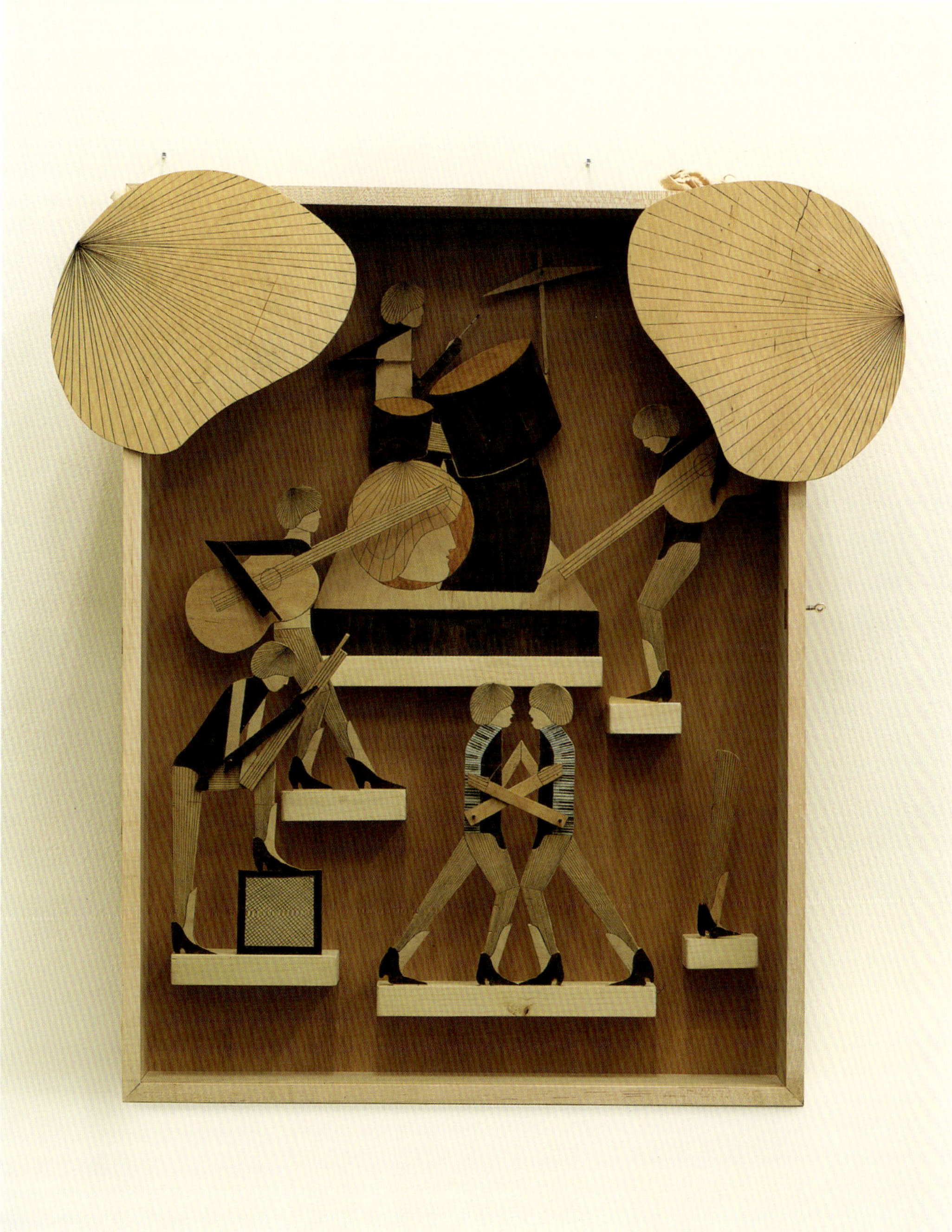

Enrico David Untitled (puppets: we are the mods), 2003

Anna Barriball Window, 2002

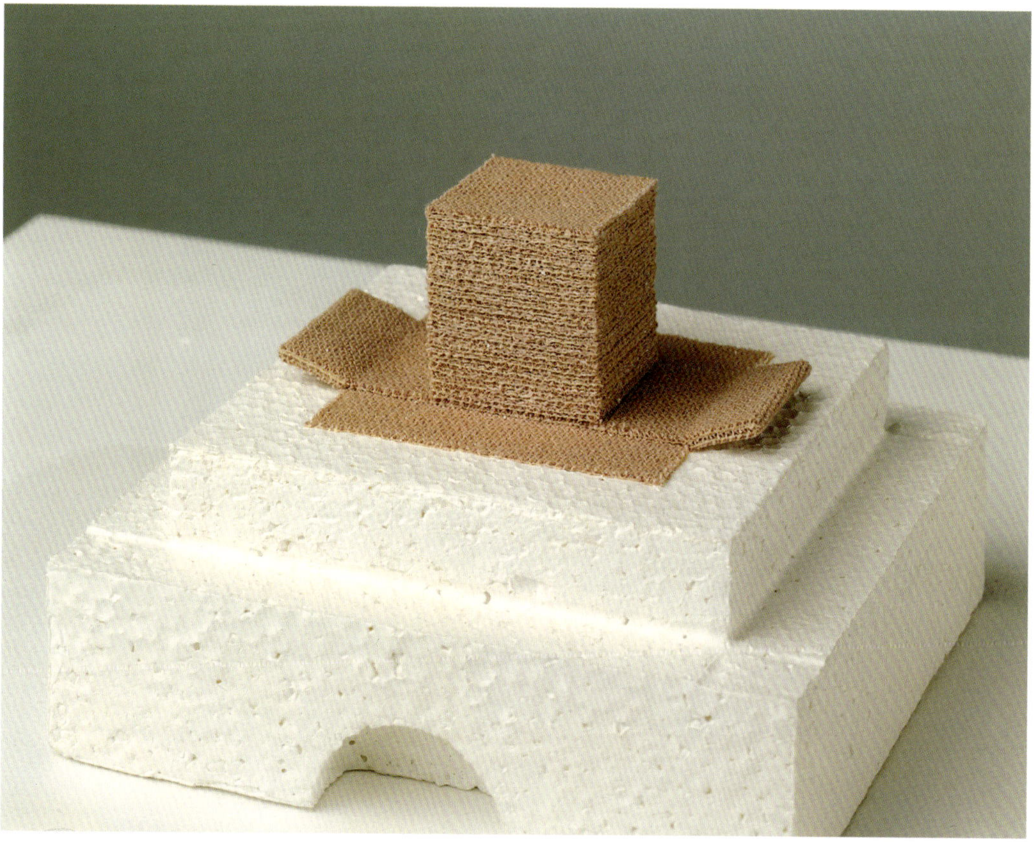

Martin Creed Work No.78, 1993

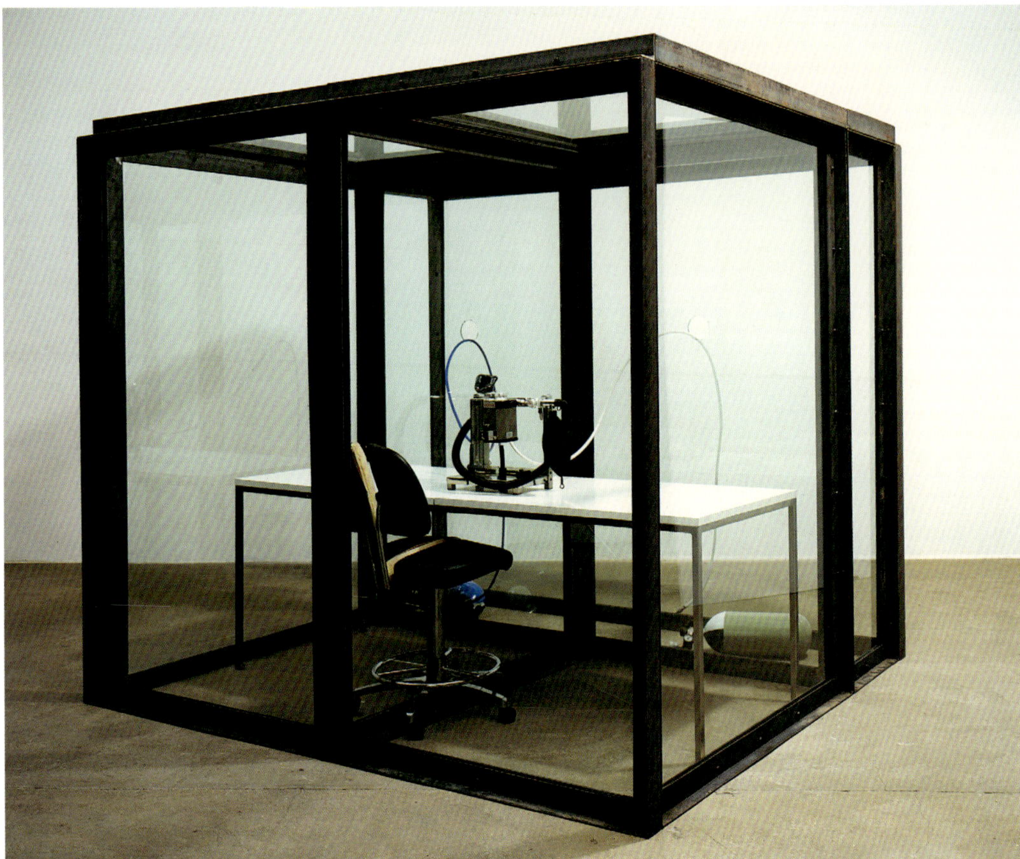

Damien Hirst He Tried to Internalise Everything, 1992–1994

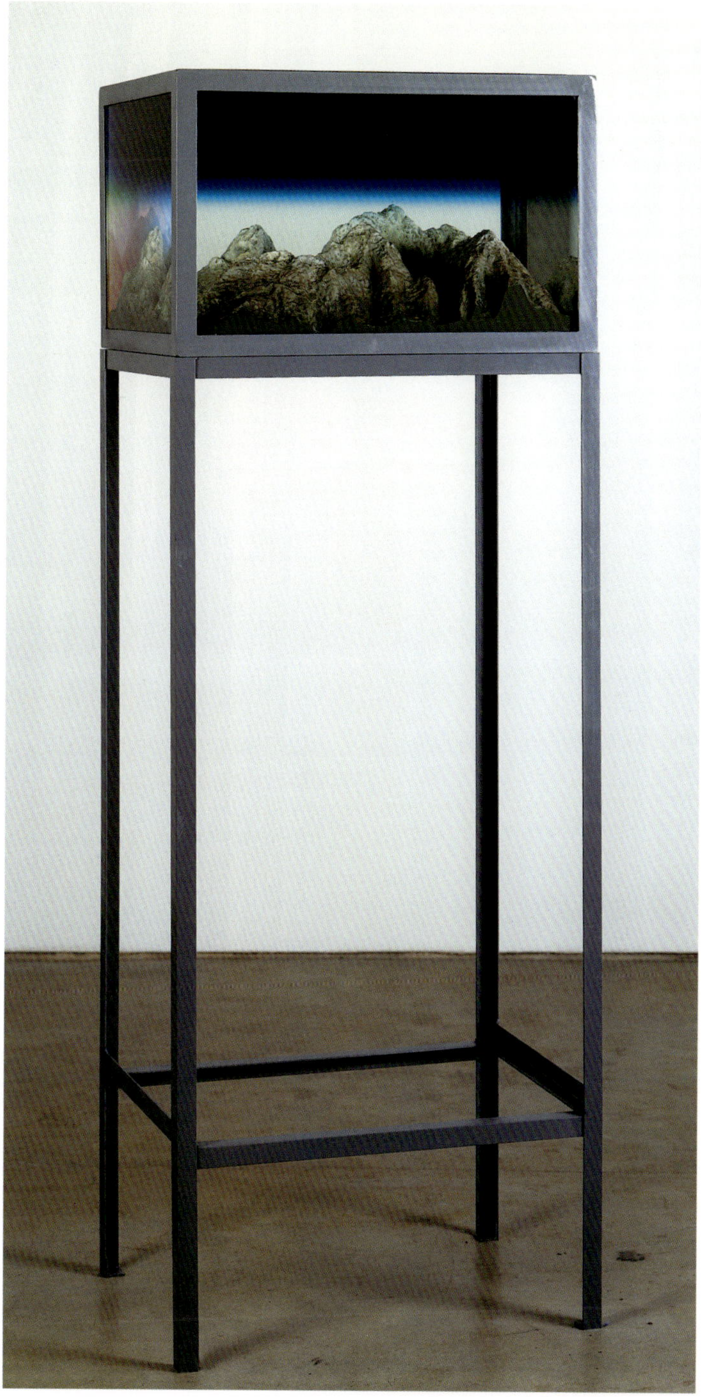

Mariele Neudecker Stolen Sunsets, 1966
overleaf **Tim Head** State of the Art, 1984

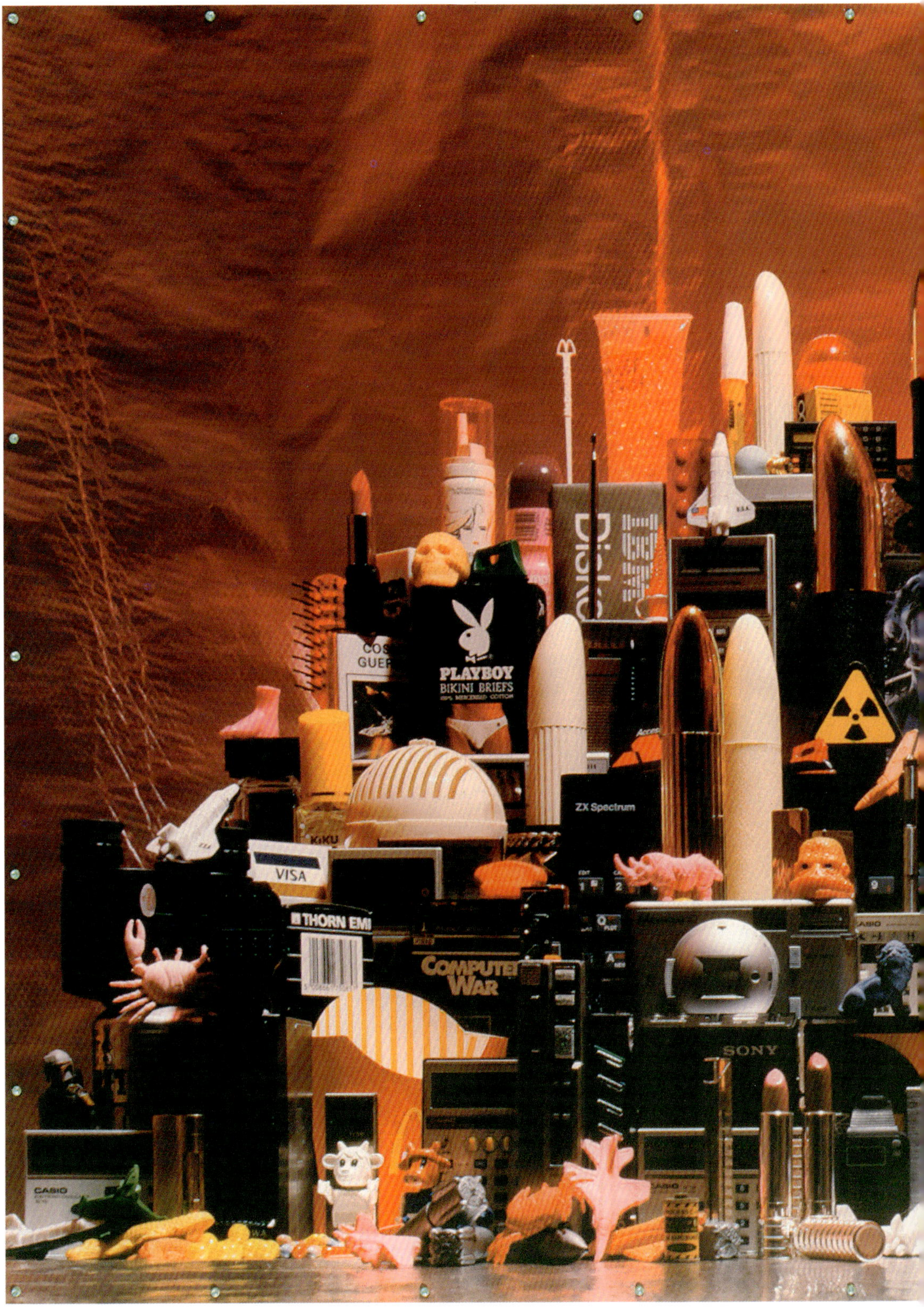
PLAYBOY
BIKINI BRIEFS
VISA
THORN EMI
ZX Spectrum
SONY
CASIO

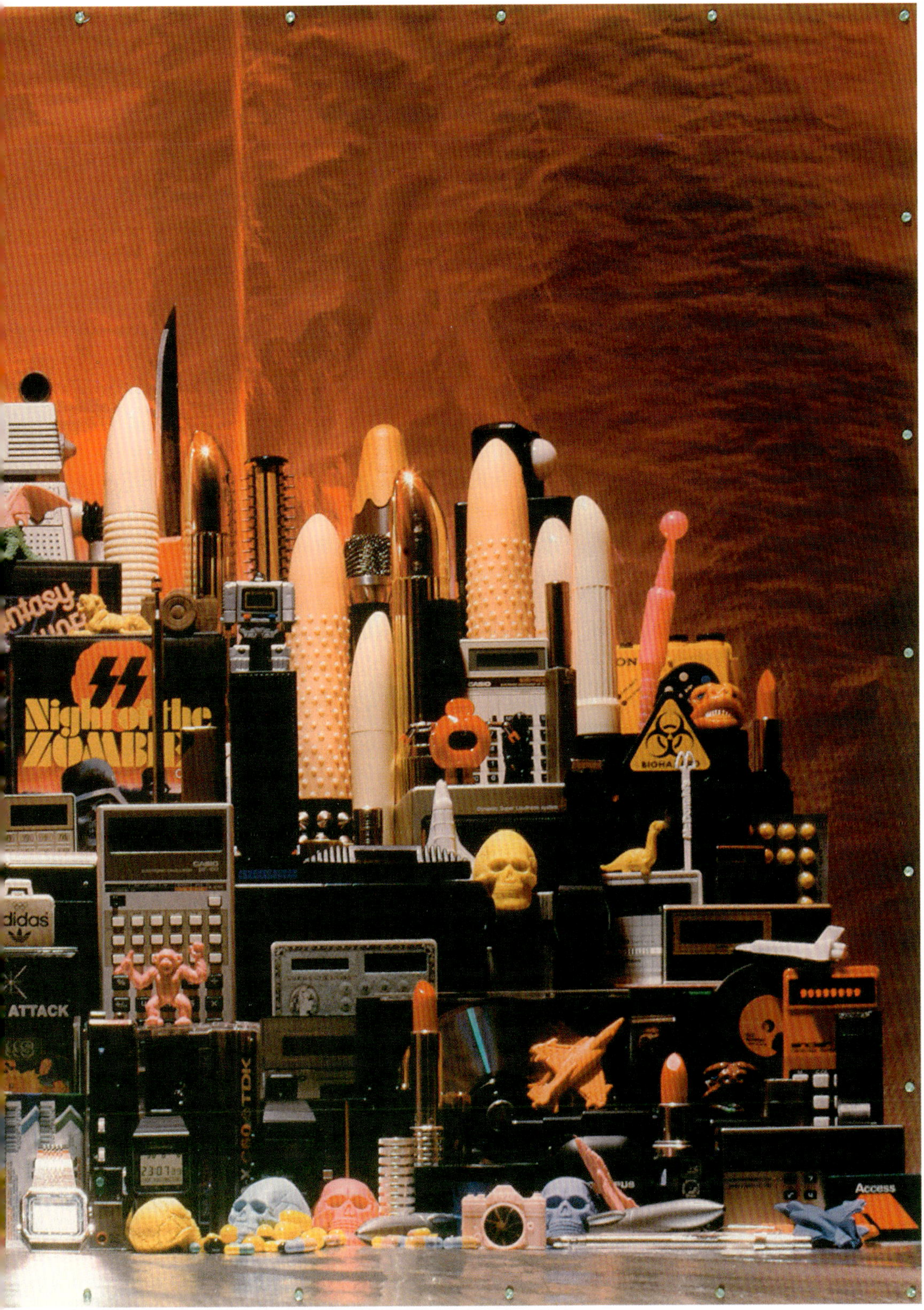

Night of the
ATTACK
TDK
Access
CASIO

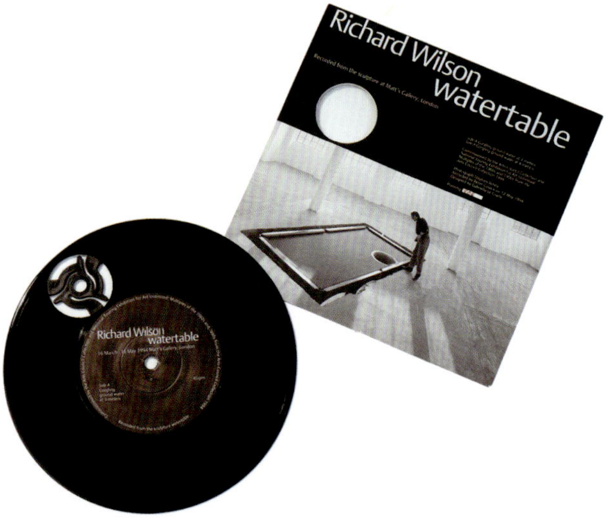

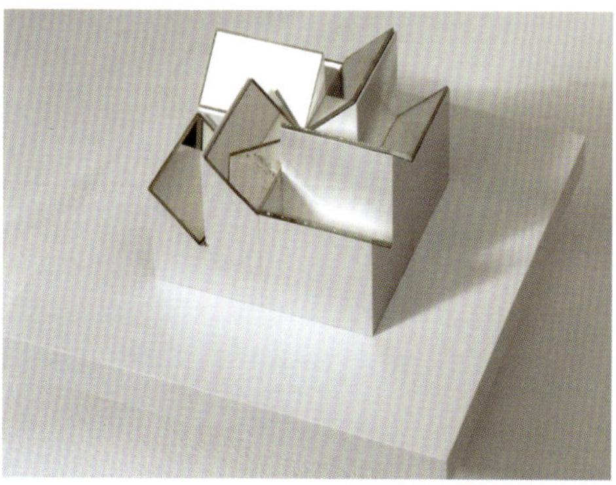

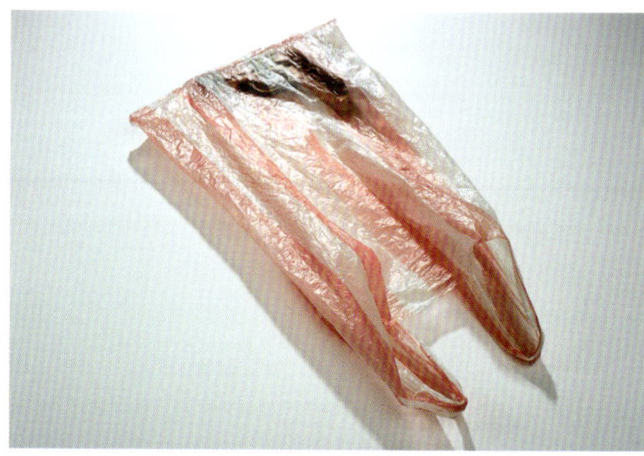

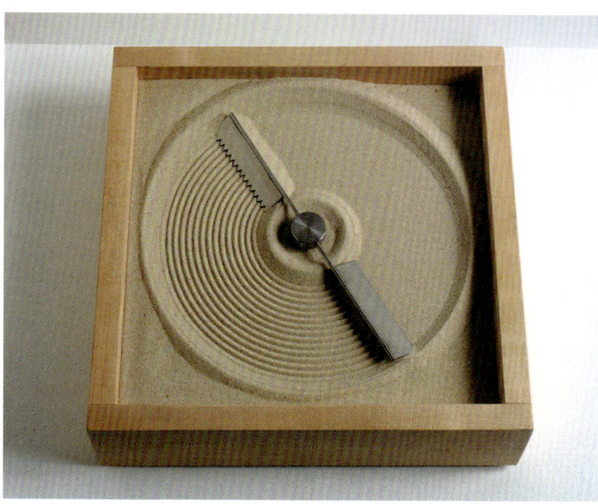

top **Richard Wilson** Watertable, 1994
centre, left **Mary Martin** Rotation (Not limited), 1968
centre, right **Christine Borland** Carrier, 1994
bottom **Mona Hatoum** + and -, 1988

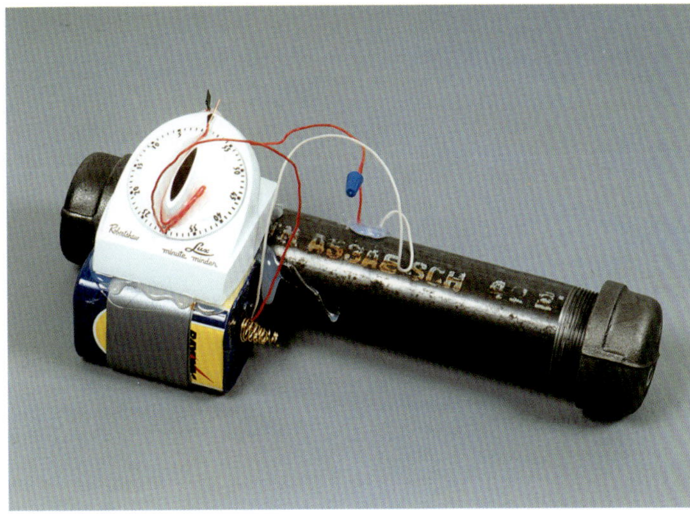

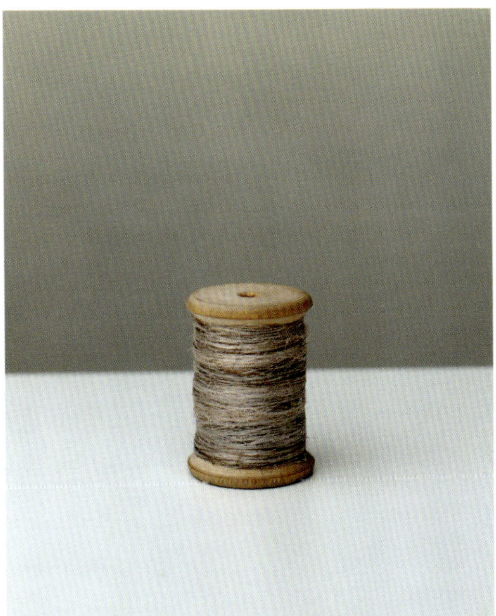

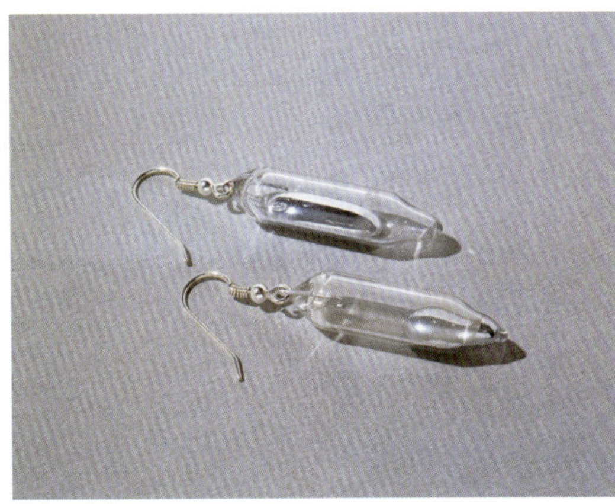

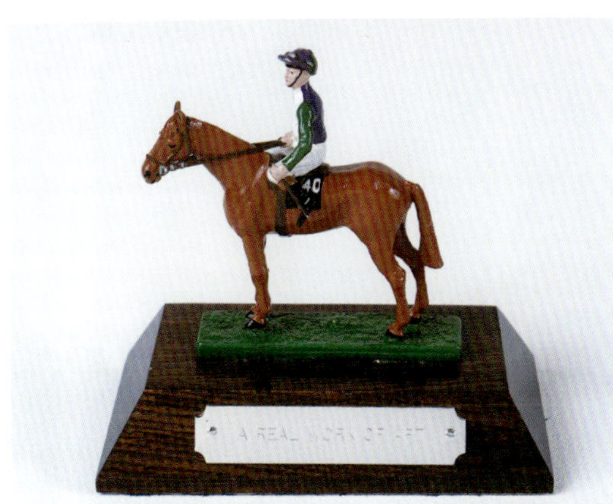

top **Gregory Green** Pipe Bomb # 3 (LA), 1993
centre, left **Kathy Prendergast** The End and the Beginning, 1996
centre, right **Lucia Nogueira** One and Three, 1994
bottom **Mark Wallinger** A Real Work of Art, 1994

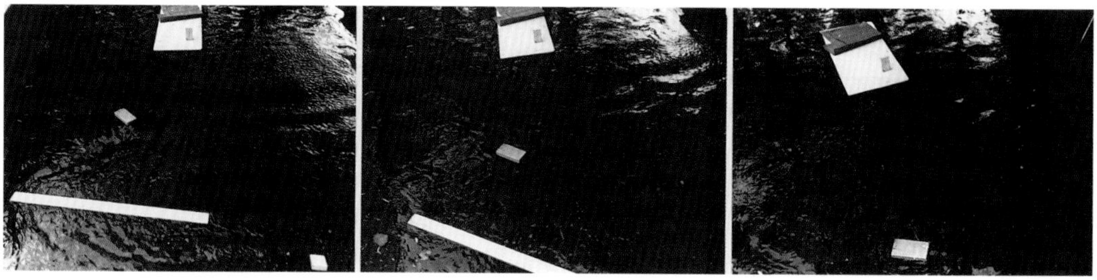

Bruce McLean Floataway Piece Beverly Brook, Barnes 1967, 1967

PRINT.

Section A.

Questionnaire.

1. Suppose this question. Is this piece of paper an art work?

2. Then n individuals whose status as an art work is established are examined for comparison with this piece of paper.

3. It may be the case that this piece of paper possesses some properties which some of the n individuals also possess. Perhaps some very general property. For example, the property of being a 3D material entity. But whilst this may possibly be counted as a necessary property of a thing being counted as an art work, and certainly of a thing being counted as an art object, it is obviously not a sufficient property.

4. There are millions of pieces of white paper, all very similar to this one (before this discourse was printed on it), all of which possess this property, but there is no assertion attached to them that they are to be counted as art works. (Although a formal precedent has been set in early conceptual works for an assertion such as 'All pieces of plain white paper are to be counted as art works', to be taken up. Although this possibility would eliminate inter white-pieces-of-paper comparisons, it would still leave us with the outstanding white-pieces-of-paper class to other art works class comparisons.) However, what has to be asked here, and this aside from inter white-pieces-of-paper comparisons, is, what is the especial property (if any) that this piece of white paper possesses that 'allows' it to be singled out as an art work?

5. Is there a property possessed by some things in the world which can be identified as art (as 'being art'), or even the property of art (this latter of course presupposing that art is a property of things)?

6. If art is literally made by the artist, then there cannot have been art in the world before there were artists. Did someone (the first-ever artist(s)) intend to make art? Or did he make something which was (somehow) afterwards assigned the status of arthood? Even if the latter is the case, one assumes that the intentions (perhaps allowing the twentieth century art critic's oft used penchant for 'unconscious intentions') are counted as intentions to 'make art'. On this view

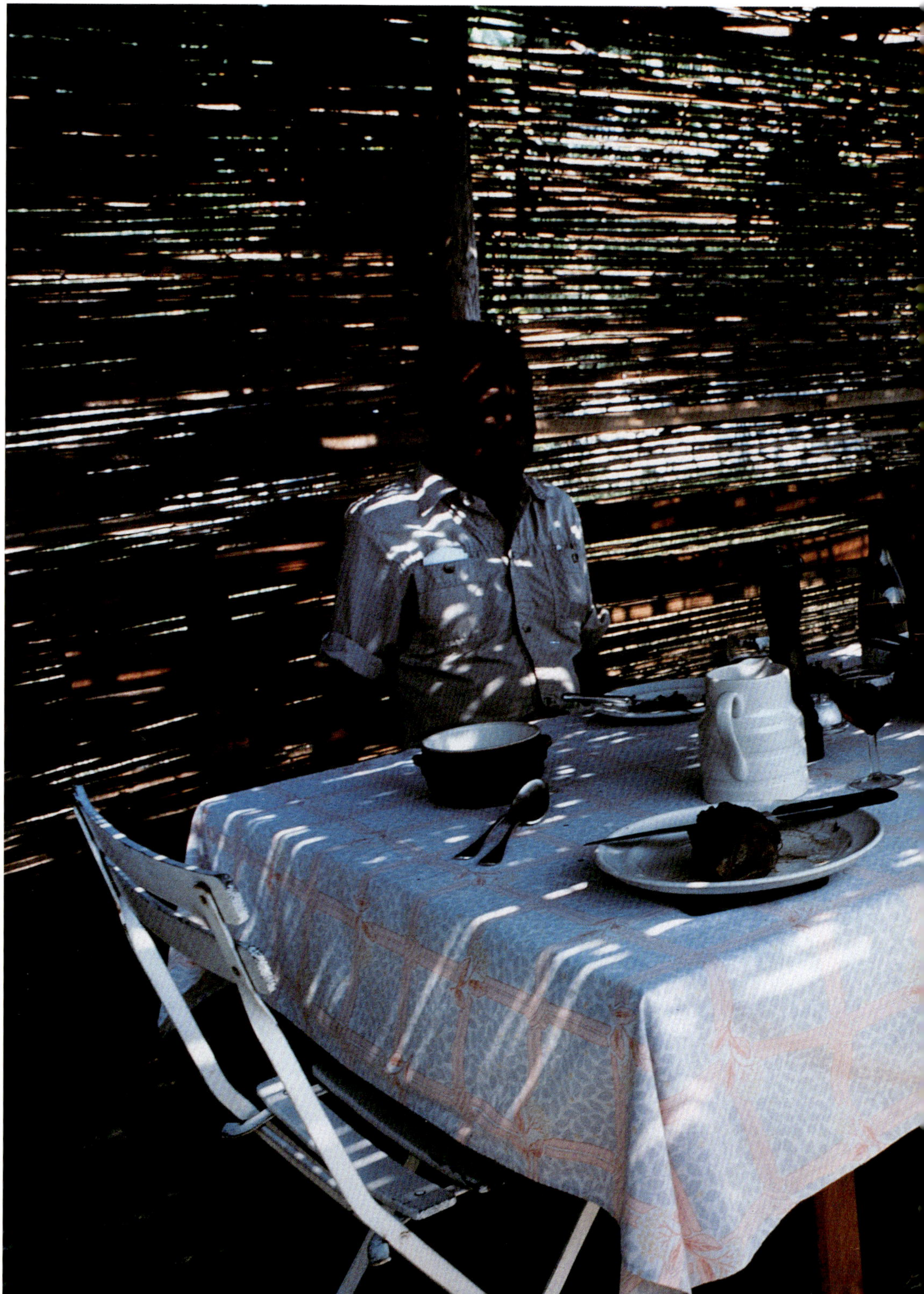

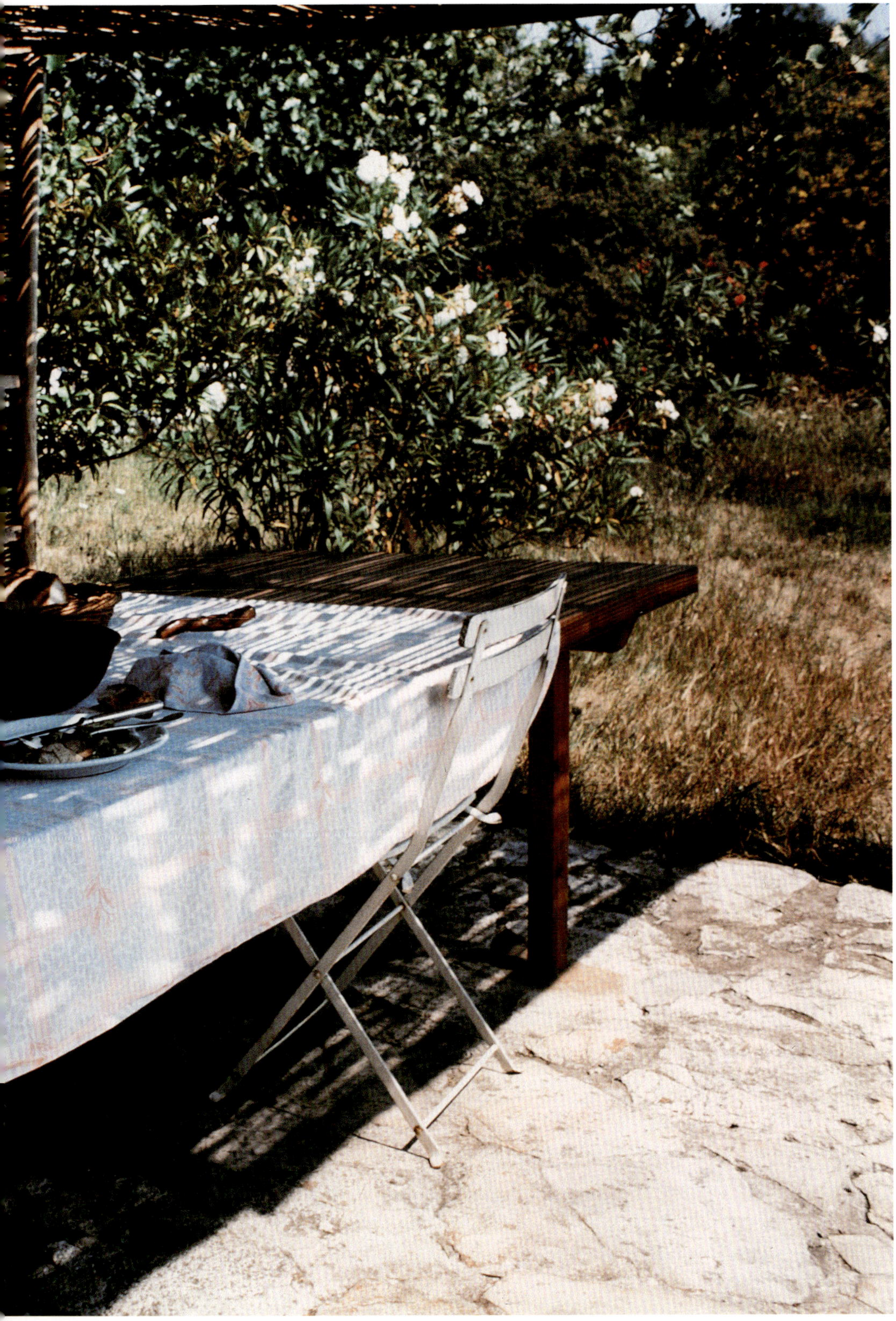

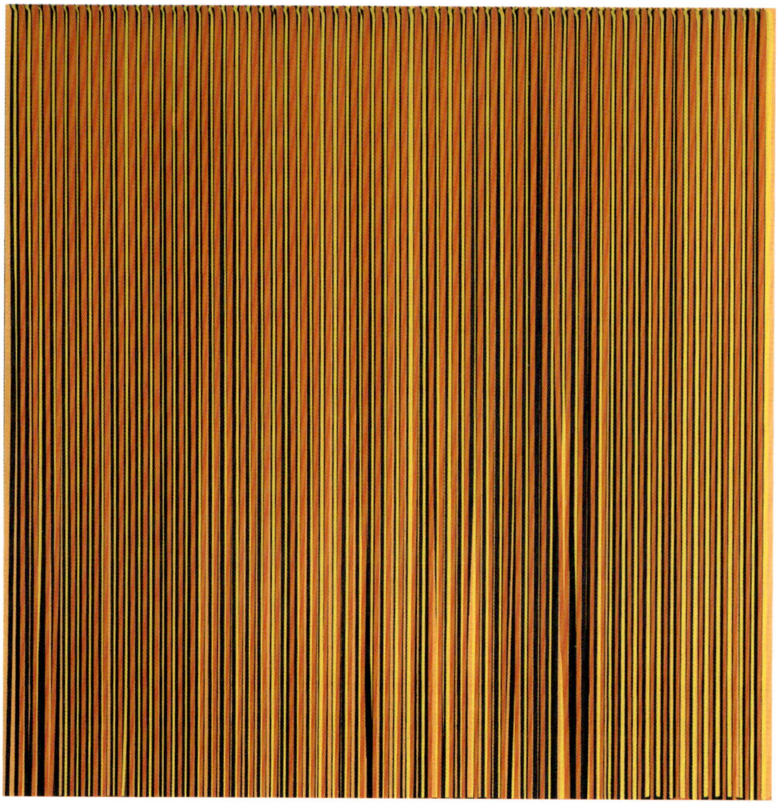

previous **Horace Ove** James Baldwin, 1984

above **Ian Davenport** Poured Lines: Light orange, blue, yellow, dark green and orange, 1995

right **Michael Craig-Martin** History Painting, 1995

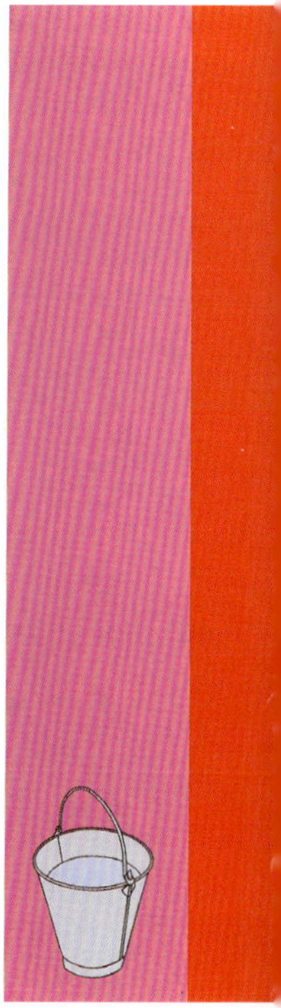

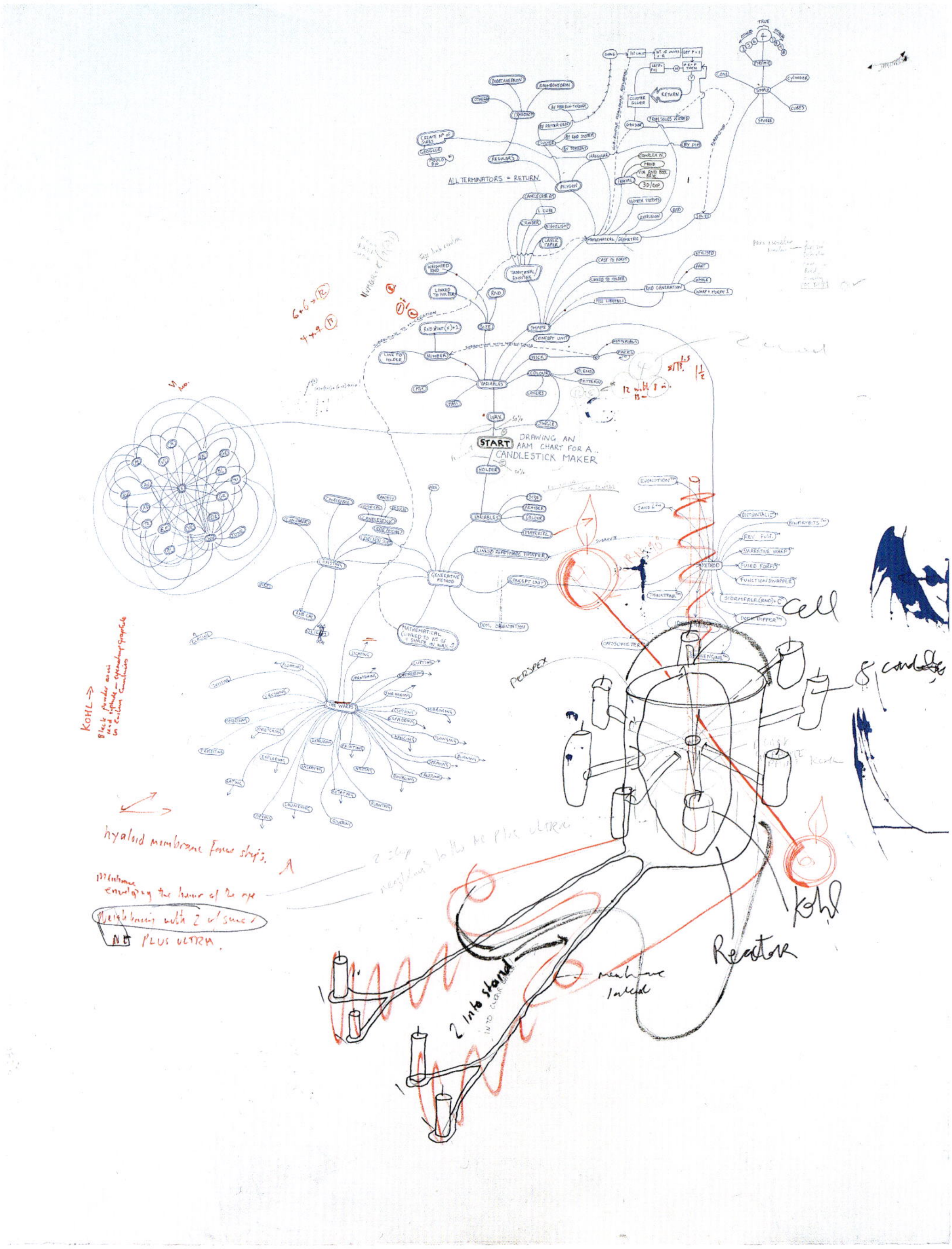

Keith Tyson Applied Artmachine Chart: Candlestick Maker, 1999

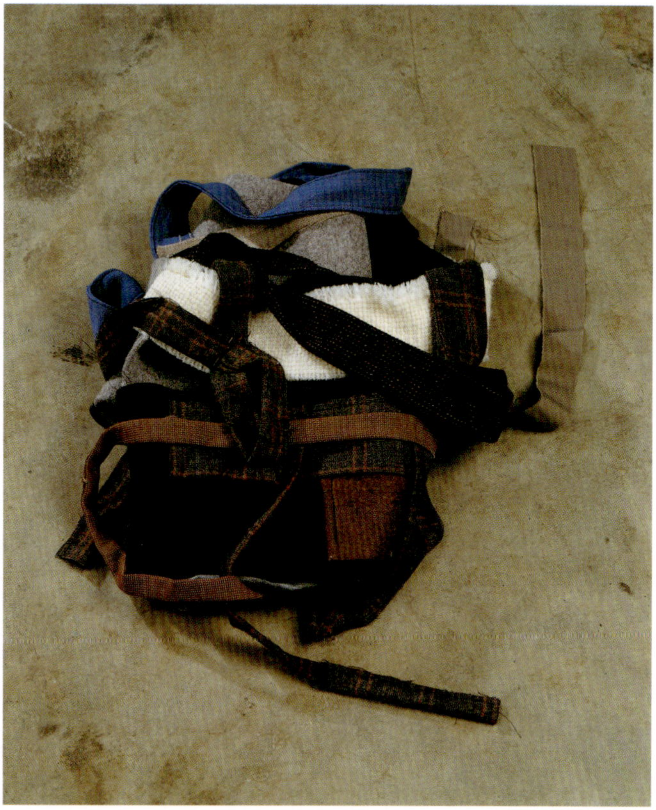

Karin Ruggaber Bag, 2004

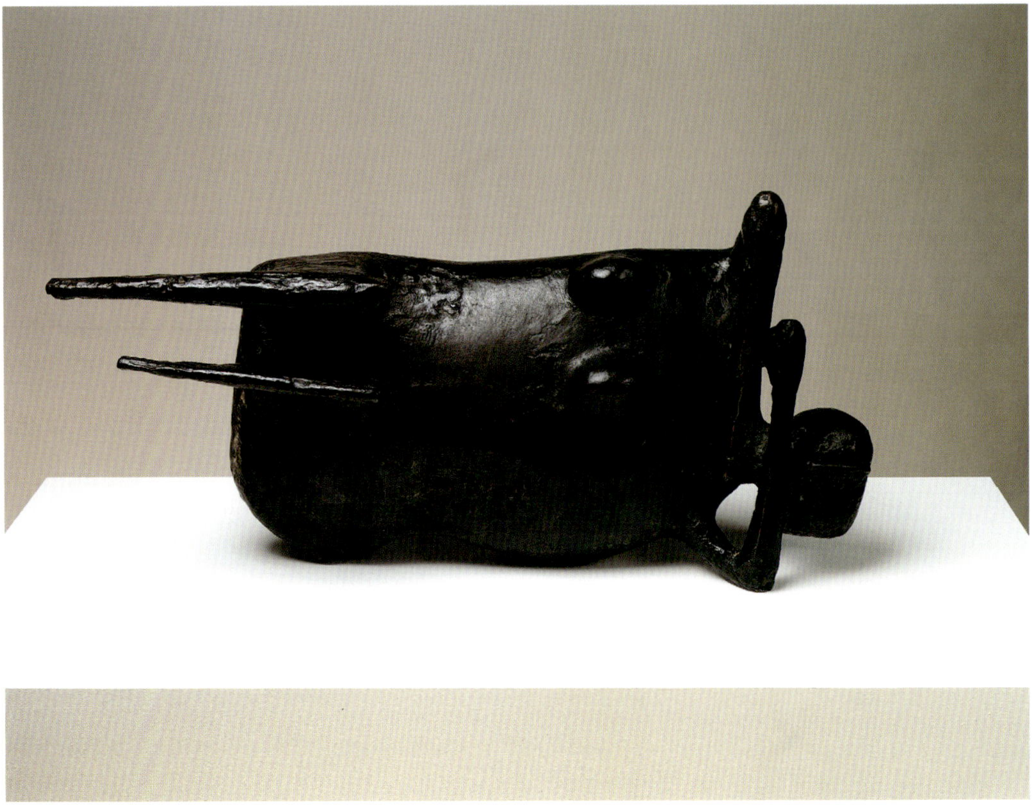

Kenneth Armitage Figure Lying on its Side (No.5), 1957

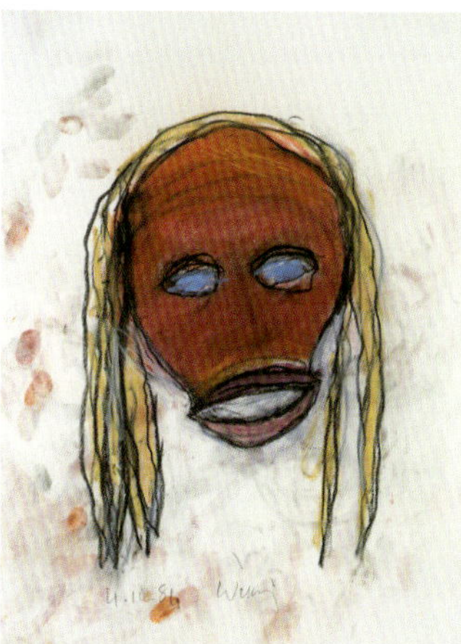

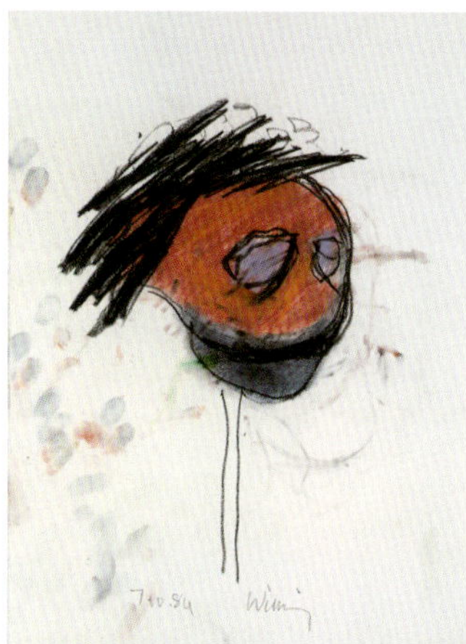

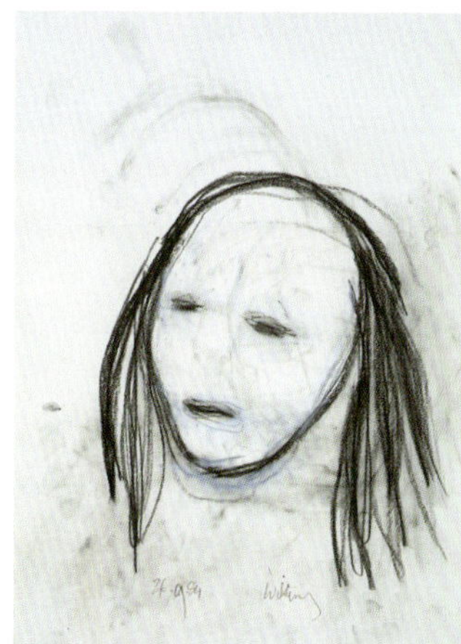

Victor Willing Mask 7.10.84, Mask 26.9.84 and Mask 4.10.84, 1984

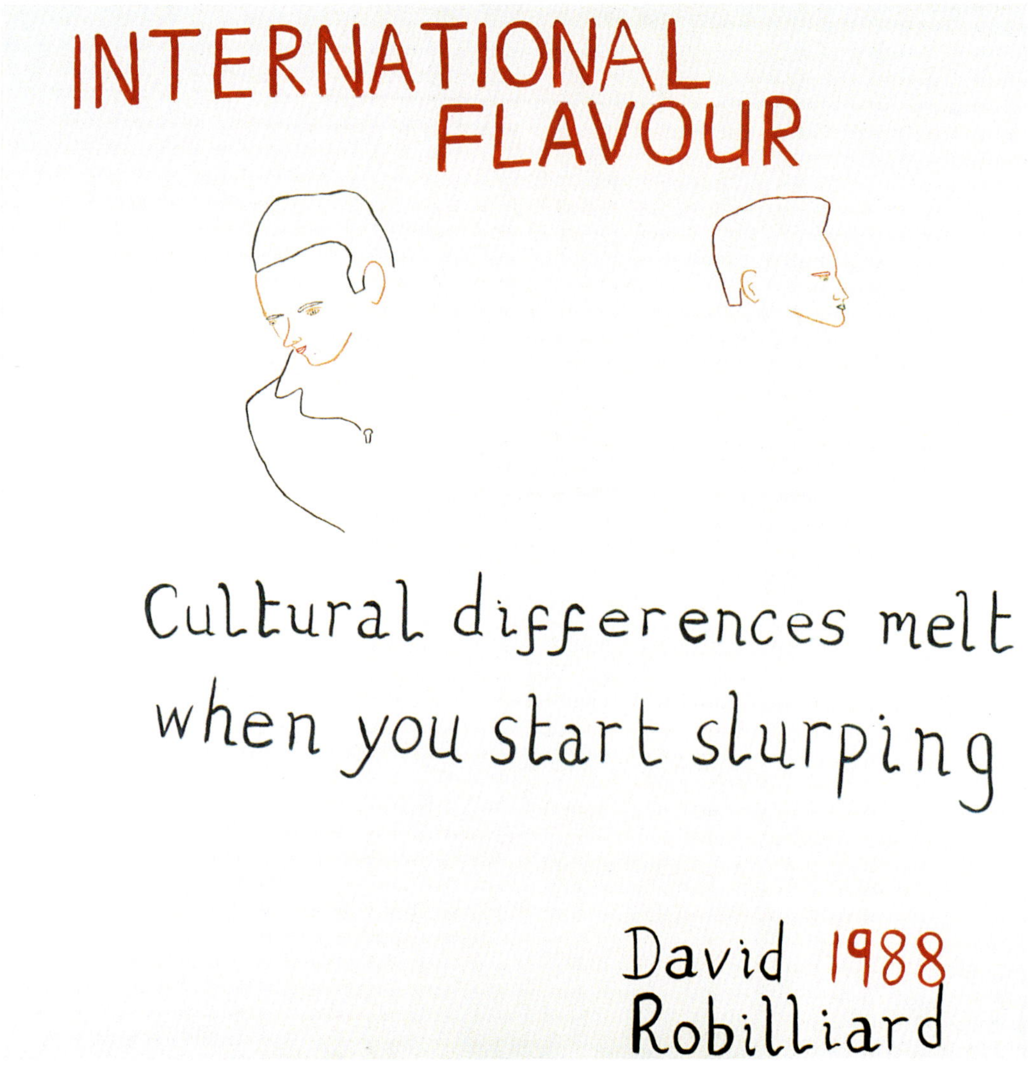

David Robilliard International flavour: cultural differences melt when you start slurping, 1988

Bob Law Bordeaux Black Blue Black, 1977

overleaf **Colin Lowe and Roddy Thomson** Swallow Seed Menu, 2003

Swallow Seed Restaurant

presents

Who wants what, gets what you re given, don t speak with your mouthful, take your elbows off the table, etc, etc.

We have no pride in ourselves or our family, so why should we worry. We don't worry. Everything we find in our kitchens is freshly murdered to your requests and prejudice is brought to bare on our rice and our housewives rices.

Free Home Delivery

(within the week, if you live next door, if not tough shit)

****

Open 3 days a week, most weeks, no weekend service available, sometimes no service available. 5.00 pm - 6.15 pm

DON T SWALLOW WHOLE DISHES

*Don t Swallow dishes were unoriginally brought into this country on the back of a hound after the quarantine laws were loosened. History shows that a kitten and some cattle from **The Roswell Incident** became romantically involved. (SERVED WITH JAM RAGS)*

DON T SWALLOW SPECIAL 7.90
Real fowl chicken, coated in drizzle, frosties & wormfood, left to stand next to sink, for the *night* hunt.

SWALLOW THE KINGS SPECIAL 7.95
Faintly drawn out slices of an excuse, in a thick *HariKari* sauce, gobbed on with a spite friccassèe. (sweet shit).

ROOT CANAL WAG TAG 5.20
Servicing the maiden head, hold the condom as you withdraw the condom and embedded in a tart, chew on a misanthrope.

BLOOD CLOT 5.30
Diced carrot on a bed of custard with salami and spaghetti hoop dreams embroiled in a basket (ball).

PUPPET MASTERSROKE 4.75
The Mystery of child birth and it s magic millennium mud pie. Lesbians adopt a son and call him Barry , *throw him to the lions* , i.e. the school bully.

R.U.STARTIN

UNPLUCKED CHICKEN 0.90
UNPLUCKED CHICKEN (sill kickin) 0.85
LONG DAY IN FACTORY 3.85
CHICKEN/LAMB LUMPET (per lump) 0.20
MUTTON JEFF 1.20
LOW CALORIE LITTLE ENGLAND STARTERS* 5.00
MIXED VEGAN & CHOP allow to chat 2.95
FRIES 1.00
CHIPS 0.50
HUNGRY JOES 0.25

**This dish has recently been taken off the menu due to it s simplicity.*

SWALLOW SEED COLD HAND DISHES

Cold Hands, consists of a tepid insistent on barely digestible ingredients nobody else would touch with a Barge Pole . Every Shaving has been masticated in the mouths of babes. Sultanas, grapes, apricots and plums that have fallen from the tree are not included in these recipes but can be found on pizzas in the gutter behind the restaurant.

SWALLOW SEED SPECIAL COLD HAND 7.45
Behind the couch old toffees, newspapers from the Gulf War and mini sausages from a Birthday party come lurching out of the darkness in an apparent approximation of edible school dinners

SQUID IN AGONY COLD HAND 4.95
Blight soup combined with essence of a saltless sea tossing uneasily on a hospital bed after your circumcision operation renders you unable to have children

MOOT POINT COLD HAND 4.95
An enormous dish compacted into an Oxo cube the size of a Rubik s cube. Smell the tarragon and the terror of 19, ner, ner, 19 year old men dropping Napalm Death 12 singles on Vietnamese Red scum

WHAT COLD HANDS YOU VE GOT 4.60
Egg fried cold shoulders dunked in huge vats of mindless compromise. Mix in some rosemary & Bowel Quake , some taramasalata & mutt chutney. Add some Singapore No Fun , and devour your girlfriend from the waste down

SWALLOW IT ALL, DON T SPILL A DROP

JAIL BAIT 15.90
Sizzling hot, acts as an aphrodisiac, cannot wait to leave the restaurant, with your wallet!

MEAT IN PASREY, SPELT WRONG 5.40
Hegelian biscuits, in a rich port solitude with can t stand losing you dumplings, combined with ligaments of oxen stewed by fool.

NUGGET LOVE 4.90
Old testament sushi, let the love in, swill it round yer gob and spit it out of your severed soul. The single cell orgasm sprinkled on the class spite cakes goes well with a stone cold reality.

CORN ON THE COPIA 4.55
A massive Daddy Long legs peruses your dome. Crack off the shell revealing the spine diamonds, which can be dipped in ***The Human Shish***. (Don t eat the eyes).

DON T AL
CHEF S

HAM NARCOLEPS
Mark of the Beast under th
in an unbearably thick sau
though this may be, Floren
swabs mushy pea lives bac
cartilage, surrounded by a

BUFFED BAKED A
A flaky skinny thing is jolt
boiled in brine and made t
A masectomied left breast
fine dust and laid to rest in

WHOLE AFGANI
Middle class sausages, in a
diseased beef, saved from
Bournemouth Bombing . N
covered in dust and a blank

CHUCK IT &

CHICKEN COME BY
Comedy noses are ground
months producing a kind o
onions and some thousand
etched in skimmed stones,
and one is in danger of a n

AGGRO & LEMON
Plonk the Spirit of an Arti
swell ead of a guinea fowl,
pancake, it s Mother bleats
charred remains and we all

PISS ON YOUR OW
More of a puddle than a so
work causes your weekend
right off, it rains, a comput
France, mud is slung, garlic
nails for a week, ending in

DEATH WARMED
Take out the hatred in men,
a lady, try on your fathers t
Universe shudders. Do not
around the edge of the plate
hard swallow away. Bare b

SWALLO
GARDEN SI
OUR S

TANDOORI LIAR .
A cheap shot in a poor life,
grilled over forty years.

THE CHEF ISN T S
Diced ambition, grated
over a disastrous first date r

STYLE OVER CON
Big butter-kissed docker, sl
funny, collapsed near the si

LAMB CONQUISTA
A Napoleonic Jew of a med
Over-burdened with garlic a

HOORAY HENRY C
Comes in a turtle neck soup
and accompanied by some

A NEST OF VIPERS
Rat-spider toast, dribbling i
it s intelligence at the back
for it s birthday, never quite rec

SLAG - MISFIT . . .
This dish won t boil over th
repeated mouthfuls the ten
what not combine to bring

ALLOW THE
IALITIES

. . . . .5.90
alp,
ng
gale
row
fish salad.
ANCE 5.25
s fur,
livin .
o a
an owl
ESS PUDENDA 6.95

pit
n Hot)

CK IT DISHES

PONCE 3.05
six
d
iefs
prejudice
scenario.
OODLES 3.50
e
o a

each day.
S 2.99
at
a
n

mood.
. . . . .2.99
he warmth of
and the
e mice heels
cifer is only a
spoonerism.

ED BACK
LITIES ARE
ALITY

. . . . .7.85

. . . . .7.35

RILL 7.95
uggets felt
eltzer extra).
. . . . .6.90

wish.
TER BED 3.55
iculous cravat
Bear slurry.
. . . . .4.60
, keeps
te, waiting
e trauma.
. . . . .4.80
, but on
a and
cream up.

ABSOLUT NIGHT BUS DRINKS LIST

LARGER:

Intercourse Pilsner 1.50
Testosterone tenderness.

Down on Luck Lager . . . . .4 for a £1.00
The Myth of the endless can.

Tenants Super 0.90
For those in the know. Tramp Champagne!

BITTER, ALE & STOUT:

A set of descriptive terms that require elbow room,crumpled black suit, a beer tan, loose fitting memories. . . . . ***Prices vary according to income***

NEW WORLD WINES:

Dobbins Last Wretched Day 4.99
Nose like an alsation, after a long hill climb, fights like a cat, net curtains and a long let down.

Dogs Leg Farm 5.99
An illiterate, zenophobic little wine with mid-England histrionics and child hating eyes.

Sink The Bismark 7.45
Brewed in Nazi Germany during the Revulsion. Not many to go.

WHISKEY:

Old Fettered Man 9.99
Take it to bed, it s the Adult Nipple.

Bells Extra Special 14.99
Known as the Tartan Tantrum . The Flexed Thistle. Bottled Catastrophe. Red Indian Genocide Liquid.

Glen Abattoir 32.50
White as a sheet, you stalk the dungeon. Several hours later waking up in an Enfield green grocers, with a kebab inside your shirt and an anger shield that has partly dissolved your soul.
(Price includes 6 Zone Travelcard)

PORTS:

The Dover/Calais cross channel off-licence.

CIDER & PERRY:

Merrydown Original 1p
It s the alcohol that everything else is based on. Jesus apparently wept when he first tasted this!

Diamond White Hell 2p
Complicated beyond belief. Has a complete lack of respect for age or gender. A tractor couldn t pull you out the misery you re in.

Baby Shambles 3p
The Child Support Agencies Liquid Santa.

Snowball 4p
Mid-Winter geriatric warmer stroke killer.

MINERAL, WATER, GOLD & FUR:

Rain Water . . . . .God s price
Cloud, mountain, river, dam, turbine, saw mill, chemical plant, pond, through swimming pool, tap, to just add ice & a lemon.
Clear water is as illusive as clear skin.

Yellow Mineral Water . . . . .Council price
About as easy to swallow as your own piss, speaking of which.
Cup your hands when the Waiter appears.

The Liquid out of a false teeth beaker.

Glass full to brim . . . . .Grandad s price
Only available a night in advance.

Guilt On Tap . . . . .Priceless
A Glass of this *home-brew* and you might leave your wife for a man.

Alsation Smoothie . . . . .Scentless
Dog rough, with a piquant whiff.

CHAMPAGNES:

Lady Shambles . . . . .Half your salary
High pedigree, low morals, high mileage.

Lansing Black Label . . . . . . .3points on your licence
Brut, detached and sarcastic. Anti-lock brakes & twin air bags.

THE HOSTS CABINET EXHUMED:

Essential drinking for the Festive Season, or when you re in a mood.

Country Satin . . . . .15 Euros
This is a subtle blend of all the countries in the 2nd WW, some of which we haven t heard of. Ouzo, Sake, Sten Gun & Coke.

Irish Velvet . . . . .15 Paddies
Cherry Brandy, Taboo & Coke. *(Good Taxi drink).*

Welsh Rugby . . . . .15 Taffies
Advocat, Ginger Wine, Ricard, Captain Morgans.
(Bucket & a Night bus Special)

Scottish Tantrum . . . . .15 Jocks
Martini Rosso, Woodpecker, The Famous Grouse & Campari.*(Something to drink in casualty).*

SUNDRIES NOBODY WANTS

NAN 1.30
ME NAN IS DEAD 1.50
PHALLIC RIPE BANANAS 2.10
CONKERS 2.10
STRING 2.10
VINEGAR 2.10
DETENTION 2.10
BOILED HURT 1.50
SPECIAL BOILED HURT 1.50
PLASTIC SPOON 0.70
EGG FRIED COLD SHOULDER 0.60
HOPE PURIFIED 1.50
SINGAPORE NO FUN 1.50
SHARK IN BOAT MASSACRE 0.70
POORLIE 1.40
STUFFED POORLIE .1.55
WASTED OPPORTUNITY 0.70
CHICKEN-POX SCRAPINGS 0.80
HONEY ROASTED STILL-BORN 0.70
CORNED BEEF HYMEN 0.65
A VERY PLAIN CHAT 0.95
CRUSHED BY THE WHEELS
OF INDUSTRY 1.00
BUFF CHUTNEY IN PICKLE 0.40
PRAWN BUTT FUCK .0.75
GROT 0.10

SWALLOW SEED SPECIAL SET MEALS FOR ONE

C1 Contains:
Dry Onions, a Half Baked Bitterness, Frosty looks, a fish drowns with black eyes staring at you, a free burp & you ve lost me. An opened can of Cola-Cola, and a giraffe of white whine 15.30

S1 Contains:
No remorse, a Half Baked Bitterness, a dead cat from your childhood, a cup of madness, the weddingring & divorce settlement for you to sign, 2 free pappadums & mint sauce 10.30

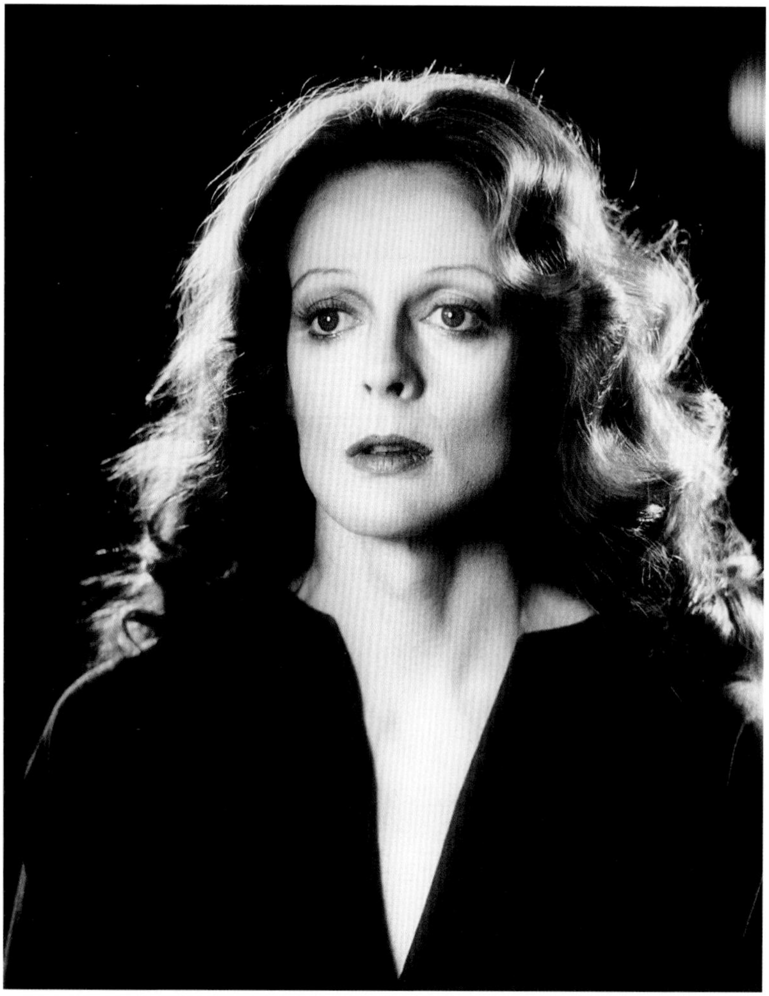

Zoë Dominic Maggie Smith as Cleopatra in 'Anthony and Cleopatra', Stratford, Ontario, 1976

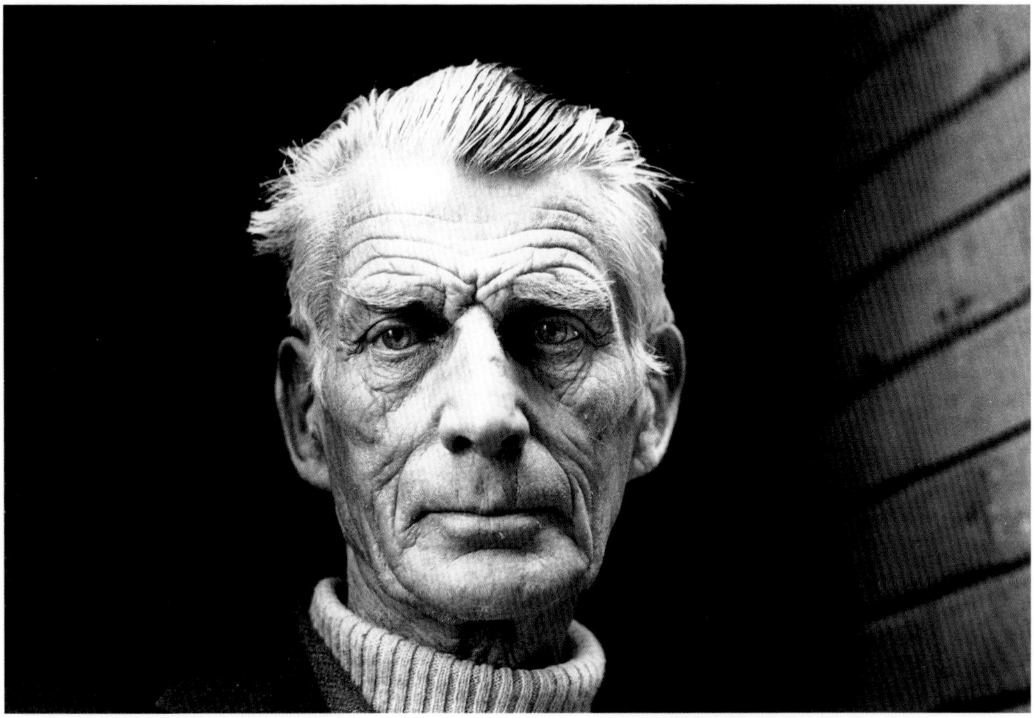

above **Jane Bown** Samuel Beckett, 1976

overleaf **Harry Diamond** Francis Bacon and Lucien Freud, 1974

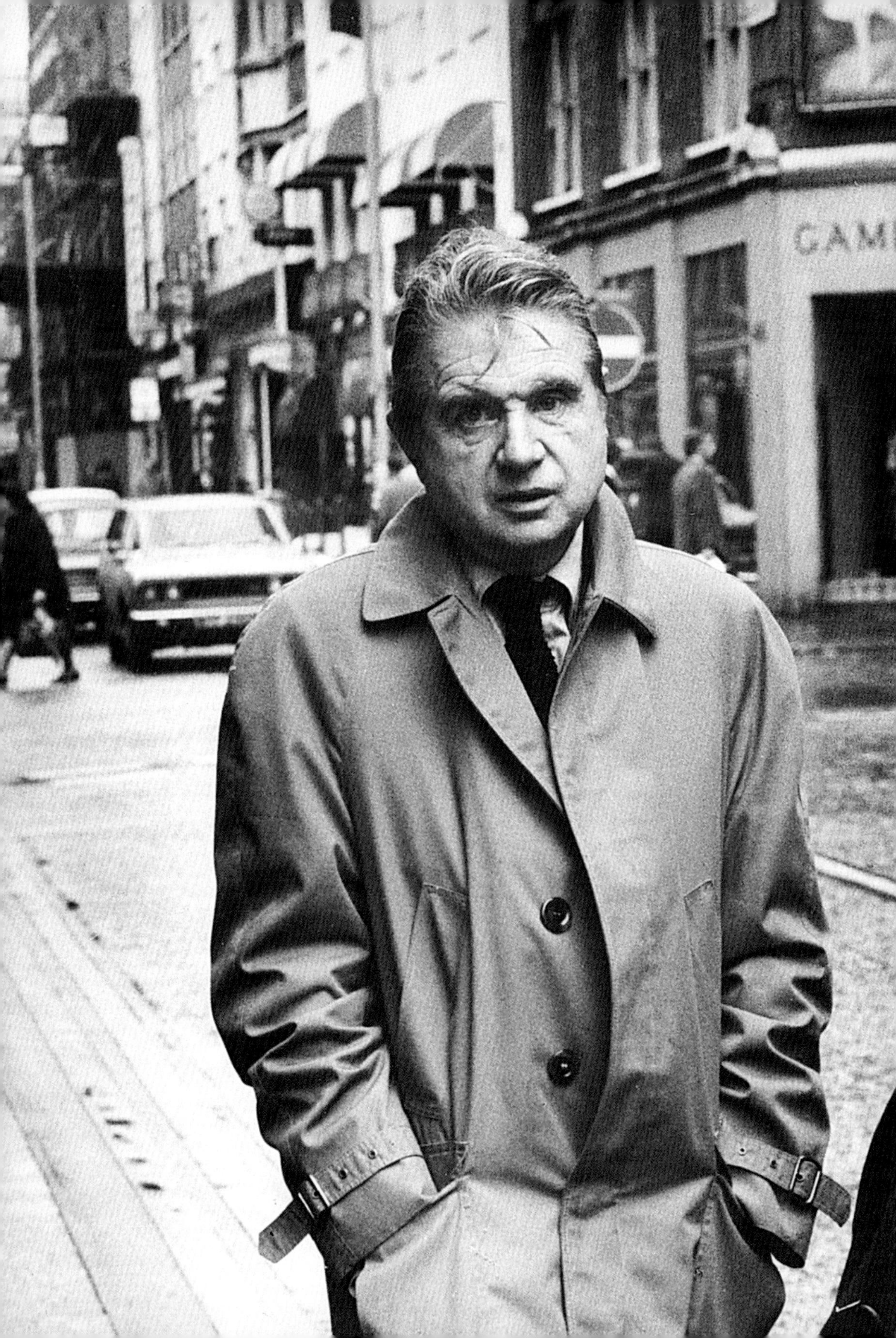

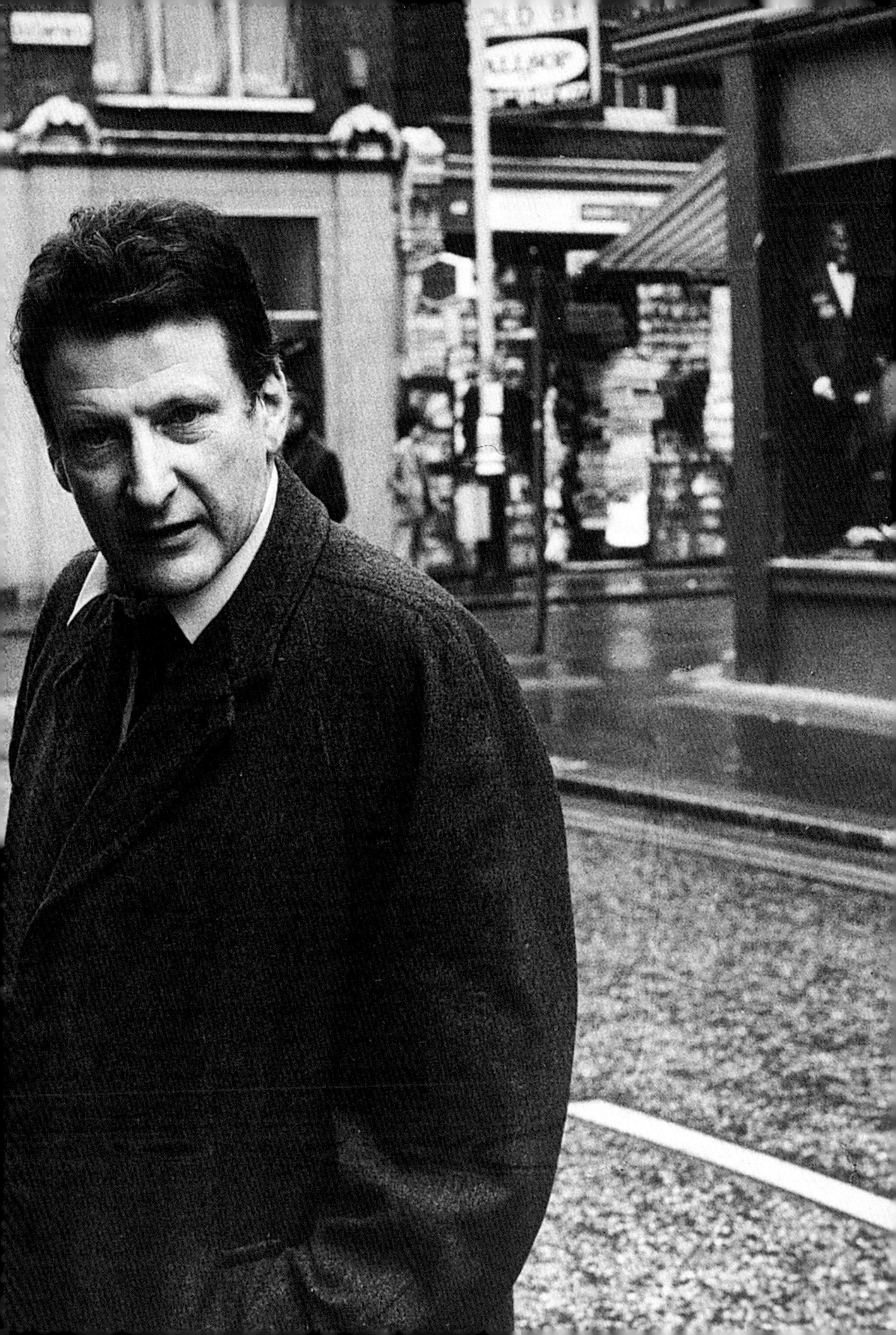

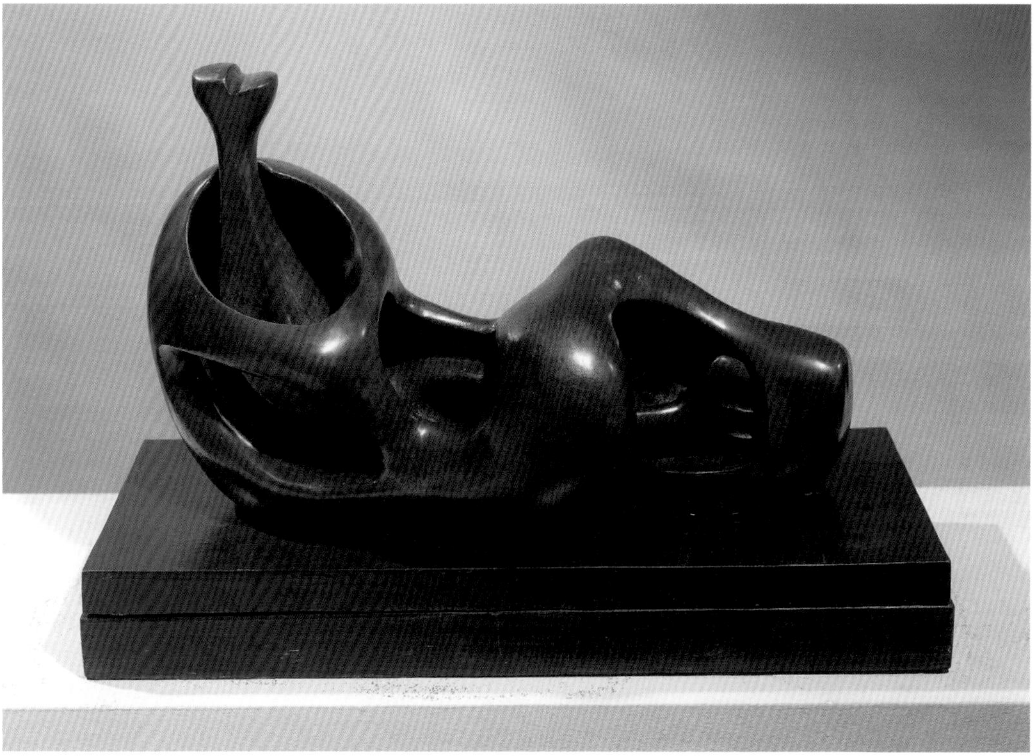

Henry Moore Working Model for Reclining Figure (Internal and External Forms), 1951

Chronology

Selected exhibitions, purchases and Arts Council Collection related events.

1940 Wartime government establishes the Council for the Encouragement of Music and the Arts (CEMA) to raise awareness of the importance of culture in a free society, to boost public morale and provide jobs for artists.

1942 With funds provided by the Pilgrim Trust, CEMA acquires 75 modern paintings and watercolours and begins to organise travelling exhibitions under the title *Art for the People*. Besides touring to regional art galleries, these are shown in cathedrals, theatres, welfare centres, factories, British Restaurants, gas and electricity showrooms, YMCA canteens, schools and art schools.

1946 Arts Council of Great Britain (ACGB), created as a successor to CEMA, receives its Royal Charter. Economist John Maynard Keynes is appointed Chairman. ACGB takes responsibility for CEMA's collection of modern British paintings; this forms the nucleus of the Arts Council Collection (ACC). ACC makes its first purchase, Edward Burra's painting *Design for a Drop Curtain* (1946).

1947 ACC acquires its first work by Barbara Hepworth, a drawing, *Reconstruction* (1947) and a painting by Ben Nicholson, *Still Life* (1946).

A Selection from the CEMA Collection of Oil Paintings (Parts I and II) includes works by Vanessa Bell, Edward Burra, Robert Colquhoun, Charles Ginner, Lawrence Gowing, Duncan Grant, Ivon Hitchens, Kenneth Martin, Bernard Meninsky, Rodrigo Moynihan, Ceri Richards, Claude Rogers, Gilbert Spencer, John Tunnard and Carel Weight.

1948 ACC acquires its first works by Henry Moore: two drawings, *Women Winding Wool* (1948) and *Seated Figure* (1934).

1949 ACC acquires its first sculpture, a bronze by Frank Dobson of a Russian ballet dancer, *Portrait Bust of Lady Keynes (Lydia Lopokova)* (1924).)

1950 Purchasing funds stand at £2,000 per annum.

A series of exhibitions from the Arts Council Collection begins touring nationally.

1951 ACGB organises three touring exhibitions for the Festival of Britain: a large anthology exhibition demonstrating the achievements of British painters over the preceding 25 years; a second exhibition to fill what are perceived to be the gaps in the first exhibition's selection; and a third, perhaps the most important for the collection, *60 paintings for 51*, for which each of the 60 artists are invited to paint a 'large' painting measuring 45 x 60 inches. Victor Pasmore's *The Snowstorm: Spiral Motif in Black and White* (1950–1951) and Prunella Clough's *Lowestoft Harbour* (1951) are among eight of the paintings acquired for ACC from this exhibition, five of which were given to municipal galleries. A major year for acquisitions with 108 works purchased in total.

Twelve sculptures are also commissioned for the festival; among them are works by Reg Butler, Lynn Chadwick, Jacob Epstein, Barbara Hepworth, Henry Moore and Eduardo Paolozzi. A ceramic study by Frank Dobson for his *London Pride* (1951) is acquired.

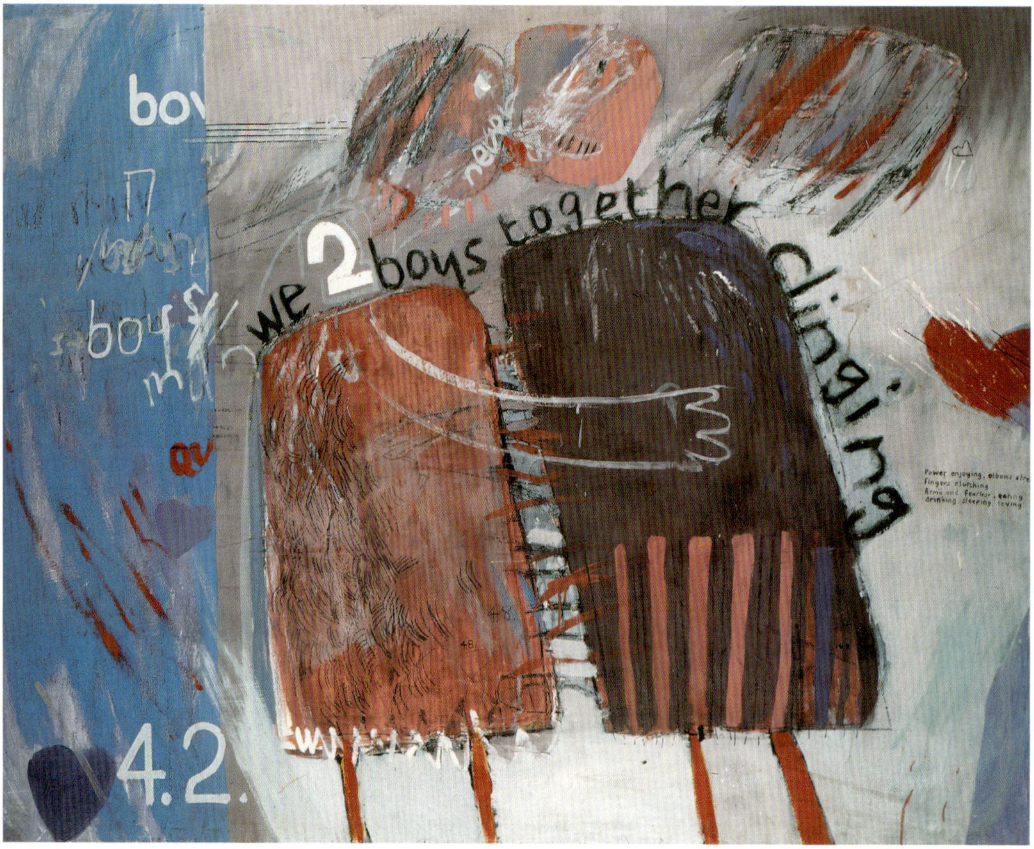

David Hockney We Two Boys Together Clinging, 1961

1952 ACC acquires a painting by Francis Bacon, *Head VI* (1949), and another by Lucian Freud, *Cock's Head* (1951).

ACC acquires an early work by Peter Lanyon, *Bicyclist in Penwith* (1952), and goes on to amass a strong holding of works by the St Ives based artists.

1953 Kenneth Clark appointed Chairman of ACGB. He had said earlier, 'It is easy to run exhibitions, and arguable that the Arts Council should have its own Collection as a supplement to that of the Tate.'

1956 ACC acquires its first painting by Frank Auerbach, *Head of E.O.W. VIII* (1956).

1958 *The Arts Council Collection of Paintings and Drawings (Parts I–IV)*. Catalogue introduction by Andrew Forge. Includes works by Edward Ardizzone, Frank Auerbach, Francis Bacon, Vanessa Bell, Martin Bloch, John Bratby, Harold Cohen, William Coldstream and Cecil Collins.

1959 ACC acquires its first work by Antony Caro, a bronze, *Woman Waking Up* (1956).

Purchasing funds stand at £4,000 pa.

1961 From the early 1960s onwards the purchasing committee focuses exclusively on contemporary art.

At the end of his time at the Royal College of Art, David Hockney asks if an earlier purchase, a small abstract painting called *November*, could be exchanged for his most important work to date: *We Two Boys Together Clinging* (1961). ACC is pleased to accept.

*New Paintings 58–61**. Catalogue introduction by Alan Bowness.

1962 ACC acquires its first painting by Bridget Riley, *Movement in Squares* (1962).

1963 As a result of ACGB touring exhibition, ACC acquires 14 works (drawings and sculptures) by Henry Moore. In the same year ACC acquires its first work by Peter Blake, *Baron Adolf Kaiser* (1961–1963).

1964 *New Painting 61–64**. Catalogue introduction by Ronald Alley.

ACC acquires its first painting by Richard Hamilton, *Portrait of Hugh Gaitskell as a Famous Monster of Filmland* (1964).

1967 Janet ('Jennie') Lee, Baroness Lee of Asheridge is appointed first Minister for the Arts.

1968 *Painting 64-67**. Catalogue introduction by John Russell.

*Sculpture 60-67**. Catalogue introduction by Norbert Lynton.

1969 *Arts Council Collection 1967–1968*. Paintings bought for ACC by Alan Bowness and Robyn Denny.

1970 Purchasing funds stand at £21,000 pa.

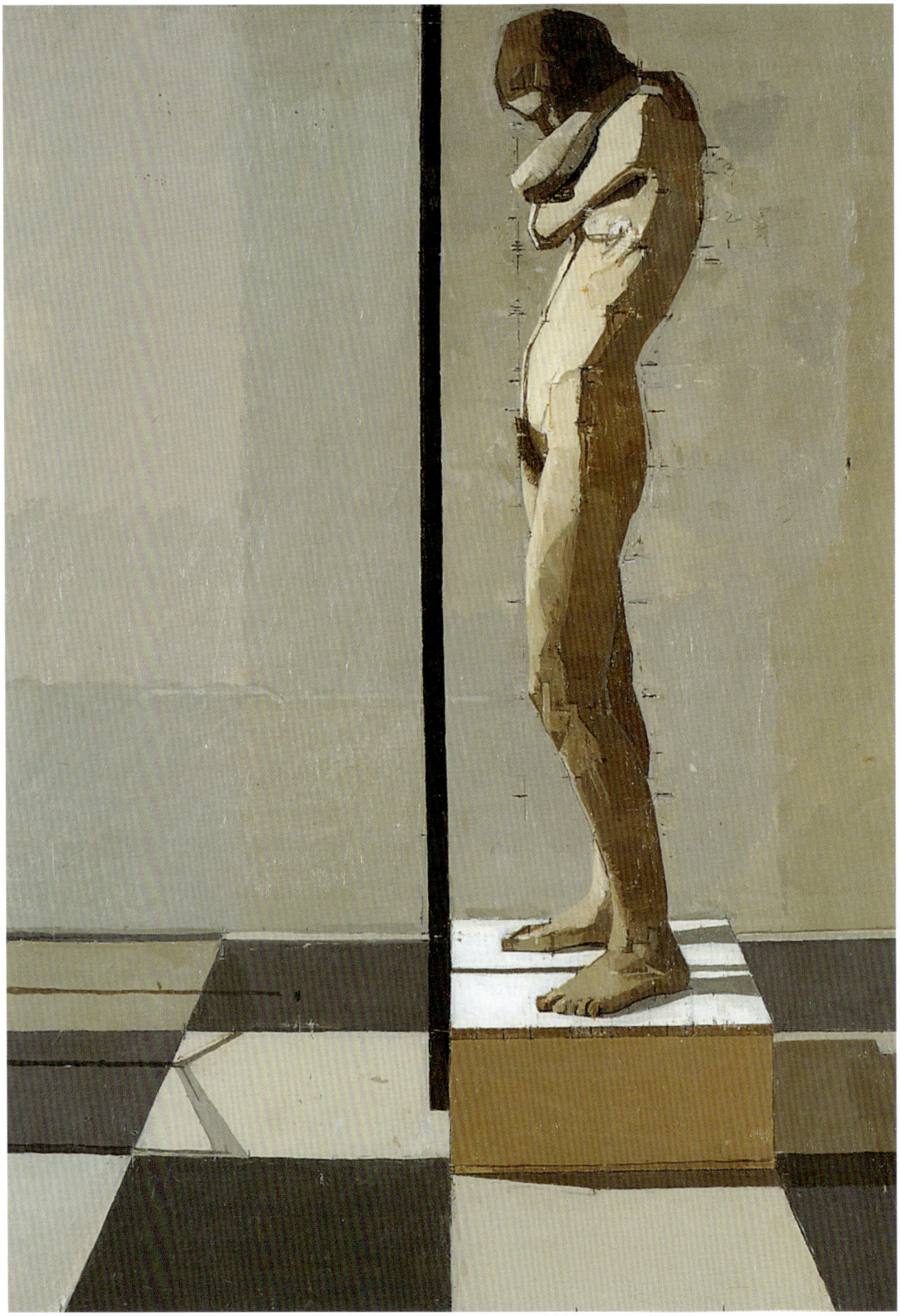

Euan Uglow Snake, 1976

1972 ACC acquisitions committee invited to buy work on specific themes for exhibition purposes e.g. *Objects and Documents*, curated by artist Richard Smith; *Eight Individuals*, curated by Bryan Roberton; *Beyond Painting and Sculpture*, curated by Richard Cork; *Art as a Thought Process*, curated by Michael Compton; *An Element of Landscape*, curated by Jeremy Rees; *11 Sculptors*, One Decade, curated by Hubert Dalwood; and *Drawings of People*, curated by Patrick George.

At the same time, ACC starts to acquire documentary photography through the Arts Council by making this a condition of its awards and bursaries, and grants for publications. The Photography Collection is held at Sheffield Polytechnic (Hallam University) and is used mainly as a teaching resource.

ACC acquires its first sculpture by Richard Long, *Stone Circle* (1972).

1973 Gilbert & George's *A Portrait of the Artists as Young Men* (1972) is the first video work to be acquired.

1975 Karen Amiel takes over from Katharine Kinnear (Sathe) as Curator of the Arts Council Collection.

The Condition of Sculpture, recent sculpture by young British and foreign artists, curated by William Tucker, held at Hayward Gallery.

1976 *The Human Clay*, curated by R.B. Kitaj, includes works bought by him especially for the exhibition. Opens at Hayward Gallery before touring nationally. Includes work by Michael Andrews, Francis Bacon, William Coldstream, Lucian Freud, Maggi Hambling, Nigel Henderson, David Hockney, Allen Jones, Leonard McComb, William Scott, Euan Uglow and Carel Weight.

1977 First *Hayward Annual**, intended to present a cumulative picture of British art as it develops, runs until 1986.

Yorkshire Sculpture Park, the first of its kind in the country is awarded £1,000 by Yorkshire Arts Association towards its opening exhibition.

Purchasing funds stand at £67,000 pa.

ACC acquires Howard Hodgkin's painting *Foy Nissen's Bombay* (1975–1977).

Stage designs in ACC are transferred to the V&A Museum.

1978 *The Constructive Context*, curated by Stephen Bann. Tour begins at Artists Market, Warehouse Gallery, London.

Joanna Drew appointed Director of Visual Arts at ACGB.

Dr Isobel Johnstone appointed Curator of the Arts Council Collection.

1979 Rudi Fuchs, Director of the Van Abbemuseum in Eindhoven, becomes the first international curator to select an ACC exhibition: *Languages: an exhibition of artists using word and image*, with works by Art & Language, Victor Burgin, Gerard Hemsworth, John Murphy, Gerald Newman, Bruce Robbins, John Stezaker and Stephan Willats.

Mary Kelly Post-Partum Document, Documentation VI:Pre-Writing Alphabet, Exerque and Diary/Experimentum Mentis VI: (On the Insistence of the Letter), 1978–1979

*The British Art Show 1**, curated by William Packer, tours to Sheffield, Newcastle upon Tyne and Bristol.

A Cold Wind Brushing the Temple, curated by George Melly.

ACC acquires first work by new generation of sculptors: Tony Cragg's *New Stones - Newton's Tones* (1978).

Publication of *Arts Council Collection: Acquisitions 1942–1978* (volume 1). 9.6 per cent of the works are by women artists.

1980 First survey exhibition of ACC, *British Art 1940–1980: The Arts Council Collection*, held at Hayward Gallery.

Nature as Material, sculpture and photography curated by Andrew Causey.

1981 ACC purchasing procedure is established: includes three guest purchasers (a curator, an artist, a critic) serving a period of 12–18 months.

A Mansion of Many Chambers, curated by David Brown.

1982 *Anthony Caro: works from the ACC*. Tour begins at Hunterian Art Gallery, Glasgow.

*Through Children's Eyes**, organised by Southampton Art Gallery, Wildground County Junior School and ACGB, with works from ACC and Southampton Art Gallery.

Purchasing funds stand at £100,000 pa

1983 *The Sculpture Show: Fifty Sculptors at the Serpentine and the South Bank**, curated by Paul de Monchaux, Fenella Crichton and Kate Blacker, held at Hayward GalleryandSerpentine Gallery.

1984 Publication of *Arts Council Collection: Acquisitions 1979–1983* (volume 2).

*The British Art Show 2**: *Old Allegiances and New Directions 1979–1984**, curated by Marjorie Allthorpe-Guyton, Alexander Moffat and Jon Thompson, tours to Birmingham, Edinburgh, Sheffield and Southampton.

The Glory of the Garden. The Development of the Arts in England: A Strategy for a Decade, ACGB's strategy document, declares that 'the Arts Council has failed to decentralise and disperse the dramatic and musical and artistic life of this country', and announces 'the largest single programme of devolution in the history of the Arts Council'. More attention is to be given to towards developing the potential of the municipal museums in partnership with local authorities.

*Home and Abroad**, an exhibition at the Serpentine Gallery, provokes hostile press when a sculpture by Richard Wentworth, *Tirana*, is associated with the sinking of the Argentinean warship, the *Belgrano*, during the Falklands War.

1985 *Beyond Appearances: sculpture for the visually handicapped and sighted to share**, organised by Nottingham Castle Museum and ACGB.

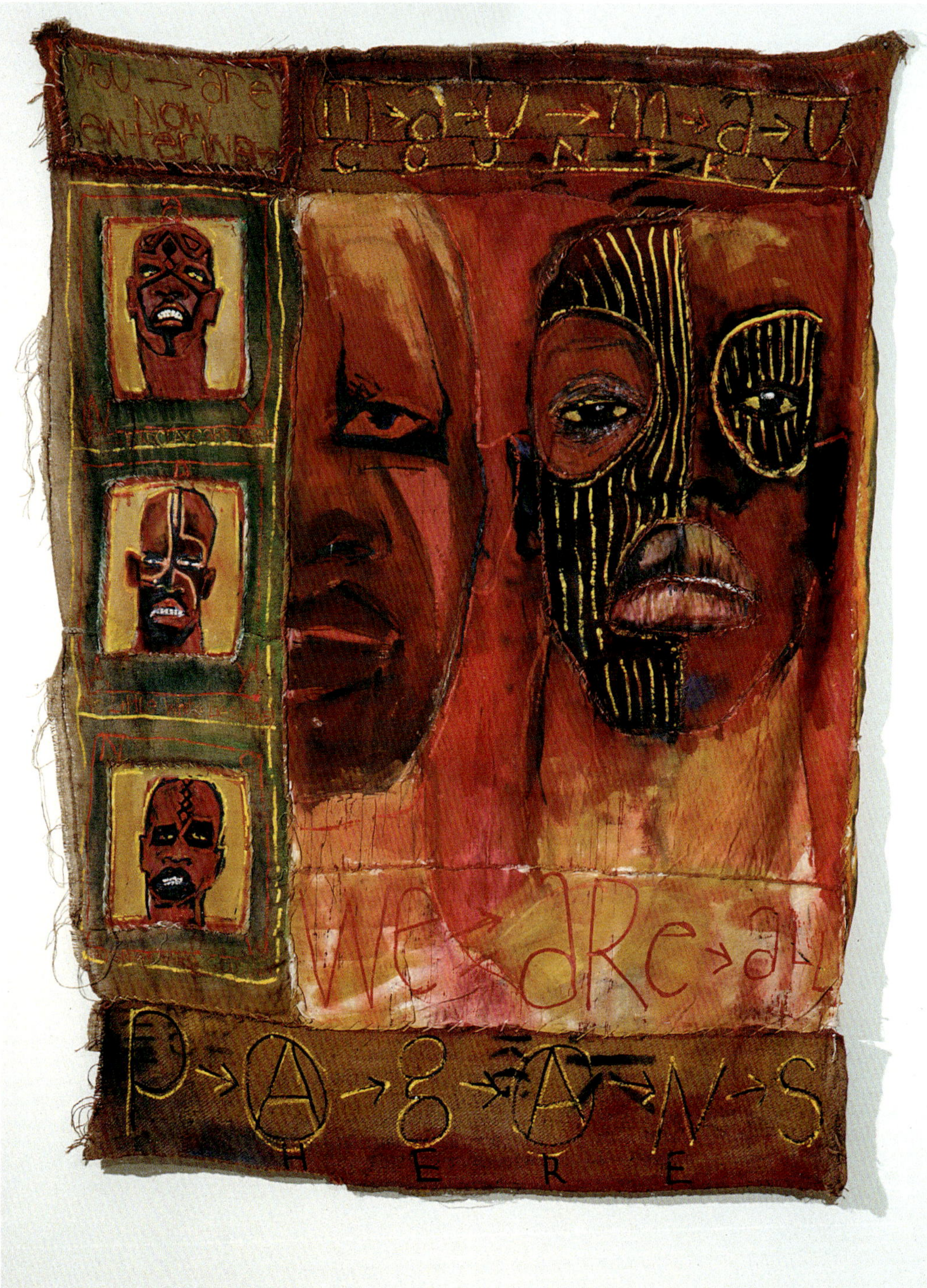

Keith Piper (You are now entering) Mau Mau country, 1983

The Contemporary Art Society celebrates its 75th anniversary. Since 1910 it has been purchasing contemporary painting and sculpture and presenting it to public galleries in Britain and the Commonwealth; it has donated over 4,000 works of art, beneficiaries include most regional galleries.

1986 ACGB transfers its exhibition-making activities – Hayward Gallery, National Touring Exhibitions and ACC – to newly formed South Bank Centre (SBC), following the Greater London Council's (GLC) demise.

1987 Sandy Nairne succeeds Joanna Drew as Director of Art at ACGB. Joanna Drew continues as first independent Director of the Hayward Gallery.

Introducing with Pleasure (selectors include Kate Adie, Clive Arrowsmith, David Attenborough, Janet Baker, Michael Clark, Shirley Conran, Roald Dahl, Peter Gill, Jean Muir, Patrick Nevin, Bruce Oldfield and Greta Scacchi).

The Experience of Landscape, curated by the ACGB's poetry librarian, Jonathan Barker. Tour begins at Derby Art Gallery.

Paula Rego's painting, *Sleeping* (1986) is acquired with financial assistance from English Estates.

1988 Publication of *Arts Council Collection: Acquisitions 1984–1988* (volume 3). The introduction notes rising prices of work and tighter budgets. 'In coming years we shall be looking for increased public funding but also to private and commercial sources. Offers of gifts or bequests of work will also continue to be welcome.'

Frank Dobson's sculpture, *London Pride*, commissioned by ACGB in 1951, is cast in bronze and sited on the South Bank in 1987, and vested in the ACC a year later.

1989 *It's a Still Life*. Tour begins at Plymouth City Museum and Art Gallery.

1990 Purchasing funds are reduced to below £80,000 pa.

Purchase of Richard Deacon's *Kiss and Tell* (1989) with the assistance of The Henry Moore Foundation and the National Art Collections Fund. It is the first work to be acquired for ACC with the direct assistance of outside agencies.

Festival of Fifty One, paintings and sculpture of 1951. Tour begins at the Royal Festival Hall.

Masterpieces from the Arts Council Collection tours to Japan.

*The British Art Show 1990 3**, curated by Caroline Collier, Andrew Nairne and David Ward, tours to Glasgow, Leeds and Hayward Gallery. Most of artists are aged under 35.

1991 *Shocks to the System: Social and Political Issues in Recent British Art*. Catalogue introduction by Neal Ascherson.

1993 Marjorie Allthorpe-Guyton succeeds Sandy Nairne as Director of Visual Arts at ACGB. Joanna Drew retires after a life-time of distinguished service. Henry Meyric Hughes succeeds her as Director of the Hayward Gallery.

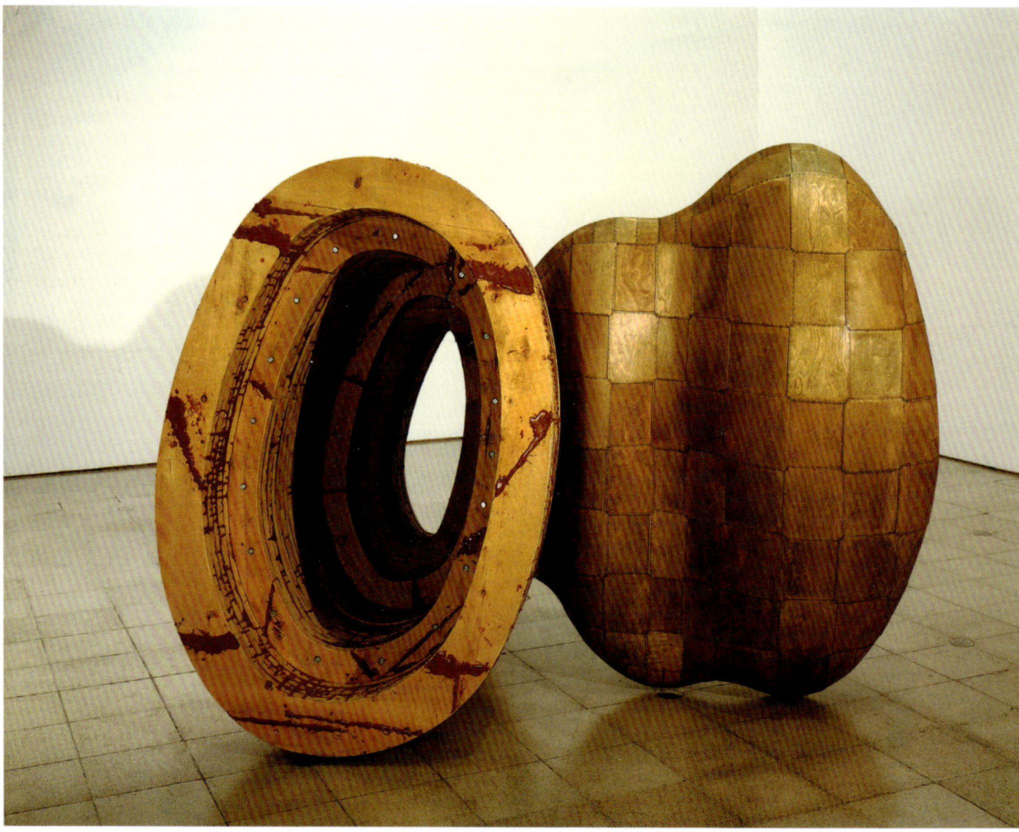

Richard Deacon Kiss and Tell, 1989

The touring exhibition *Recent British Sculpture* gives rise to a new series of exhibitions from ACC, called *Spotlights*, each focusing initially on a single work (for example, works by Tony Cragg, Richard Deacon, Anish Kapoor, Jacqui Poncelet and Kathy Prendergast).

The *Spotlight* series later concentrates on small groups of works by a single artist. It goes on to include Francis Bacon, Prunella Clough, Terry Frost, Douglas Gordon, David Hockney, Kenneth Martin, Ben Nicholson, Eduardo Paolozzi, Victor Pasmore, William Tucker, Euan Uglow and Gillian Wearing.

1994 ACGB reconfigured and replaced by the Arts Council of England (ACE).

Institute of International Visual Arts (inIVA) founded by the ACE 'to reflect a culturally diverse spectrum of artistic practices, curatorial voices and critical perspectives in contemporary art through collaborations and commissions'.

National Lottery launched and generates almost £2 billion for the arts in its first decade.

Catherine Yass commissioned to make *Portrait: Selection Committee for the Arts Council Collection*, light box and cibachrome transparency.

New multiples commissioned for the touring exhibition *Art Unlimited: Multiples of the 1960s and 1990s*.

1995 ACC acquires Antony Gormley's installation, *Field for the British Isles* (1993) with the assistance of The Henry Moore Foundation and the National Art Collections Fund.

*The British Art Show 4**, curated by Richard Cork, Rose Finn-Kelcey and Thomas Lawson, tours to Manchester, Edinburgh and Cardiff.

1996 *ACE! New acquisitions from ACC* shown at Hayward Gallery to celebrate the 50th anniversary of the founding of ACC. Tour opens at the Hatton Gallery, Newcastle, to coincide with the launch of *Visual Arts UK* in the North of England, as part of the Arts Council's nationwide project, Arts 2000.

Susan Ferleger Brades succeeds Henry Meyric Hughes as Director of the Hayward Gallery. ACC acquires Damien Hirst's sculpture *He Tried to Internalise Everything* (1992–1994) with the assistance of The Henry Moore Foundation.

The new *Select* programme of exhibitions begins with *Still Life* at University of East London. These are exhibitions curated by galleries from ACC. More than 60 galleries go on to use this programme, including Shrewsbury Museum and Art Gallery; Usher Gallery, Lincoln; Talbot Rice Gallery, Edinburgh; Oriel Mostyn, Llandudno; Newlyn Art Gallery, Penzance;Mercer Gallery, Harrogate; and the Lowry, Salford.

1998 *Fifty Years of British Sculpture* opens at Lothbury Gallery, London (a collaboration with the private sector for public display).

Head First: Portraits from the ACC, curated by Richard Shone.

The touring exhibition *Here to Stay: Purchases of the 1990s* opens at Plymouth Arts Centre.

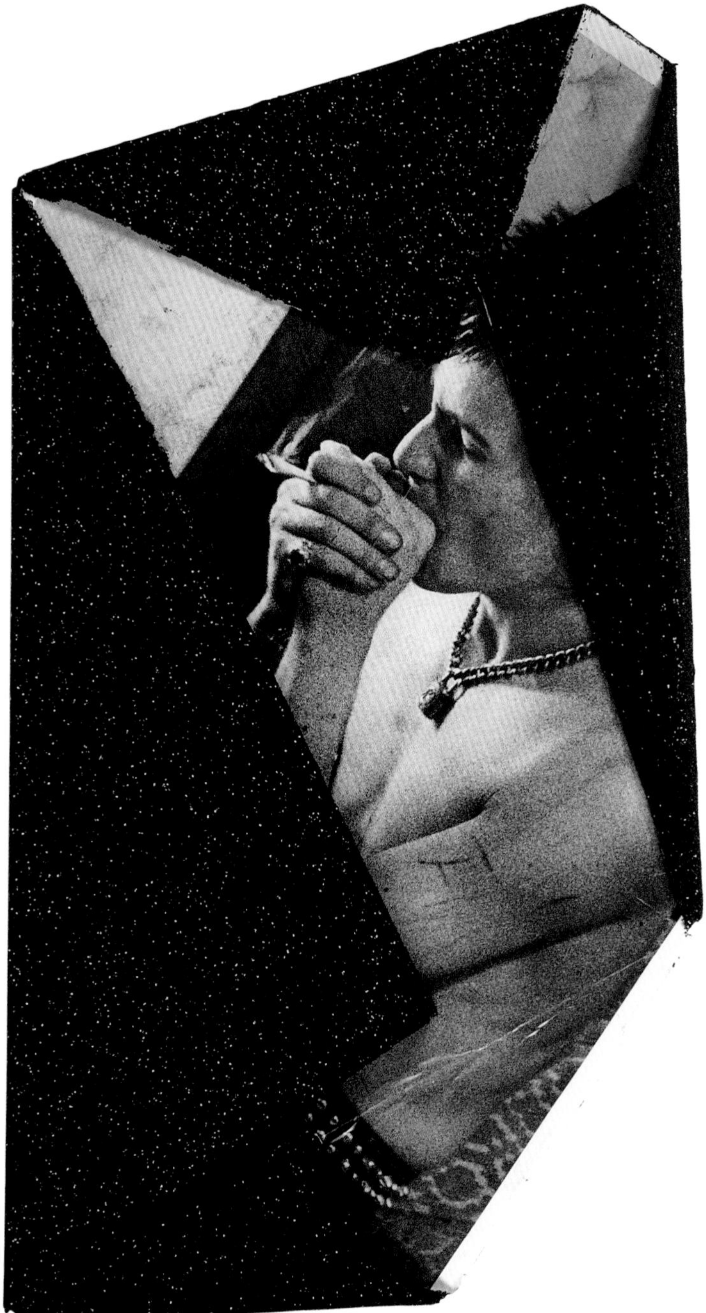

Jim Lambie Sid Vicious, 2001

The Contemporary Art Society is awarded £2.5 million from the National Lottery through Arts Council England to set up the Special Collection Scheme, enabling 15 museums throughout England to develop collections of international contemporary art and craft over five years.

1999 Photography Collection joins the rest of the ACC in London.

Charles Saatchi gives 100 works by 63 artists to the Arts Council Collection.

Select exhibition of works from the Saatchi gift opens at the Mapping, Sheffield; this is the first of several *Select* exhibitions focusing on the Saatchi gift.

Sublime: The Darkness and Light opens at the John Mansard Gallery, Southampton. Catalogue essays by Christopher Kool-Want and Jon Thompson.

2000 The biggest programme of new and refurbished museums and galleries in British history, with over £400 million of Lottery money, begins with the opening of Walsall's New Art Gallery, followed by Salford's Lowry Centre and in London the new Tate Modern at Bankside and the re-launch of the Tate Gallery on Millbank as Tate Britain.

*The British Art Show 5**, curated by Pippa Coles, Matthew Higgs and Jacqui Poncelet, tours to Edinburgh, Southampton, Cardiff and Birmingham.

2001 *Out of Line*, an exhibition of ACC drawings, opens at York City Art Gallery.

Arnolfini Collection Trust gives eight works to ACC.

2002 Charles Saatchi gives a further 34 sculptures by 18 artists to the ACC.

The Arts Council of England and 10 Regional Arts Boards merge to become Arts Council England, the single national development agency for the arts.

Words, tour begins at Plymouth City Museum and Art Gallery.

2003 Relocation of sculpture in the ACC to a new operating base at Longside, Yorkshire Sculpture Park (YSP). The space enables the Collection to meet its growing conservation and handling needs, and increases accessibility, outreach and training opportunities. Launch of new exhibitions programme at the adjacent Longside Gallery, which the Hayward Gallery shares with YSP. The project is funded by Arts Council England with the support of The Henry Moore Foundation. The refurbishment of Longside is carried out by Tony Fretton Architects. The opening is marked by the commission of a new work by Stefan Gec, *Untitled (Apollo Soyus test Project)*, double screen computer animation.

ACC acquires Richard Deacon's sculpture *Kind of Blue (A)* (2001) with the assistance of the National Art Collections Fund.

Natalie Rudd is appointed first Sculpture Curator at Longside.

Bad Behaviour, tour begins at Longside Gallery.

Purchasing funds stand at approximately £152,000 pa.

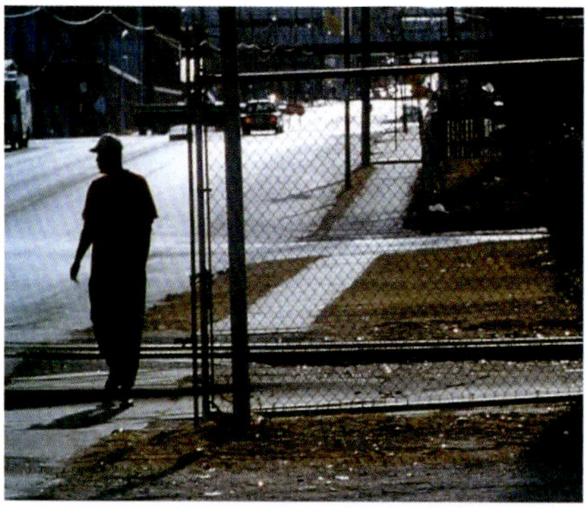

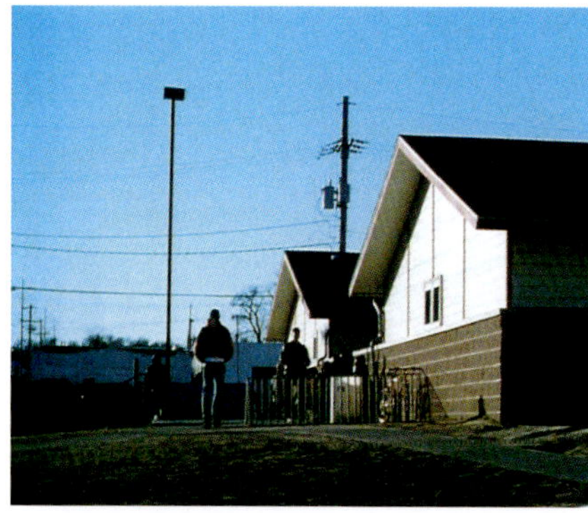

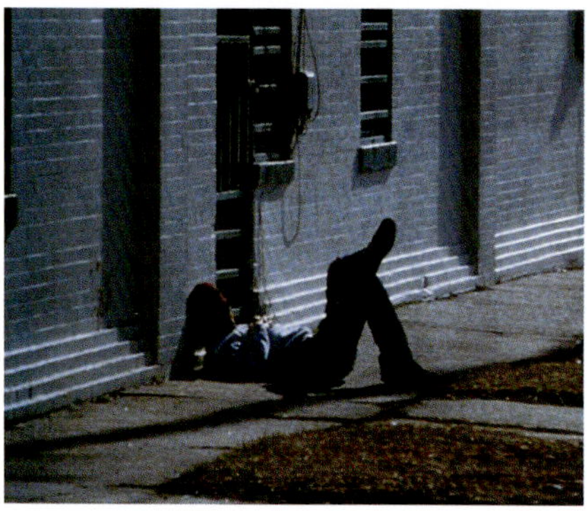

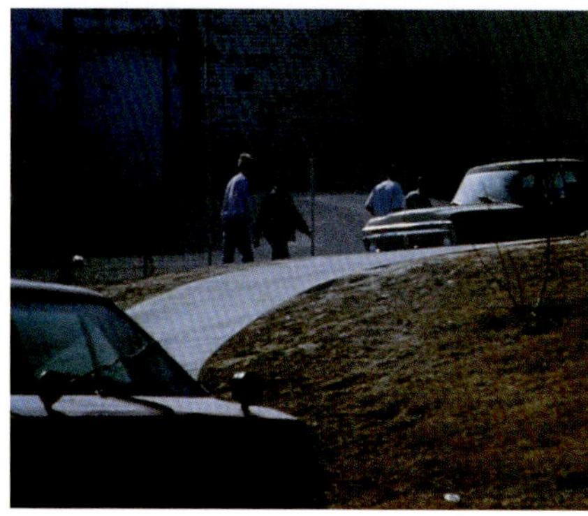

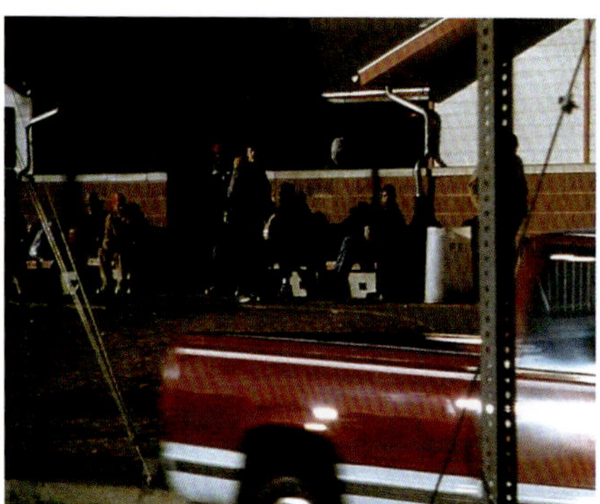

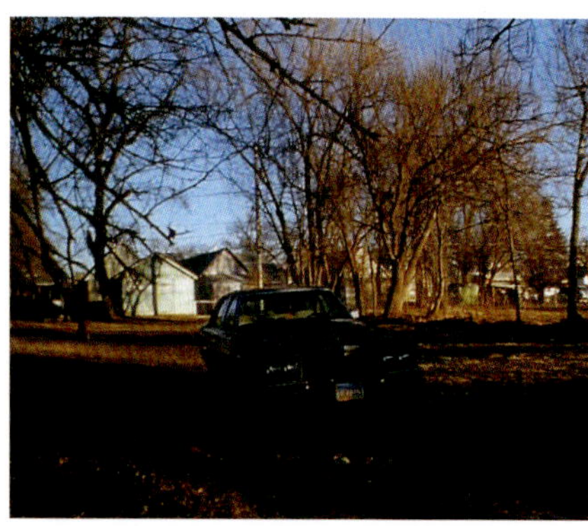

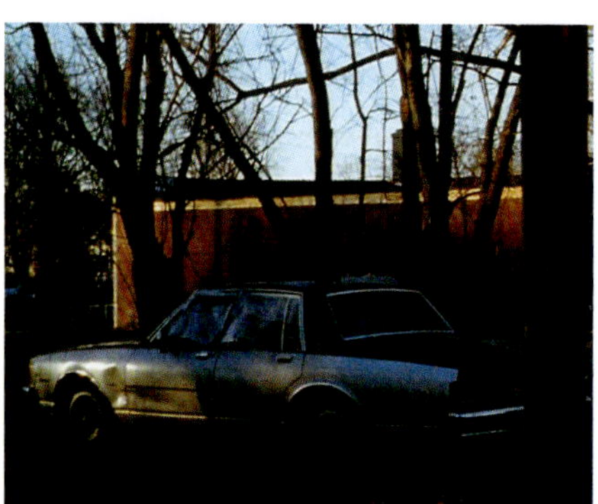

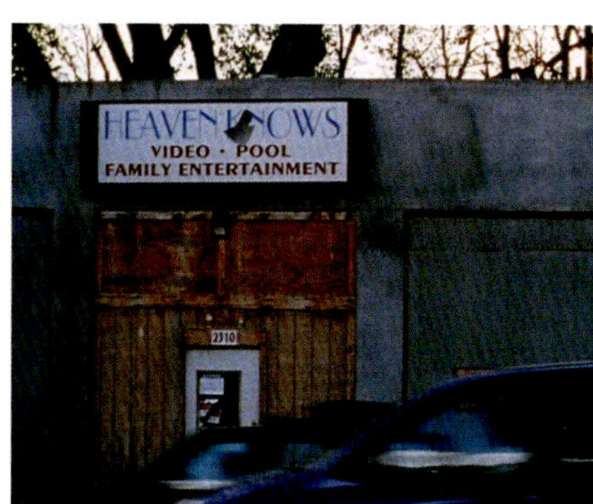
HEAVEN KNOWS
VIDEO · POOL
FAMILY ENTERTAINMENT

Publication of *Arts Council Collection: Acquisitions 1989–2002* (volume 4). 30.7 per cent of works are by women artists.

2004 Dr Isobel Johnstone retires as Curator of the Arts Council Collection after 25 years. Jill Constantine, Assistant Curator since 1994, takes over as Curator until Susan May is appointed with the new title, Head of Arts Council Collection.

Stranger than Fiction, tour begins at Leeds City Art Gallery. Catalogue text by Sukhdev Sandhu.

2005 New store opens in London for the care of ACC's two-dimensional works.

*British Art Show 6**, curated by Alex Farquharson and Andrea Schlieker, tours to Gateshead, Manchester, Nottingham and Bristol.

Size Matters, national tour begins at Longside Gallery.

2006 ACC celebrates its 60th anniversary.

Longside Gallery celebrates the anniversary with *60: Sixty Years of Sculpture in the Arts Council Collection* featuring 60 works spanning the breadth of ACC.

Spotlight on St Ives is the first *Spotlight* focusing on a group of works by several artists.

Material World, Major sculpture exhibition, including, Tony Cragg, Richard Deacon, Shirazeh Houshiary, Grayson Perry and Rachel Whiteread. Held at the Gallery of Modern Art, Glasgow.

Revelation, early works by major artists, David Bachelor, Helen Chadwick, Tracy Emin, Lucien Freud, Gary Hume and Fiona Rae. Opens at Laing Art Gallery, Newcastle and tours to Salford and Graves Art Gallery in Sheffield.

How to Improve the World: 60 Years of British Art, works from ACC, opens at Hayward Gallery, followed by a national tour.

ACE launches *Turning Point*, a 10-year strategy for the contemporary visual arts in England, following a major review of the presentation of contemporary visual arts, and commits to prioritising the visual arts.

Ralph Rugoff appointed as Director of the Hayward Gallery and Caroline Douglas is appointed Head of Arts Council Collection.

ACC launches website to allow users to find out more about ACC and to search holdings online.

* Indicate those exhibitions where only a selection of works owned by the ACC is shown.

opposite **Rosalind Nashashibi** Midwest, 2002
overleaf **Ian Hamilton Finlay** Strawberry Camouflage, 1977

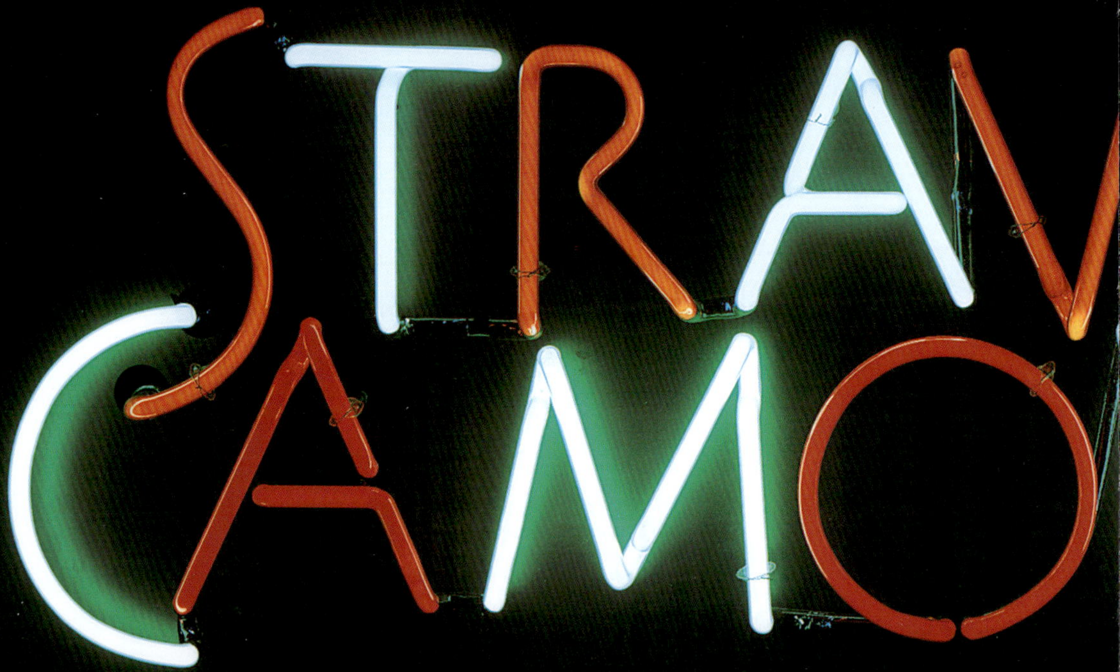
STRAV
CAMO

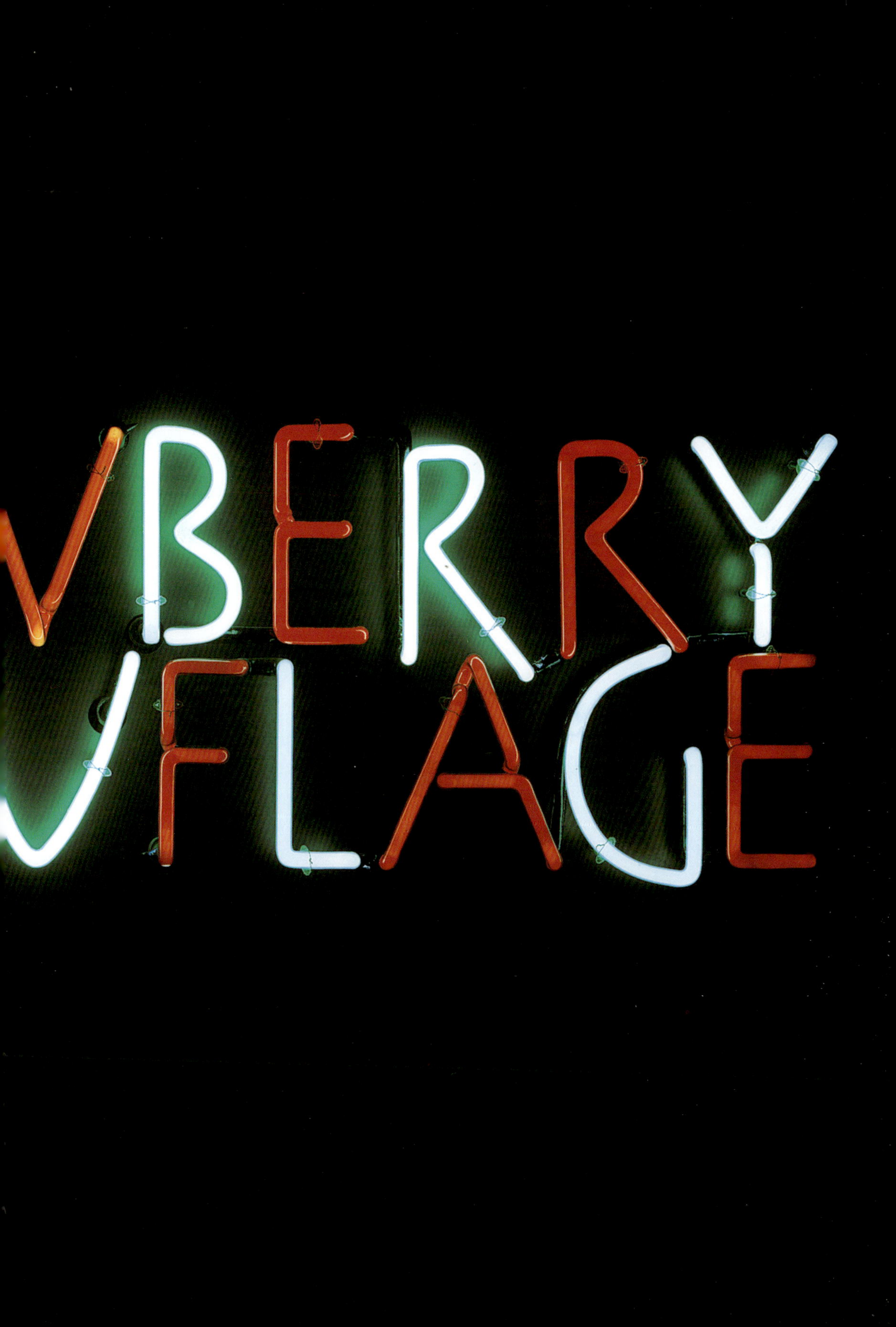
BERRY
FLAGE

List of Purchasers between 1958 and 2006

1958 James Fitton
Bryan Robertson

1959 Claude Rogers
John Russell

1960 Alan Bowness
Lawrence Gowing

1961 Keith Vaughan
Carel Weight

1962 Adrian Stokes
David Sylvester

1963 Ronald Alley
Sir Roland Penrose

1964 Lawrence Gowing
Adrian Heath
John Russell
Adrian Stokes
Joe Tilson

1965 Norbert Lynton

1966 Alan Bowness

1967 Alan Bowness
Robyn Denny
Bernard Meadows

1968 Robyn Denny
David Sylvester

1969/70 John Golding
Norbert Lynton
Bryan Robertson

1970/71 Ronald Alley
Bryan Robertson

1971/72 Hubert Dalwood
Bryan Robertson
Richard Smith

1972/73 Richard Cook
Edward Lucie-Smith
The Marquis of Dufferin & Ava

1973/74 Michael Compton
Hubert Dalwood
Jeremy Rees

1974/75 Patrick George
Bryan Kneale

1975/76 Paul Huxley
R. B. Kitaj
Bryan Kneale
Peter Turner

1976/77 Paul Huxley

1977/78 Rudi Fuchs
Bill Gaskins
George Melly

Panel members who have purchased works:
Stephen Bann
Bernard Cohen
Patrick George
John Hubbard
Ian Jeffrey
Phillip King
Jack Smith
William Varley

1978/79 Ed Barber
Derek Boshier
Andrew Causey
George Melly
Chris Steele-Perkins

Panel members who have purchased works:

Sherban Cantacuzino
Peter de Francia
Bill Gaskins
Lawrence Gowing
Adrian Henri
John Hubbard
Ian Jeffrey
Phillip King
Myles Murphy
Duncan Robinson
The Lady Vaizey

1979/80 Derek Boshier
Julian Spalding

1980/81 Julian Spalding
David Brown

1980/82 Sirkka-Liisa Konttinen
Griselda Pollock
Roger Taylor

1981/82 Frank Constantine
Adrian Heath
Ursula Hoff
Shelagh Wakely

1982/83 Prunella Clough
Malcolm Hughes
John McEwan

1983/84 Bruce Bernard
Rose Garrard
John Spurling

1984/85 Lynne Cooke
Richard Cork
David Elliott

1985/86 Barry Barker
Timothy Hyman

1986/87 Sonia Boyce
Mike Tooby
Alison Wilding

1988/89 John Lyons
John Maine
Boyd Webb

1990/92 Mel Gooding
Susan Hiller

1992/94 Shirazeh Houshiary
Vong Phaophanit
Adrian Searle

1994/96 Simon Linke
Nima Poovaya-Smith
Richard Shone

1996/98 Sacha Craddock
Susan Daniel-McElroy
Cornelia Parker

1998/2000 Guy Brett
Pavel Büchler
Yinka Shonibare

2000/02 David Batchelor
Mariele Neudecker
Mark Sealy

2002/04 Michael Archer
Susan Collins
Keith Hartley

2004/06 Willie Doherty
Mustafa Hulusi
Polly Staple

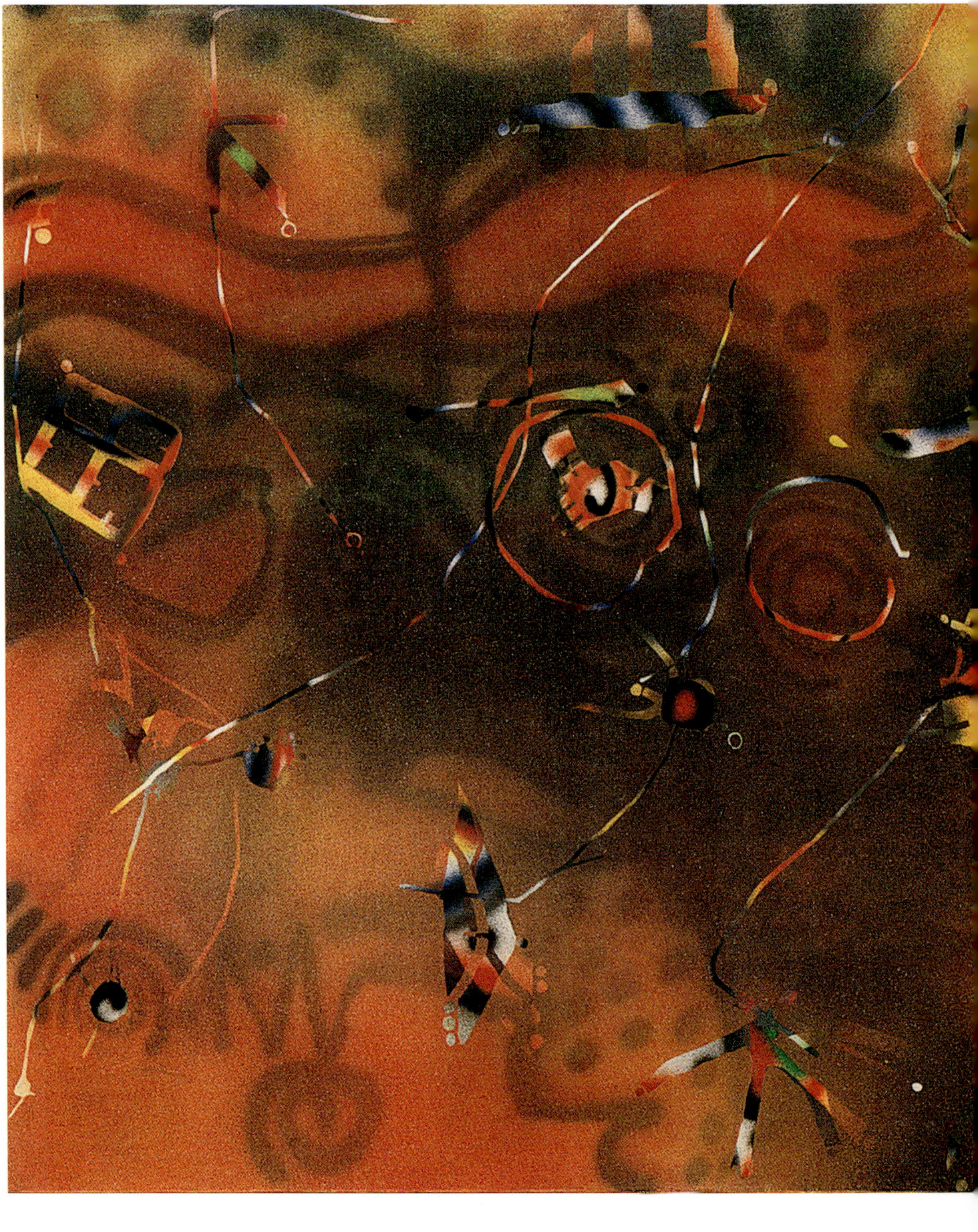

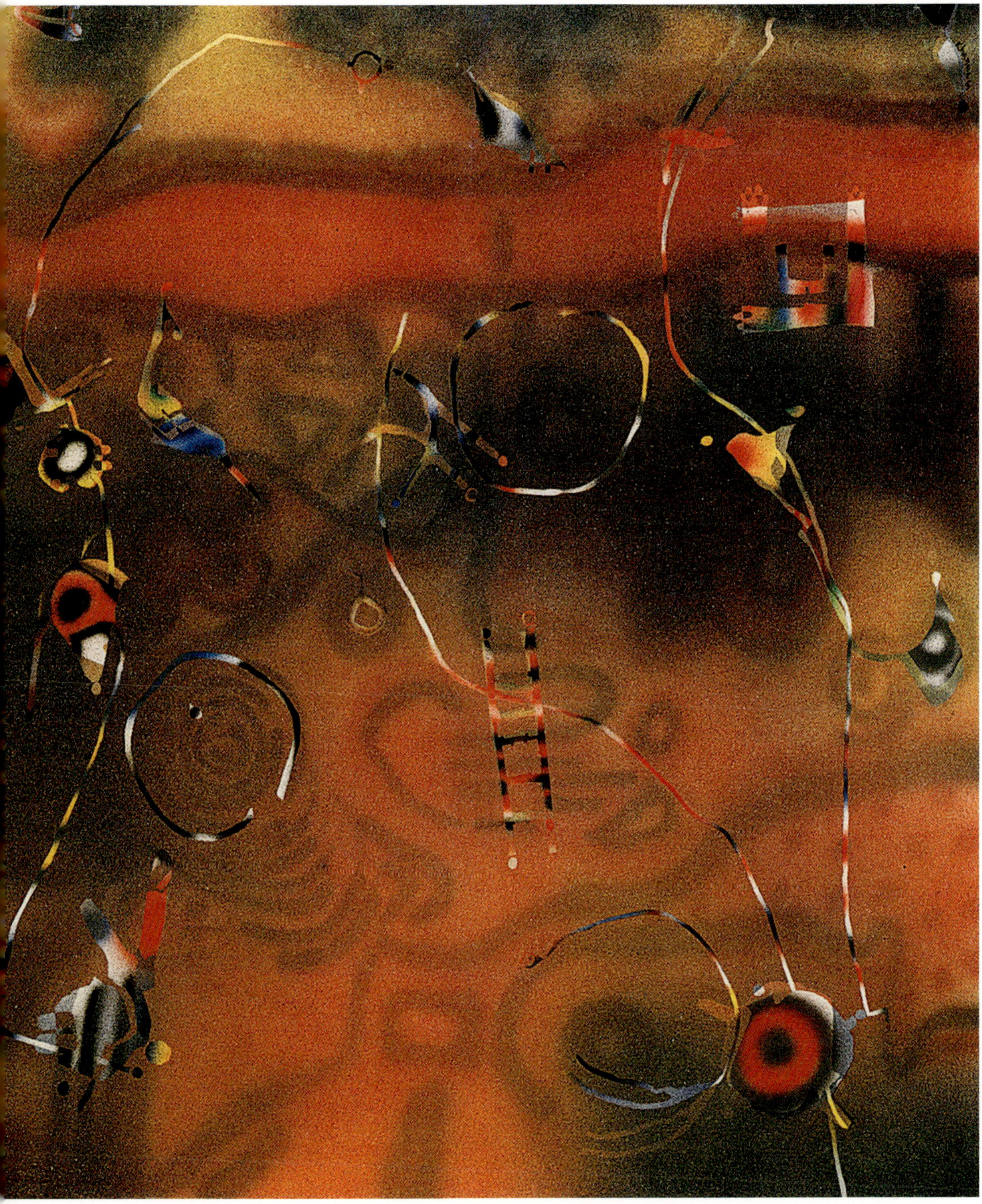

above **Balraj Khanna** Coming from Rajasthan, 1984

overleaf **David Shrigley** These and others will be there to greet you at the airport..., 1997

THESE AND OTHERS WILL BE THERE TO GREET YOU AT THE AIRPORT

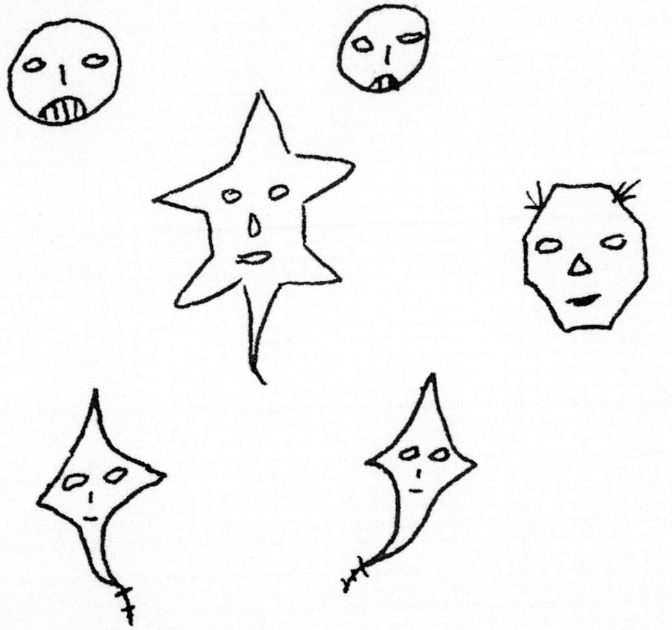

BUT THEY DON'T SPEAK ENGLISH SO YOU'D BETTER BRING YOUR PHRASEBOOK

List of Works

All measurements are in centimetres, height x width x depth. Page references are to illustrations in this book. All works are from the Arts Council Collection, Hayward Gallery, South Bank Centre, London. All galleries unless otherwise stated are in London.

p. 72
Roger Ackling (b. 1947)
Five Hour Cloud Drawing, 1980
Sunlight on cardboard
62.4 x 75.2
Purchased from Lisson Gallery, 1981
AC 4041

p. 52
Rasheed Araeen (b. 1935)
Green Painting I, 1985–1986
Mixed media; 173 x 226
Purchased from the artist, 1987
AC 5458

p. 148
Kenneth Armitage (1916–2002)
Figure Lying on its Side (No. 5), 1957
Bronze
38.1 x 82.5 x 22.3
Purchased from the artist, 1958
AC 450
© The Kenneth Armitage Foundation

pp. 34–35
Keith Arnatt (b. 1930)
Is it Possible for me to do Nothing as my Contribution to this Exhibition?, 1970
Text on paper
76.2 x 101.6
Purchased from the artist, 1973
AC 1288

p. 141
Art & Language
(Terry Atkinson b. 1939; Michael Baldwin b. 1945) *Print (Two sections A & B)*, 1966
Letterpress on paper
37.2 x 109.7
Purchased from Lisson Gallery, 1974
AC 1320

p. 99
Frank Auerbach (b. 1931)
Euston Steps - Study, 1980–1981
Oil on hardboard
122.6 x 152.7
Purchased from Marlborough Fine Art, 1982
AC 4055

p. 90
Gillian Ayres (b. 1930)
Lure, 1963
Oil on canvas
152.4 x 152.4
Purchased from Hamilton Gallery, 1963
AC 705

p. 2
Francis Bacon (1909–92)
Head VI, 1949
Oil on canvas
93.2 x 76.5
Purchased from Hanover Gallery, 1952
AC 230
© Estate of Francis Bacon/DACS

p. 132
Anna Barriball (b. 1972)
Window, 2002
Pencil on paper
55.5 x 51
Purchased from Frith Street Gallery, 2004
ACC 9/2004

p. 112
John Berger (b. 1926)
Scaffolding - Festival of Britain, 1950
Oil on canvas
76.2 x 50.8
Purchased from the artist, 1950
AC 169

Bruce Bernard (1928–2000)
Lucian Freud with painting of Leigh Bowery, 1990
Bromide print
33 x 48.5
Purchased from Peralta Pictures, 1995
ACC 30/1995

pp. 120–121
Leigh Bowery and Nicola Bateman posing for 'And for the Bridegroom', 1993
No. 1 from a triptych
C-type print
30.3 x 45.7
Purchased from Peralta Pictures, 1995
ACC 32/1995

Leigh Bowery posing with painting by Lucian Freud, 1994
C-type print
45.8 x 31.4
Purchased from Peralta Pictures, 1995
ACC 31/1995

Sue Tilley posing in Lucian Freud's studio, 1995
C-type print
30.9 x 45.8
Purchased from Peralta Pictures, 1995
ACC 33/1995

pp. 40–41
Zarina Bhimji (b. 1963)
Here was Uganda, as if in the vastness of India, 1999–2001
Cibachrome on aluminium
122.4 x 173.4
Purchased from Norwich Gallery, 2001
ACC 40/2001

p. 104
Peter Blake (b. 1932)
Boy Eating a Hot Dog,
1960–1965
Acrylic on board
36.5 x 40.7
Purchased from Robert Fraser Gallery, 1965
AC 817

p. 95
David Bomberg (1890–1957)
Trendrine, Cornwall, 1947
Oil on canvas
81.3 x 106.7
Purchased from Lilian Bomberg, 1957
AC 446

p. 46
Henry Bond and **Liam Gillick**
(b. 1966, b. 1964)
11th February 1992; Evacuation and closure of Whitehall and surrounding area due to discovery of suspected device. Trafalgar Square, 1992
R-type photograph
30 x 21
Purchased from the artists, 1993
ACC 6/1993

p. 138
Christine Borland (b. 1965)
Carrier, 1994
De-activated gun and polythene; 51 x 21 x 3.2
Purchased from the artist, 1994
ACC 40/1997

p. 155
Jane Bown (b. 1925)
Samuel Beckett, 1976
Silver bromide print; 22.9 x 34.1
Purchased from the artist, 1978
ACP 0064

p. 49
Martin Boyce (b. 1967)
Dark Unit and Mask, 2003
Wood, steel, paint, altered Arne Jacobson Series 7 and Ant Chair parts
40 x 60 x 169
Purchased from roma roma roma, 2004
ACC 48/2003

pp. 56–57
Ian Breakwell (1943–2005)
Photo-text piece 1, 1972
Photograph and ink on board
8.9 x 31.9
Purchased from the artist, 1972
AC 1801

pp. 56–57
Photo-text piece 2, 1972
Photograph and ink on board
8.9 x 47.9
Purchased from the artist, 1972
AC 1802

pp. 56–57
Photo-text piece 3, 1972
Photograph and ink on board
10 x 60.7
Purchased from the artist, 1972
AC 1803

Photo-text piece 4, 1972
Photograph and ink on board
8 x 48.6
Purchased from the artist, 1972
AC 1804

Photo-text piece 5, 1972
Photograph and ink on board
10.2 x 61
Purchased from the artist, 1972
AC 1805

p. 100
Stuart Brisley (b. 1933)
1=66,666 (March 1983 – Georgiana Collection VI), 1983
Wood, steel, plaster, leather, nylon, cloth and paper
217 x 500 x 81
Purchased from Lewis Johnstone Gallery, 1983
AC 5222

p. 109
Glenn Brown (b. 1966)
Decline and Fall, 1995
Oil on canvas on board
58.4 x 54.6
Purchased from Karsten Schubert, 1995
ACC 9/1995

p. 68
Angela Bulloch (b. 1966)
Pink Chance Corner, 1990
Perspex, glass, metal, electric light and plastic
2 spheres, each 30 (diameter)
Purchased from Interim Art, 1993
ACC 9/1992

p. 123
Victor Burgin (b. 1941)
Possession, 1976
Photo-lithographic print
84 x 120
Purchased from the artist, 1980
ACC 13/1980

p. 119
Reg Butler (1913–1981)
Girl and Boy, 1951
Iron
200.7 x 66.5 x 84
Purchased from the artist, 1951
AC 203

p. 111
Gillian Carnegie (b. 1971)
Mono, 2005
Oil on board
73.3 x 58.7
Purchased from Cabinet
Gallery, 2005
ACC 3/2006

pp. 70–71
Anthony Caro (b. 1924)
Slow Movement, 1965
Painted steel
144.8 x 299.7 x 61
Purchased from Kasmin
Gallery, 1965
AC 821

pp. 18–19
Patrick Caulfield (1936–2005)
Sculpture in a Landscape, 1966
Oil on board; 121.9 x 213.3
Purchased from Robert Fraser
Gallery, 1967
AC 889

p. 89
Dining Recess, 1972
Oil on canvas; 274.5 x 213.5
Purchased from Waddington
Galleries, 1974
AC 1431

p. 103
Lynn Chadwick (1914–2003)
The Seasons, 1955
Iron
53.3 x 30.5 x 27.9
Purchased from the
Contemporary Art Society,
1956
AC 398
Arts Council Collection,
Hayward Gallery/The
Bridgeman Art Library

p. 36
John Coplans (1920–2003)
*Self Portrait (Upside
Down No. 1)*, 1992
Silver gelatin print on aluminium
3 parts, total 220 x 114.5
Purchased from London
Projects, 1996
ACC 9/1996

pp. 86–87
Tony Cragg (b. 1949)
New Stones – Newton's Tones,
1978
Plastic and metal; 6 x 366 x 244
Purchased from Lisson
Gallery, 1979
AC 1992

pp. 144–145
Michael Craig-Martin (b. 1941)
History Painting, 1995
Acrylic on canvas; 183 x 366
Purchased from Waddington
Galleries, 1995
ACC 25/1995

p. 133
Martin Creed (b. 1968)
Work No. 78, 1993
Elastoplast, polystyrene,
paper and cardboard
2.2 x 6.8 x 4.9
Purchased from Marc Jancou
Gallery, 1994
ACC 13/1997

Work No. 117, 1995
Audio cassette; 108 x 69 x 17
Purchased from the artist, 1995
ACC 42/1995

Work No. 123, 1995
Plastic, metal (sound), 3 parts
3 parts, each height 4.6,
diameter 9.3
Gift of Charles Saatchi, 1999
ACC 158/1998

p. 144
Ian Davenport (b. 1966)
*Poured Lines: Light orange,
blue, yellow, dark green
and orange*, 1995
Household paint on canvas
213.4 x 213.4
Purchased from Waddington
Galleries, 1995
ACC 38/1995

p. 131
Enrico David (b. 1966)
*Untitled (puppets:
we are the mods)*, 2003
Wood, glass and paint
85 x 65 x 12
Purchased from Galerie
Daniel Buchholz, Cologne,
2005
ACC 15/2005
Image courtesy Galerie
Daniel Buchholz, Cologne

p. 168
Richard Deacon (b. 1949)
Kiss and Tell, 1989
Epoxy, resin, timber,
plywood and steel
175 x 233 x 162
Purchased from Lisson
Gallery, with assistance from
The Henry Moore Foundation
and the National Art
Collections Fund, 1990
ACC 55/1989

pp. 8–9
Jeremy Deller (b. 1966)
The History of the World, 1998
Screenprint
66 x 112
Purchased from Paul Stolper,
1998
ACC 6/1998

Harry Diamond (b. 1924)
Langdale St, 1970
Silver bromide print
25 x 20.5
Purchased from Whitechapel
Art Gallery, 1977
ACP 0446

Self Portrait, 1973
Silver bromide print
24.2 x 19.2
Purchased from Whitechapel
Art Gallery, 1977
ACP 0447

pp. 156–157
Francis Bacon and Lucian Freud, 1974
Silver bromide print
16.4 x 24
Purchased from Whitechapel
Art Gallery, 1977
ACP 0449

The Empty Pint Blues, 1974
Silver bromide print
18.5 x 24
Purchased from Whitechapel
Art Gallery, 1977
ACP 0453

p. 110
Peter Doig (b. 1959)
Red Deer, 1990
Oil on canvas
237.5 x 182.6
Purchased from the artist, 1992
ACC 86/1991

p. 154
Zoë Dominic (b. 1920)
Maggie Smith as Cleopatra in 'Anthony and Cleopatra', Stratford, Ontario, 1976, 1976
Silver bromide print
38.4 x 30.6
Purchased from the artist, 1978
ACP 0262

p. 82
Tracey Emin (b. 1963)
Why I Never Became a Dancer, 1995
Betacam sp video projection
Running time: 6 mins, 40 secs
Purchased from White Cube, 1998
ACC 65/1997

p. 81
Rose Finn-Kelcey
Glory, 1983
Production in collaboration with Steven Hawley and Harry Walton
U-matic
Running time: 15 mins
Purchase Award, 1983
AC 5325

pp. 128–129
Barry Flanagan (b. 1941)
Sand/Muslin, 1966
Sand and muslin
15.5 x 104.5 x 75
Purchased from Rowan
Gallery, 1969
AC 1061

p. 130
Heap 4, 1967
Hessian filled with sand
15 parts, total size 60 x 131 x 100
Purchased from Rowan
Gallery, 1969
AC 1062

p. 13
Lucian Freud (b. 1922)
Girl in a Green Dress, 1954
Oil on canvas
32.5 x 23.6
Purchased from Daily Express
Exhibition, 1955
AC 363

p. 92
Terry Frost (1915–2003)
Ginger and Purple 'Chirpy', 1966
Oil on canvas
144.8 x 91.4
Purchased from the artist, 1967
ACA 44

p. 127
Gilbert & George
(b. 1943, b. 1942)
A Portrait of the Artists as Young Men, 1972
Videotape (transferred to DVD) and framed certificate
Running time: 8 mins
Purchased from Nigel
Greenwood, 1973
AC 1281

Gordon's Makes Us Drunk, 1972
Videotape (transferred to DVD) and framed certificate
Running time: 9 mins
Purchased from Nigel
Greenwood, 1973
AC 1280a

p. 126
Smash, 1977
Black and white photographs
302.5 x 252
Purchased from Anthony
d'Offay Gallery, 1981
ACC 1/1981

p. 108
Douglas Gordon (b. 1966)
Painting No. 19: Mark Rothko / Betty Parsons, 1992
Acrylic on canvas
100 x 66
Purchased from the artist, 1992
ACC 98/1991

p. 139
Gregory Green (b. 1959)
Pipe Bomb # 3 (LA), 1993
Metal, plastic, glue,
wire and paint
34.3 x 10.2 x 14.6
Gift of Charles Saatchi, 2002
ACC 31/2002

p. 115
Lucy Gunning (b. 1964)
Climbing Around My Room,
1993
Betacam sp video tape
Running time: 7 mins, 30 secs
Purchased from the artist, 1995
ACC 22/1995

Sunil Gupta (b. 1953)
Humayan's Tomb from
the series *Exiles*, 1987
C-type photographic print
48.2 x 48.2
Purchased from the artist, 1988
ACP 2004

India Gate from the series
Exiles, 1987
C-type photographic print
48.2 x 48.2
Purchased from the artist, 1988
ACP 2005

p. 124
Lodhi Gardens from the series
Exiles, 1987
C-type photographic print
48.2 x 48.2
Purchased from the artist, 1988
ACP 2007

Pragati Maidan from the
series *Exiles*, 1987
C-type photographic print
48.2 x 48.2
Purchased from the artist, 1988
ACP 2007

p. 59
Richard Hamilton (b. 1922)
Portrait of Derek Jarman,
1996-1997
Colour pigment transfer print
39.4 x 39.4
Purchased from Richard
Salmon Gallery, for the Elton
John AIDS Foundation, 1997
ACC 3/1997

pp. 174–175
Ian Hamilton Finlay
(1925–2006)
Strawberry Camouflage, 1977
Neon on board; 40.8 x 137 x 12.5
Purchased from the artist, 1977
AC 1830

p. 125
Siobhán Hapaska (b. 1963)
Heart, 1995
Rosewood veneer, MDF
and audio components
291 x 76 x 18.5
Purchased from Entwistle
Gallery, 1997
ACC57/1997

p. 138
Mona Hatoum (b. 1952)
Measures of Distance, 1988
Betacam sp video
Running time: 15 mins
Purchased from the artist, 1999
ACC 14/1999

+ and -, 1994
Wood, metal and sand (kinetic)
8 x 30 x 30
Purchased from the artist, 1999
ACC 44/1997

p. 135
Tim Head (b. 1946)
State of the Art, 1984
C-type colour print ; 183 x 274
Purchased from the artist, 1984
ACP 2008

p. 107
Nigel Henderson (1917–1985)
Head of a Man, 1956–1961
Oil and photographic
processes on card
152.4 x 121.9
Purchased from Anthony
d'Offay Gallery, 1977
AC 1849

p. 48
Barbara Hepworth (1903–1975)
Icon, 1957
Mahogany; 45.7 x 35.6 x 30.5
Purchased from Gimpel Fils
Gallery, 1958
ACC 3/1958
© Bowness, Hepworth Estate

p. 93
Spring, 1966
Bronze, string and
painted interior
76.8 x 50.8 x 38.1
Purchased from the artist, 1967
AC 869
© Bowness, Hepworth Estate

pp. 96–97
Patrick Heron (1920–1999)
*Green Painting with
White Disc*, 1964
Oil on canvas; 122 x 152.3
Purchased from Waddington
Galleries, 1964
AC 761
© The Estate of Patrick
Heron/DACS 2006

pp. 30–31
Susan Hiller (b. 1942)
Wild Talents, 1997
Video (and laser disc)
installation
Running time: 60 mins;
dimensions variable
Purchased from Wigmore
Fine Art, New York, 1998
ACC 10/1998

p. 102
Roger Hilton (1911–1975)
February - March 1954, 1954
Oil on canvas
127 x 101.6
Purchased from the artist, 1959
AC 445

pp. 16–17
Roger Hiorns (b. 1975)
Nunhead, 2004
Engines, steel and copper
sulphate
170 x 141.5 x 122
Purchased from Corvi-Mora,
2005
ACC 1/2006

p. 134
Damien Hirst (b. 1965)
*He Tried to Internalise
Everything*, 1992-1994
Glass, steel, foam, rubber,
vinyl, plastic, and wood
213 x 213 x 305
Purchased from White Cube,
with assistance from The
Henry Moore Foundation,
1996
ACC 21/1995

p. 160
David Hockney (b. 1937)
*We Two Boys Together
Clinging*, 1961
Oil on board; 121.9 x 152.4
Purchased from the artist, 1961
ACC 5/1961

p. 77
John Hoyland (b. 1934)
20.5.68, 1968
Acrylic on canvas
198.1 x 367 cm
Purchased from Waddington
Galleries, 1969
AC 1070

p. 51
Paul Huxley (b. 1938)
Untitled No. 32, 1964
Acrylic on canvas
172.7 x 172.7
Purchased from Rowan
Gallery, 1965
AC 785

p. 32
Anish Kapoor (b. 1954)
Untitled, 1995
Stainless steel
140 x 93 x 85 cm
Purchased from Lisson
Gallery, with assistance from
The Henry Moore Foundation
1997
ACC 63/1996

p. 164
Mary Kelly (b. 1941)
*Post-Partum Document,
Documentation VI: Pre-
Writing Alphabet, Exerque and
Diary/Experimentum Mentis
VI: (On the Insistence of the
Letter)*, 1978-1979
Slate and resin
18 parts, each 35.6 x 27.9
Purchased from the artist, 1981
AC 5000

pp. 178–179
Balraj Khanna (b. 1940)
Coming from Rajasthan, 1984
Acrylic on canvas
168 x 304
Purchased from the artist, 1991
ACC 28/1990

p. 88
Phillip King (b. 1934)
Point X, 1965
Fibreglass and polyester
182.9 x 188 x 152.4
Purchased from Rowan
Gallery, 1967
AC 898

p. 98
Leon Kossoff (b. 1926)
*Children's Swimming Pool,
Autumn 1972*, 1972
Oil on board
182.9 x 213.4
Purchased from Fischer Fine
Art, 1978
ACC 7/1978

p. 170
Jim Lambie (b. 1964)
Sid Vicious, 2001
Printed poster on foamboard
with black glitter
43 x 60 x 20
Purchased from Sadie Coles
HQ, 2001
ACC 3/2001

p. 101
John Latham (1921–2006)
Shaun II, 1958
Assemblage on canvas
252.7 x 116.8 x 30.5
Purchased from the artist, 1966
ACA 28

p. 151
Bob Law (1934–2004)
Bordeaux Black Blue Black,
1977
Acrylic on canvas
152.5 x 160
Purchased from Lisson
Gallery, 1979
AC 2002

p. 26
Mark Leckey (b. 1964)
Parade, 2003
Videotape
Running time: 32 mins
Purchased from Cabinet
Gallery, 2005
ACC 4/2006

p. 58
Andrew Logan (b. 1945)
Homage to the New Wave,
1977
Metal, resin, glass and stone
124 x 22.8 x 16
Purchased from Whitechapel
Art Gallery, 1977
AC 1820

p. 74
Richard Long (b. 1945)
Stone Circle, 1972
Stones
14 x 426.7 x 426.7
Purchased from the artist, 1972
AC 1211

p. 117
Camilla Løw (b. 1976)
7, 2004
Perspex, enamel and metal
260 x 40 x 50
Purchased from Sutton Lane,
2004
ACC 3/2005

pp. 152–153
Colin Lowe and **Roddy Thomson**
(b. 1966, b. 1965)
Swallow Seed Menu, 2003
Wood, paper, plastic,
felt and steel
42.7 x 50 x 6
Purchased from Sadie Coles
HQ, 2003
ACC 12/2003

p. 3
Sarah Lucas (b. 1962)
Eating a Banana, 1990,
from the series *Self Portraits*,
1990–1998
Iris print
78 x 82
Purchased from Sadie Coles
HQ, 2000
ACC 3/2000

Divine, 1991, from the series
Self Portraits, 1990–1998
Iris print; 78.8 x 90.8
Purchased from Sadie Coles
HQ, 2000
ACC 4/2000

Self Portrait with Mug of Tea,
1993, from the series *Self
Portraits*, 1990–1998
Iris print; 92.7 x 75
Purchased from Sadie Coles
HQ, 2000
ACC 6/2000

Self Portrait with Knickers,
1994, from the series *Self
Portraits*, 1990–1998
Iris print; 98 x 73.1
Purchased from Sadie Coles
HQ, 2000
ACC 7/2000

Fighting Fire with Fire, 1996,
from the series *Self Portraits*,
1990–1998
Iris print; 97 x 73.3
Purchased from Sadie Coles
HQ, 2000
ACC 10/2000

Human Toilet II, 1996, from
the series *Self Portraits*,
1990–1998
Iris print; 97.7 x 71.4
Purchased from Sadie Coles
HQ, 2000
ACC 9/2000

Self Portrait with Fried Eggs,
1996, from the series *Self
Portraits*, 1990–1998
Iris print; 98.2 x 73.7
Purchased from Sadie Coles
HQ, 2000
ACC 8/2000

Got a Salmon On #1, 1997,
from the series *Self Portraits*,
1990–1998
Iris print; 98 x 72.5
Purchased from Sadie Coles
HQ, 2000
ACC 12/2000

Self Portrait with Skull, 1997,
from the series *Self Portraits*,
1990–1998
Iris print; 97.3 x 70.8
Purchased from Sadie Coles
HQ, 2000
ACC 11/2000

Human Toilet Revisited, 1998,
from the series Self Portraits,
1990–1998
Iris print; 81.5 x 77.3
Purchased from Sadie Coles
HQ, 2000
ACC 15/2000

Smoking, 1998, from the series
Self Portraits, 1990–1998
Iris print; 97.3 x 71.6
Purchased from Sadie Coles
HQ, 2000
ACC 13/2000

Summer, 1998, from the series
Self Portraits, 1990–1998
Iris print; 84.5 x 77.2
Purchased from Sadie Coles
HQ, 2000
ACC 14/2000

p. 113
Kenneth Martin (1905–1984)
Endless Configuration, 1964
Oil on board
160.7 x 122.9
Purchased from the artist, 1964
AC 742

p. 138
Mary Martin (1907–1969)
Rotation (Not limited), 1968
Polystyrene and mirror
9 x 13 x 13; Purchased from
Unlimited, Bath, 1970
PR 163
© The Mary Martin Estate

p. 140
Bruce McLean (b. 1944)
Floataway Piece Beverly Brook, Barnes 1967, 1967
Black and white photograph
mounted on card; 16.2 x 66.4 cm
Purchased from Situation
Galleries, 1974
AC 1356

2 Mud and Water Pieces Beverly Brook, Easter 1967, 1967
Black and white photograph
mounted on card; 17 x 49.5
Purchased from Situations
Gallery, 1974
AC 1355

p. 64
Steve McQueen (b. 1969)
Bear, 1993
16mm film/u-matic video
transfer to Betacam sp
video tape
Running time: approx. 10 mins
Purchased from Anthony
Reynolds Gallery, 1995
ACC 116/1995

pp. 42–43
Gustav Metzger (b. 1926)
Historic Photographs: To Crawl Into – Anschluss, Vienna, March 1938, 1996–1998
Black and white photograph
on foamex with cloth cover
approx. 286.3 x 400
Purchased from the artist, 1997
ACC 62/1996

p. 158
Henry Moore (1898–1986)
Working Model for Reclining Figure (Internal and External Forms), 1951
Bronze
33 x 52 x 17.1
Purchased from the artist, 1963
ACC 7/1963
Reproduced by permission of
The Henry Moore Foundation

Time-Life Screen (Working Model), 1952
Bronze
43.2 x 111.1 x 20
Purchased from the artist, 1964
AC 725

Head of a King, 1952–1953
Bronze
58.4 x 48.3 x 20.3
Purchased from the artist, 1963
ACC 5/1963

Working Model for Knife-Edge Two Piece, 1962
Bronze; 44.5 x 58.4 x 22.9
Purchased from the artist, 1963
ACC 6/1963

p. 192
David Musgrave (b. 1973)
Overlapping Figures, 2001
Acrylic; 0.3 x 96 x 57
Purchased from greengrassi,
2001
ACC 41/2001

p. 17
Rosalind Nashashibi (b. 1973)
Midwest, 2002
Betacam
Running time: 11 mins
Purchased from the artist,
2004
ACC 44/2003
© the artist and Sinibad Films
Ltd

p. 135
Mariele Neudecker (b. 1965)
Stolen Sunsets, 1966
Steel, glass, dye, fibreglass,
enamel, acrylic, water, salt
and varnish
180 x 65 x 45
Gift of Charles Saatchi, 1999
ACC 227/1998

p. 12
Ben Nicholson (1894–1982)
Contrapuntal February 25–'53, 1953
Oil on board
167.6 x 121.9
Purchased from Penwith
Gallery, St Ives, 1953
AC 286
© Angela Verren Taunt 2006 All
rights reserved, DACS

p. 139
Lucia Nogueira (1950–1998)
One and Three, 1994
Glass, mercury, phosphorus,
paint, platinum, velvet and
cardboard
2 earrings, each 5.2 x 1 x 1.8;
box 3.1 x 8.1 x 8.1
Purchased from the artist, 1994
ACC 46/1997

p. 15
Chris Ofili (b. 1968)
Popcorn Shells, 1995
Paper collage, oil, polyester
resin, map-pins, elephant dung
and 2 elephant dung props
182.9 x 121.9 x 15.8
Purchased from Victoria
Miro Gallery, 1996
ACC 58/1995

p. 20
Julian Opie (b. 1958)
This is Fiona, 2000
Continuous computer film on CD-ROM, computer and wall mounted screen
Purchased from Lisson Gallery, 2001
ACC 45/2000

p. 118
The Otolith Group
(Anjalika Sagar, b. 1968; Kodwo Eshun, b. 1968; Richard Couzins, b. 1965)
Otolith, 2006
Betacam
Running time: 23 mins
Purchased from the artists, 2006
ACC 14/2006

pp. 142–143
Horace Ove (b. 1939)
James Baldwin, 1984
Cibachrome print
26.6 x 39.4
Purchased from the artist, 1989
ACP 2071

p. 106
Eduardo Paolozzi (1924–2005)
The Cage, 1951
Bronze
148 x 75.6 x 75
Purchased from the artist, 1951
AC 201

p. 105
The Frog, 1958
Bronze
68.6 x 81.3 x 86.2
Purchased from the artist, 1963
AC 661

p. 34
Victor Pasmore (1908–1998)
The Snowstorm: Spiral Motif in Black and White, 1950–1951
Oil on canvas
119.4 x 152.4
Purchased from the artist, 1951
ACC 3/1951

p. 60
Oliver Payne and **Nick Relph**
(b. 1977, b. 1979)
Mixtape, 2002
DVD
Running time: 23 mins
Purchased from Gavin Brown's Enterprise, New York, 2002
ACC 57/2002

p. 78
Peter Peri (b. 1971)
Pageant, 2005
Mixed media on canvas
102 x 76.5
Purchased from Counter Gallery, 2005
ACC 7/2006

p. 166
Keith Piper (b. 1960)
(You are now entering) Mau Mau country, 1983
Acrylic and hessian on canvas
246.5 x 192
Purchased from Mappin Gallery, Sheffield, 1984
AC 5346

p. 73
Ingrid Pollard (b. 1953)
Pastoral Interlude, No. 4, 1988
Hand-tinted silver print and text
51 x 51
Purchased from the artist, 2000
ACC 56/1999

p. 139
Kathy Prendergast (b. 1958)
The End and the Beginning, 1996
Human hair and wood
5.5 x 4 x 4
Purchased from Kerlin Gallery, Dublin, 1997
ACC 21/1996

p. 11
Bridget Riley (b. 1931)
Movement in Squares, 1961
Emulsion on board; 122 x 122
Purchased from Gallery One, 1962
ACC 6/1962

p. 150
David Robilliard (1952–1988)
International flavour: cultural differences melt when you start slurping, 1988
Acrylic on canvas
182.5 x 182.5
Purchased from the artist, 1988
ACC 17/1988

p. 37
Donald Rodney (1961–1998)
In the House of My Father, 1997
Photographic print on aluminium; 122 x 153
Purchased from the Trustees of the Estate of Donald Rodney, 1999
ACC 59/1997

p. 114
Eva Rothschild (b. 1972)
Heavy Cloud, 2003
Wood, plastic and paint
200 x 190 x 175
Purchased from Modern Art, 2005
ACC 14/2005

p. 147
Karin Ruggaber (b. 1969)
Bag, 2004
Felt, tweed, wool and cotton
50 x 30 x 10
Purchased from greengrassi, 2005
ACC 5/2005

pp. 24–25
Tim Scott (b. 1937)
Round Midnight, 1961
Glass and emulsion paint on wood
121.9 x 198.1 x 121.9
Purchased from the artist, 1967
ACA 76

p. 75
William Scott (1913–1989)
Dark Brown, Orange and White, 1963
Oil on canvas
160 x 173
Purchased from Hanover Gallery, 1963
AC 691

David Shrigley (b. 1968)
Take off ... , 1997
Marker on paper
15 x 10
Purchased from Galleri Nicolai Wallner, Copenhagen, 1999
ACC 36/1999

p. 180
These and others will be there to greet you at the airport ... , 1997
Marker on paper
15 x 10
Purchased from Galleri Nicolai Wallner, Copenhagen, 1999
ACC 37/1999

At the earliest point of early morning ... , 1998
Marker on paper
24 x 21
Purchased from Galleri Nicolai Wallner, Copenhagen, 1999
ACC 34/1999

Compare our prices against our competitors ... , 1998
Marker on paper
24.5 x 26
Purchased from Galleri Nicolai Wallner, Copenhagen, 1999
ACC 32/1999

p. 122
See the little creature in the giant cage ... , 1998
Marker on paper
24 x 21
Purchased from Galleri Nicolai Wallner, Copenhagen, 1999
ACC 33/1999

The road to beasthood ... , 1998
Marker on paper
24 x 20.5
Purchased from Galleri Nicolai Wallner, Copenhagen, 1999
ACC 35/1999

p. 33
Maud Sulter (b. 1960)
Calliope from the series Zabat, 1989
Cibachrome print
152.4 x 121.9
Purchased from the artist, 1991
ACC 11/1990

Terpsichore from the series Zabat, 1989
Cibachrome print
152.4 x 121.9
Purchased from the artist, 1991
ACC 100/1991

(bookmark)
Mark Titchner (b. 1973)
The Invisible Republic, 2006
Fibreglass
850 x 180
Purchased from Vilma Gold, 2006
ACC 13/2006

p. 91
William Tucker (b. 1935)
Thebes, 1966
Painted wood
121.9 x 137. 2 x 203.2 cm
Purchased from Rowan Gallery
AC 765

p. 146
Keith Tyson (b. 1969)
Applied Artmachine Chart: Candlestick Maker, 1999
Ballpoint pen, felt-tip pen, ink and pencil on paper
157 x 126
Purchased from Anthony Reynolds Gallery, 2000
ACC 16/2000

p. 162
Euan Uglow (1932–2000)
Snake, 1976
Oil on canvas
49.5 x 35
Purchased from the artist, 1976
AC 1586

p. 139
Mark Wallinger (b. 1959)
A Real Work of Art, 1994
Wood, polyurethane plastic, brass, felt and enamel paint
12 x 12.8 x 7.3
Purchased from Anthony Reynolds Gallery, 1994
ACC 35/1997

p. 116
Gary Webb (b. 1973)
Mirage of Loose Change, 2001
Chrome, steel, plastic, granite, wood and neon light
108 x 132 x 47
Purchased from The Approach, 2001
ACC 2/2002

p. 61
Richard Wentworth (b. 1947)
Toy, 1983
Galvanised and tinned steel
31 x 41 x 62.5
Purchased from Anthony Reynolds Gallery, 1984
ACC 1/1984

p. 61
London, 1999. Making do and getting by., 2000
Unique photograph; 72 x 94
Purchased from Lisson Gallery, 2001
ACC 60/2000
Tirana, 1999. Occasional geometries., 2000
Unique photograph
74 x 92
Purchased from Lisson Gallery, 2001
ACC 61/2000

p. 85
Rachel Whiteread (b. 1963)
Untitled, 1993
Bronze; 6.3 x 6.3 x 20.3
Purchased from Karsten Schubert Gallery, 1994
ACC 37/1997

p. 38
Alison Wilding (b. 1948)
Untitled, 1980
Zinc and brass foil
24 x 131 x 160.5
Purchased from the artist, 1980
AC 3097

pp. 6–7
Cathy Wilkes (b. 1966)
She's Pregnant Again, 2005
Televisions, aluminium, water, petrol, pram, sink, towel, phone, salad bowls, mirror, jar, battery, saucer, shoe, fabric, thread and painting
Dimensions variable
Purchased from The Modern Institute, Glasgow, 2005
ACC 8/2006

p. 149
Victor Willing (1928–1988)
Mask 26.9.84, 1984
Pastel and charcoal on paper
37.8 x 28.4
Purchased from Bernard Jacobson Gallery, 1985
AC 5360
All works by Victor Willing are © Bernard Jacobson

p. 149
Mask 4.10.84, 1984
Pastel and charcoal on paper
38 x 28.2
Purchased from Bernard Jacobson Gallery, 1985
AC 5361

p. 149
Mask 7.10.84, 1984
Pastel and charcoal on paper
38 x 28.2
Purchased from Bernard Jacobson Gallery, 1985
AC 5362

p. 138
Richard Wilson (b. 1953)
Watertable, 1994
Vinyl and printed card
18 x 18
Purchased from the artist, 1994
ACC 48/1997

p. 76
Isaac Witkin (1936–2006)
Vermont III, 1964–1965
Painted steel and stainless steel
86.4 x 274.3 x 80
Purchased from Waddington Galleries, 1966
AC 883
© The Estate of Isaac Witkin

p. 6
Bill Woodrow (b. 1948)
Armchair and Paraffin Heater with Campfire, 1981
Plastic and metal
Total area variable
Purchased from Lisson Gallery, 1981
ACC 3/1981

p. 45
Cerith Wyn Evans (b. 1958)
'Diary: How to improve the world (you will only make matters worse) continued 1968 (revised)' from 'M' writings '67–'72 by John Cage, 2003
Chandelier, flat screen monitor, morse code unit, computer
Purchased from White Cube, 2003
ACC 41/2003

pp. 62–63
Carey Young (b. 1970)
Lines Made by Walking (after Richard Long), 2003
Slide projection
175 x 263
Purchased from IBID Projects, 2003
ACC 43/2003

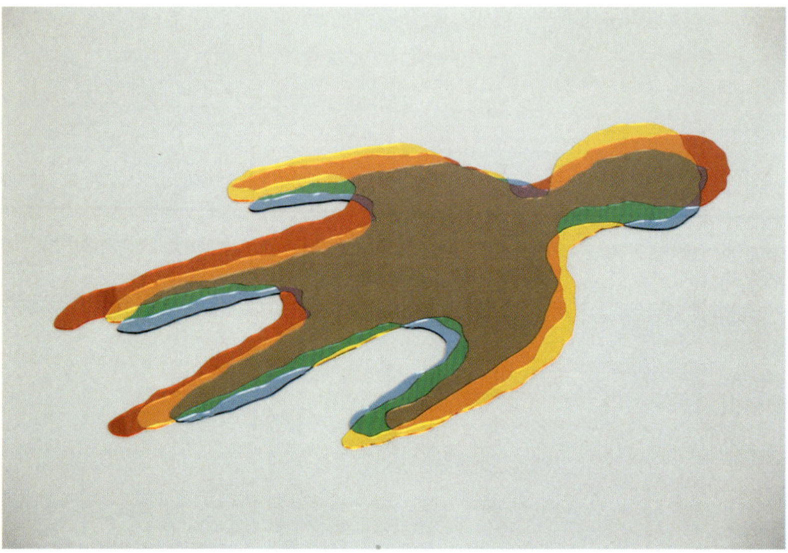